PEOPLE POWER

A USER'S GUIDE TO DEMOCRACY

Dan Jellinek
Illustrations by Harry Venning

CORGI BOOKS

TRANSWORLD PUBLISHERS
61–63 Uxbridge Road, London W5 5SA
A Random House Group Company
www.transworldbooks.co.uk

PEOPLE POWER
A CORGI BOOK: 9780552167864

First published in Great Britain
in 2013 by Bantam Press
an imprint of Transworld Publishers
Corgi edition published 2014

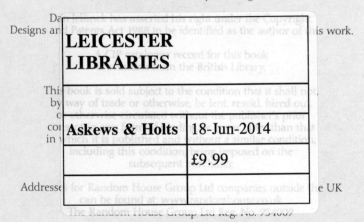

LEICESTER
LIBRARIES

Askews & Holts	18-Jun-2014	
	£9.99	

The Random House Group Limited supports the Forest Stewardship Council®
(FSC®), the leading international forest-certification organisation.
Our books carrying the FSC label are printed on FSC®-certified paper.
FSC is the only forest-certification scheme supported by the leading
environmental organisations, including Greenpeace. Our paper procurement
policy can be found at www.randomhouse.co.uk/environment

Typeset in Nofret by
Kestrel Data, Exeter, Devon.
Printed in Great Britain by Clays Ltd, St Ives plc

2 4 6 8 10 9 7 5 3 1

MIX
Paper from
responsible sources
FSC® C016897

To Gillian, Ezra and Frida – my people, my power

Contents

Burning down the house

Whenever an election comes around, so many people seem to become angry and depressed. 'I'm not going to bother voting for anyone this time,' they say. 'They're all as bad as each other. What's the point?'

Of course, there may be all sorts of good reasons to be angry with some things that politicians have done since the last election. Or not done. But not to vote? That is to vastly overreact to whatever anger people might have about politicians – like burning down a house because you don't like some of the furniture in it. And not just any old house: the one in which all of us live and, we had better hope, the only one in which we will ever live.

It's heartbreaking to see how casually so many people are able to toss away one of their most precious possessions. Our right to vote is not just precious because so many people have been killed or injured fighting for it, from the Suffragettes to countless soldiers and civilians killed in two world wars. Or that so many people in other countries would – and do – give their lives and their freedom every day in the struggle to tear that right from the hands of the people who rule over them, from Bahrain to China. Our right to vote is the steadily beating heart of our democracy, and of our freedom. It's not the only important part of living in a free democracy – this book describes many others, from a free press to independent courts – but it is a hugely important part. The fact that a new government must be elected every few years, in a secret vote by its citizens, is a massive protection against corruption and general uselessness. In a democracy, if the people in charge do things we don't like, we can boot them out. Of course, politicians can still do unpopular things while they are in power. No government will ever deliver all the changes in society we would like to see, not least because no two people would like to see the same things happening. But come the next election, if most people are dissatisfied or can be persuaded that another way might be worth trying, the government will suffer.

In any case, if it can be right for one person not to vote, surely it could be right for nobody to vote? But imagine if there was an election and nobody *did* vote. Although the count would not take long, there would be a problem. Who would be in charge? No one would have any legal or moral right to rule. Ultimately, we would be at the mercy of whatever regime could fight its way to the top. Government without election means domination by the biggest, baddest, most ruthless creatures in the political jungle.

It may well be that most people who don't vote take it for granted that most other people *will* vote, and so everything will carry on fine and their own vote will be there for the times when they might fancy using it again. But that's a dangerous game to play, whittling away at our politicians' right to rule and reducing their representativeness.

This is not a simple problem to solve: there are many reasons why people may not vote or engage with our democracy. One of the saddest reasons is that many people are struggling simply to get by and think that no politician alive could help to improve their situation. After all, why is it that despite the fact that everyone can vote and hence has a little share of power, there are still such yawning gaps between the haves and the have-nots, which never seem to disappear?

For example, the wealthiest tenth of households in Great Britain own more than 40 per cent of the nation's overall wealth, according to figures published in December 2012 by the Office for National Statistics.

On the other hand, there do seem to have been advances for everyone in the days of modern democracy. While men and women in the highest socio-economic group – in other words, richer people – can still expect to live up to seven years longer than those in the lower socio-economic groups, one recent Equality and Human Rights Commission report found that the average girl born in Britain today has a life expectancy almost double that of a girl born a hundred years ago, from less than fifty years to more than ninety years. According to the report, 'this remarkable increase is a testament to medical breakthroughs, changes in the British economy, and improvements in diet and housing that have revolutionised life over the past century'.

Other general trends include growing average material wealth and growing home ownership; and the narrowing of the earnings gap between men and women.

'Britain has become a fairer place,' the commission concludes. 'However, the evidence shows clearly that whatever progress has been made for some groups in some places, the outcomes for many people are not shifting as far or as fast as they should.'

Overall it is a complex picture. While we have moved a long way from Victorian times when child labour, servitude and ill-health were the norm, life is still very hard for many people in Britain today.

It is a big step, however, and a dangerous one, to offer the many real social problems that remain in the UK today as a reason to attack democracy itself. Because, as this book will try to show, a vote is not the end of the rights and freedoms we enjoy as citizens of a democracy. Many, like our freedom of speech, freedom of the press and the right to a fair trial, exist all the time, elections or no elections, and they are essential for finding out about, exposing and trying to alleviate the social problems we all face. And if we reject democracy, we reject all those other freedoms as well.

That is the purpose behind this book: to explain how democracy in the UK works, in the hope that if we understand it better, we can help make it work better.

A free vote will never create a perfect world, since a perfect world cannot be created. But it has been shown time and again – from Hitler's Germany to Soviet Russia – that democracy is much better equipped to tackle the serious problems we face – to identify them, debate them openly and try to address them – than any other system that has ever been seen in the real world.

As Winston Churchill famously said: 'Democracy is the worst form of government, except all those other forms that have been tried from time to time.'

He made this remark in a 1947 House of Commons debate on reforming the House of Lords – a subject still rumbling on today. At that time, Churchill was no longer Prime Minister but Conservative leader of the Opposition, and the Labour government had introduced a Parliament Bill to cut the amount of time the Lords could delay the passing of laws from two years to one year.

Deputy Prime Minister Herbert Morrison (Peter Mandelson's grandfather) said the subject was 'an important constitutional issue . . . [for] a progressive government'. At this, one Conservative MP called out: 'Progressing backwards.'

The debate was heated. The government said the unelected House of Lords – which at the time had a huge Conservative majority – had too much potential to block the passing of laws by an elected Labour government, which was undemocratic. 'Governments should be appointed to do things,' said Morrison.

The Conservatives objected that, in reducing the powers of the Lords to scrutinize the work of the Commons, an important constitutional safeguard was being scrapped. In any case, the Lords had never actually been unreasonably obstructive, they said.

Churchill, who had missed the first day of the debate due to a heavy cold, appeared on day two 'under some protest from my medical adviser'. But true to form, he was in fighting mood as he turned his fire on Prime Minister Clement Attlee.

'As a free–born Englishman, what I hate is the sense of being at anybody's mercy or anybody's power, be he Hitler or Attlee,' he thundered, melodramatically. 'We are approaching very near to dictatorship in this country.'

The passage containing his famous comment on democracy pulsates with Churchill's unique, visceral eloquence. 'It is not Parliament that should rule; it is the people who should rule through Parliament . . . The object of the [previous] Parliament Act, and the spirit of that Act, were to give effect, not to spasmodic emotions of the electorate, but to the settled, persistent will of the people. What they wanted to do they could do, and what they did not want to do they could stop. All this idea of a handful of men getting hold of the State machine, having the right to make the people do what suits their party and personal interests or doctrines, is completely contrary to every conception of surviving Western democracy . . . All this idea of a group of super men and super-planners . . . making the masses of the people do what they think is good for them, without any check or correction, is a violation of democracy. Many forms of government have been tried, and will be tried in this world of sin and woe. No one pretends that democracy is perfect or all-wise. Indeed, it has been said that democracy is the worst form of government except all those other forms that have been tried from time to time; but there is the broad feeling in our country that the people should rule, continuously rule, and that public opinion, expressed by all constitutional means, should shape, guide, and control the actions of Ministers who are their servants and not their masters.'

Churchill's argument was that the Lords needed strong powers to prevent unfair actions by governments between elections – 'a handful of men getting hold of the state machine'. Attlee disagreed, saying that this implied that 'the brake is more important than the engine'.

Other speakers on the government side were angered by the suggestion that the members of an unelected House of Lords could be considered to be the last defenders of the will of the people.

Terence Donovan, the then Labour MP for Leicester East, added that, in a functioning democracy, there are many ways that the public can make their views and feelings known to politicians in the long gaps between general elections. 'There are by-elections, public meetings, the Press, petitions, the reception that Members of Parliament get when they attend meetings in their own constituencies, and, if the House likes, I will throw in local municipal elections,' Donovan said.

In the end, the government won its vote, the Bill ended up as law and the powers of the Lords were reduced. But as well as giving us Churchill's famous view of democracy, this sixty-five-year-old debate provides a fantastic introduction to some of the main concepts behind this book.

One of these is that it is important to realize that our democracy, and how it works, is not set in stone. Although many of its principles have remained unchanged for centuries, most of the detail about how it works has changed over the years out of all recognition. What is more, any part of it could still be changed again at any time.

The balance between the power of the government, the power of Parliament and the power of the people, for example, is as important for us to think about and debate today as it ever was.

Those people who say that because things sometimes seem hopeless then democracy as a whole has failed should also remember that their very ability to discuss how to improve the way things are exists only because they are living in a democracy. According to bitter human experience, if they did want to remove democracy, as soon as they got what they wanted they would have to stop talking about it. Because, as we will see later on, once people do not have a choice of governments to vote for, the regime in power must prevent freedom of speech to crush dissent. Totalitarian power is maintained by state control over the media.

A disturbing event that took place in China in January 2013 offers a powerful example. Journalists at a major newspaper, the *Southern Daily*, were reported across the world to have gone on strike when, just before publication, government censors removed an article calling for reform. The shock of this story was not that the censorship had happened but that the strike had happened, and that we had heard about it, in a country where open dissent is usually stamped out ruthlessly before it takes hold.

But what happened next? No one knows. Mysteriously, the protest

– or, at least, coverage of the protest – fizzled out. Some journalists were reported to have been bundled into police vans and spirited away. The paper went back to publication. No one can be interviewed, no investigations mounted or reports published. The protests have simply disappeared, as if they never took place. This is more shocking than the strike itself, but less surprising: without democracy, what could anyone do about it?

None of this is to say that nothing bad or repressive ever happens in a democracy. Like all human endeavours, the way any particular democracy works can never be perfect, so we do always need to keep trying to improve our system. It was only just over eighty years ago that women in Britain gained the same voting rights as men; and we are still debating issues of core importance to how our democracy works, such as devolution or independence for the different parts of the UK; how our systems for making new laws could be improved; and where the monarchy fits into a modern Britain.

But the best place to start trying to improve our democracy is to appreciate what we already have of value, and see how we can go about making it even better. And the first step in trying to change things for the better must be to try to understand how they work now, and that is where this book is intended to help. Piece by piece, it looks at the main components of our democracy: how the UK works as a society; how we can make our voices heard; and the ways we can get more engaged.

What are the pieces of this puzzle? They include free and fair elections, and how they are run; political parties, and the role they have in shaping government; the two historic Houses of the UK Parliament, and how they are adapting to the modern world; the devolution of power to Scotland, Wales and Northern Ireland; the role of the monarchy in the modern world; Cabinet government and collective responsibility; the civil service and its careful codes of conduct; the importance of an independent justice system; freedom of speech and the media, as a new regulatory system begins to take shape; the right to protest, within reason; the true democratic meaning and extent of the internet revolution; and our place in Europe, post-euro crisis. Inevitably, in a single book which covers so much ground, there will be gaps. It has not been possible, for example, to examine in depth the workings of each devolved part of the UK. As the book also covers areas that are changing all the time, there will also be some sections that have already become at least partly out of date.

But I hope this will not matter too much, because above all this is a book about principles. It is not an academic book, or a book for political experts. It is certainly not a party-political book. It is a book for everyone.

What it aims to be is an inspiration for new thoughts, new conversations and new positive actions. By running through the basic elements of the system we have, examining them and explaining how they work, it is an attempt to show that democracy is a many-faceted, delicate and precious construction, built by everyone, for everyone.

So if it helps you look deeper, find out more and become involved, then it will have worked. If it helps to show that history is alive, that our system is changing, will continue to change, and that at least some of the power to shape it rests in your own hands, then it will have worked. We will come back to these ideas at the end of the book. The rest is up to you.

Chapter 1

A potted history of people power

The soldiers wheeled round on their horses, the sun sparkling off their unsheathed sabres. In front of them stood a huge crowd, uneasy but determined: thousands upon thousands of men, women and children standing shoulder to shoulder, defiantly holding their bright banners as high as they could. The flags were sewn with messages, the simplest of which was just one word: 'REFORM'. Most protestors were unarmed; a few clutched bricks and stones, useless against mounted troops.

Time stood still.

The soldiers themselves were uneasy – they had not signed up for this – until the shout rang out: 'Have at the flags', and they charged, sabres whirling at poles and cloth and everything else in their path. Heads, arms and bodies were battered and slashed as chaos, shrieks and the sound of thundering hooves filled the air. It was steel against flesh, a massacre; and the soldiers carved their bloody path through to arrest the leaders of the protest in St Peter's Field on 16 August 1819. But no one can kill an idea, and by the end of that day the idea of democracy in Britain was stronger than ever.

The word 'democracy' comes from two words in ancient Greek: *demos* meaning 'people' and *kratos* meaning strength, authority or power. People power. Its *Oxford English Dictionary* definition is a bit longer: 'Government by the people; that form of government in which the sovereign power resides in the people as a whole, and is exercised either directly by them (as in the small republics of antiquity) or by officers elected by them.

In modern use, often more vaguely denoting a social state in which all have equal rights, without hereditary or arbitrary differences of rank or privilege.'

There are three parts to this definition. First, that power is owned by everybody together; second, that it can either be exercised directly or by people we elect; and third, that it has come to mean we all have equal rights.

Direct democracy – where everyone has a say directly, rather than through elected representatives – is not used much in modern Britain beyond general elections, referendums and *The X Factor.* Most key decisions are taken by elected representatives, or people who report to elected representatives. Today, this group includes MPs (Westminster), MSPs (Scotland), AMs (Wales) and MLAs (Northern Ireland); local councillors; elected mayors; police commissioners in England and Wales; and school governors (parent council members in Scotland). At the same time, we still have a monarchy, though it has little power left to exercise of its own free will, as we will see later.

The word 'republic' is also mentioned in the Oxford dictionary definition. A republic is another term for a state where the government is elected; it also usually refers to one with an elected president as the 'first citizen', and not a monarch. Some unelected governments like to use the word too, or misuse it, like the elite group of people controlling the so-called People's Republic of China – but as they are in fact undemocratic, no one can argue with them.

The Greek city-state of Athens and its surrounding region of Attica between 500 and 300 BC is usually considered the birthplace of democracy. It was where the word itself was invented, after all. The Athenian system was undemocratic in modern terms, because women were not allowed to vote and there was slavery (slaves could not vote either, though this was not their biggest concern). But its principles among free men were recognizably democratic.

Nearly every week, several thousand of the free male citizens of Attica (out of an eligible population estimated at anywhere between

20,000 and 60,000) gathered on a hill called the Pnyx, and an official cried out: 'Who wishes to address the assembly?'

In this mob (the word 'Pnyx' was derived from *piknos*, meaning 'crowded'), anyone could put up their hand. Older men were allowed to speak first, and people who were clearly experts on a subject were favoured over people who were clearly not, who were jeered off.

By modern standards, a great deal of power was delegated to ordinary – or even random – people. The Athenian court system appointed huge juries – at times, more than a thousand strong – and no judges, in court cases which were never allowed to last for more than a day. Some jobs in the civil service were carried out by citizens selected at random, by drawing lots, to prevent corruption. Such random civil servants were appointed in teams to make sure there would always be enough who were competent and motivated.

Despite all this, the Athenians still faced one of the biggest problems encountered by democracies today: that of getting enough people to take part to make sure everyone's views and needs were represented. They tried all sorts of things. On debate days, shops were closed; people were allowed to gather only near the Pnyx; and some were even paid to join in the debates. At one stage, officials resorted to using long ropes stained with red dye to herd people up to the hill. Anyone found with the dye on them was fined. As the playwright Aristophanes wrote in *The Acharnians*, people still tried to escape: 'They are gossiping in the marketplace, slipping hither and thither to avoid the vermilioned rope.' His character Dicaeopolis, an unusually keen citizen, gets to the Pnyx ahead of everyone else and finds himself alone: 'I groan, yawn, stretch, break wind, and know not what to do.'

The problem of engaging large numbers of people in a democratic system is the same today, and the result of many people not being engaged is the same too: where fewer people exercise their rights, the outcome becomes less fair for everybody – less democratic.

History shows too that these rights have been extremely hard won, bit by bit, battle by battle. At the heart of the development of British democracy have been two key areas of struggle: the struggle to strengthen the powers held by an elected Parliament, and the struggle to ensure that Parliament represents everyone in the country, or as many people as possible.

There are many other parts to a democracy and many other struggles, as the rest of this book will show: but the battle for fair votes has always been among the hardest fought.

The Athenian model died away following its loss of independence as a city state, and across Europe aristocracy – government by a few elite people, usually the wealthiest landowners – became the norm, generally within the framework of monarchy.

In Britain and Ireland, early systems of government between around AD 800 and 1700 developed as separate monarchies or kingdoms (and aristocracies) in England, Scotland, Wales and Ireland before gradually coming together, by choice or otherwise.

The kingdoms of England and Scotland chose to be united in 1707 as the Kingdom of Great Britain. There had been several attempts previously to unite the two, both by wars in the thirteenth and fourteenth centuries (when the English were repelled by the Scots) and peacefully, by negotiation.

The two kingdoms had shared a monarch for much of the period since 1603 when King James VI of Scotland inherited the English throne from his distant relative Queen Elizabeth I. But it took more than a hundred years of delicate talks – a slippery wrestling match between hopes and fears on both sides – to pull off a union. In 1706 the two finally agreed and separately passed their own laws leading to union the following year.

The Principality of Wales had already been incorporated into England in 1284. Before that, it had been a nation of warring kingdoms, though united by a distinct culture and language. But when England joined the Kingdom of Great Britain in 1707, Wales came too.

The monarchy in Ireland was invaded and subsumed by the English monarchy in the late twelfth century. It was managed as a separate realm until becoming part of the United Kingdom of Great Britain and Ireland in 1801 – the forerunner to the modern UK.

The Republic of Ireland regained its independence in 1922, with Northern Ireland remaining – controversially for many – in the United Kingdom. And so we are today: the United Kingdom of Great Britain and Northern Ireland.

In early monarchies, kings and queens sat on top of a hierarchical social pyramid, with power and wealth handed down within each level from one generation to the next. There were customs and traditions governing how much tax should be paid up to each higher level in the pyramid, but just like modern-day unelected leaders, monarchs tended to push the limits of this as far as they could – and it was dangerous to argue.

In the thirteenth century, the most powerful aristocrats, clergymen and barons reached the end of their patience with King John and the amount of money he demanded. In 1215 they came together to petition the enforcement of a 'charter of liberties' to set new limits on the king's behaviour. Backed into a corner, King John signed up to this Magna Carta – the 'Great Charter' – some of which remains law to this day. As well as an order stopping the king taking wood from any forest, there are clauses which codify a legal system that would work more independently and could not be so easily ignored by the monarch.

One of the legal principles set out in Magna Carta (though it did not originate there) is that of 'habeas corpus', which protects people from being put in prison without good reason by forcing the authorities to produce any prisoner in court and explain why they are being held. Other clauses relate to people's rights to a fair trial.

Magna Carta also stipulated that any new taxes set by the monarch had to be agreed by an advisory council (again, this idea did not originate here, but it was refined). Members of this council included the most powerful landowners, and they were not elected but summoned by the king himself; even so, it was a step towards greater power-sharing.

So Magna Carta did not so much represent power to the people as power away from the monarch, to a Great Council. Over time this would gradually become a larger Parliament with more and more power of its own – and which would also become more and more controlled by and responsive to ordinary citizens.

The next step in this direction was taken fifty years later by another rebel baron, Simon de Montfort. Locked in a power struggle with Henry III, in 1265 De Montfort set up his own separate rule-making Parliament – the first English Parliament to feature elected representatives. Though De Montfort was killed the same year and his Parliament rejected by the King, Henry's successor Edward I gradually came to accept the presence of 'commoners' in Parliament and as time went on De Montfort's idea slowly took shape as a formal second 'house' of Parliament, known as the Commons.

The first elected representatives were of two kinds: 'knights of the shire' elected from each county (two per shire), and 'burgesses' elected from borough constituencies, which existed only in certain places deemed to be worthy of more power or influence. Early elections are thought to have been fairly inclusive (for men) in terms of allowing most male adults to vote, but in 1430 a law was passed limiting the vote in counties to people who owned land that brought in a rent of at least 40 shillings per year (women could not own land, so this cemented their exclusion from the vote).

As Parliament grew in power and began to challenge monarchs more and more often on issues such as the handing of trade monopolies to their cronies, battles over the method of election or appointment to Parliament and the balance of power between Commons, Lords and monarchy gradually became the key to the development of democracy in the UK.

The power struggle flared up dramatically through the English Civil War of 1642–51 between Parliamentarians and Royalists, with the triumph of the Parliamentarian army; the short-lived ascent to power of the controversial and puritanical MP for Cambridge, Oliver Cromwell;

and the restoration of the monarchy in 1660 (after which Cromwell's corpse was dug up again and beheaded).

At the heart of the Civil War was a passionate debate about everybody's right to a fair say in government. Although Cromwell's New Model Army had deposed the monarchy, opinion was divided in its ranks about how far a new society should be governed by concepts such as votes for all (men) – including for soldiers, who had, after all, died for the cause – or whether power should remain in the hands of a smaller, property-owning elite.

At the forefront of the debate was a movement of reformers known as the Levellers – a label given to them by their enemies to over-dramatize their position. The Levellers drew up an 'Agreement of the People', a manifesto of demands including the right to vote for all men over the age of twenty-one (except for servants, beggars and, naturally, Royalists); that the law should proceed in English, not Latin; and the abolition of imprisonment for debt. Over two months in 1647 in a small church in Putney, West London, these demands were debated between the Levellers and the leaders of the New Model Army.

As often seems to be the case when major political reform is proposed, most of these suggestions ended up being ignored at the time, but the open discussion of democratic ideas had a much longer life of its own. With the Putney Debates, new seeds had been planted.

Although the monarchy was eventually restored, the power of Parliament was growing, slowly but surely. The subsequent 'Glorious Revolution' of 1688, in which one king (James II, also known as James VII of Scotland) was replaced by another (William of Orange – William III of England and Ireland and William II of Scotland), stemmed from a revolt planned by Parliament. This brought with it a new Bill of Rights limiting the power of the monarch – forbidding the monarch to dispense with Acts of Parliament or to maintain a peacetime army without Parliament's consent, for example – and new democratic rights for the people. These included the right to petition; the right to free election of MPs; and that freedom of speech inside Parliament 'ought not to be impeached or questioned in any court or place out of Parliament'. The latter meant that MPs could not be prosecuted for what they say in Parliament, for example under the libel laws – an important privilege that remains today, encouraging complete freedom of speech in Parliament.

Despite this home-grown progress, events elsewhere ultimately generated some of the strongest forces for change in British democracy.

The fight for American independence followed by the French Revolution towards the end of the eighteenth century raised a democratic tidal wave which many thought would sweep the world – the Arab Spring of its day. The United States Constitution, drawn up in 1788, marked the birth of a new state based on individual freedom and human rights; and the separation of powers between a lawmaking body (Congress), a governing body (a federal government headed by a President), and an independent judiciary (headed by a Supreme Court).

In a Britain struggling to come to terms with industrialization – characterized for many by back-breaking work, poverty and under-representation – political unrest grew rapidly, fuelled by these exciting developments elsewhere. Supporters of democracy – labelled 'radicals' – were opposed by anti-revolutionaries or 'loyalists', who felt that any major upheaval would lead to anarchy and disaster.

As in Tiananmen Square in Beijing and Tahrir Square in Cairo in more recent times, these power struggles soon became violent, and in 1819 the horrific event described at the start of this chapter took place in St Peter's Field, Manchester. In what became known as the Peterloo Massacre – an ironic reference to the Battle of Waterloo – tens of thousands of people had gathered to demand greater parliamentary representation. Despite the fact that they were peaceful and unarmed, their numbers alarmed local magistrates and orders were given to arrest the leaders. When the demonstrators closed ranks to prevent this happening, sabre-wielding cavalrymen hacked their way into the defenceless crowd, killing a dozen people and wounding hundreds more. Some soldiers did try to stop the carnage, but were powerless to do so in the panic and pandemonium.

The massacre gave rise to the establishment of a newspaper: the *Manchester Guardian*, whose founder John Taylor saw that the spread of news was the key to further political reform. The written word has long been linked to struggles for democratic freedom: in the time leading up to Peterloo – though he did not live to see the massacre take place – lived the writer and activist Thomas Paine, who in 1791 wrote *The Rights of Man*, a defence of the principles of the French Revolution. This beautifully written book – stingingly sarcastic and often hilariously funny – speaks out with a startling power. It makes use of some simple examples. Imagine yourself in a small group of people thrown together in any situation – down a coal mine, say, or in a village community. What would you feel would be the best way of organizing yourselves to support each other? Should everyone be consulted? Should everyone have a say? And if so, why should running a country be any different?

Why do we need any society in the first place? The answer, suggested Paine, is that everyone has different skills and talents, and so in a fair group everyone should be allowed to specialize. 'No one man is capable, without the aid of society, of supplying his own wants.' A good system should try to pool everyone's skills and supply everyone's needs: to Paine, this was the meaning of democracy.

By contrast, a Parliament like the one there was at that time, made up of just a few vested interests – the landowners' – behaved like 'a criminal sitting in judgement upon himself', said Paine. Farmers worked harder than anyone and paid huge sums in taxes – and yet because they rented their land they couldn't vote, unlike landowners, however lazy and debauched. How could this be right?

In the face of growing pressure stoked by Paine and other radicals, after Peterloo and with new riots breaking out in London, Bristol, Nottingham and across the land, the British political establishment saw which way the wind was blowing.

The Representation of the People Act 1832 – also known as the Reform Act 1832 – granted seats in the House of Commons to the industrial towns of the north and removed the small, formerly influential seats that had become known as 'rotten boroughs' for their unfair influence and corruption. Many of these constituencies had once been populous but had since become almost deserted, leaving just a few voters who could easily be bribed or threatened by powerful local landowners or rich families. The result was that positions in Parliament could be bought. Some fifty-seven rotten boroughs – each returning two MPs – were abolished in the Reform Act.

The Act increased voter numbers from about 400,000 to 650,000 by reducing the value of property men needed to own to vote, but this was not a big increase in a population of 14 million. It still meant only the wealthiest 14 per cent of men were able to vote, and there remained a big imbalance in geographical representation in Parliament for the new industrial towns of central and northern England and of Scotland.

Unsurprisingly, therefore, it was with huge rallies in the cities of Glasgow, Birmingham and Manchester a few years later, in 1838, that one of the largest British reform movements after the Levellers – Chartism – sprang into life.

The Chartists were a group of radical activists and workers united behind a People's Charter of six demands:

1. All adult men should have the vote.
2. MPs should not have to own property.
3. The House of Commons should be elected every year.
4. Constituencies should have roughly equal numbers of voters.
5. MPs should be paid, to allow poorer people to stand for election.
6. Voting should be by secret ballot, to avoid corruption and intimidation.

Many Chartists also supported other social reforms such as limiting factory work to ten hours a day, and votes for women. Even more unusually for political movements at the time, there was a leading black Chartist activist – William Cuffay, a tailor from London.

Cuffay was a trade unionist who became president of the London Chartists. The son of a freed slave, he once referred to fellow tailors at a Chartist meeting as 'brother slaves', signalling how ordinary working people of the time were shackled by the system. Britain had ruled the slave trade illegal only in 1807 and outlawed it within the empire in 1833, so the jibe was powerful. The Chartists also borrowed some of the methods used successfully by the slave trade abolitionists, including the compilation of mass petitions.

And 'mass' is definitely the word. In 1842 the Chartists presented to Parliament a National Petition of the Industrious Classes carrying a staggering 3,317,752 signatures: about a third of the entire adult population of England, Scotland and Wales at the time. According to a report in the movement's *Northern Star* newspaper, the petition was carried to Parliament on huge rolls by thirty bearers leading a procession two miles long. Once there, 'the huge framework was found much too large to enter, and it had to be broken up. The Petition was carried in lumps and bundles and strewed all over the floor of the House. It looked as if it had been snowing paper.'

You might think that politicians would have had to take notice of such a mammoth protest, but a motion for the Chartists to present their case to the Commons was defeated by 287 votes to 49. Over the next few years more violence followed, with many activists imprisoned or (like Cuffay) transported to Australia, and the movement died away.

In the longer term, however, its effects were felt. In 1858, the property-owning qualification for MPs was abolished – point two of the People's Charter – and point six, the secret ballot, was introduced soon after.

Before secret ballots, vote-rigging was rife. One document in the National Archives dating from 1854 describes election bribery, nineteenth-century style: an outraged letter to Home Secretary Lord Palmerston from Samuel Baraclough of Tamworth in Staffordshire listed the offering of various gastronomic inducements for votes in the town's elections. 'I am prepared at any time your Lordship thinks fit', thundered Baraclough, 'to prove to your Lordship that not only Ale but a Pig was offered for a vote for Mr Shaw the present Mayor. I can also prove to your Lordship that the person who offered the Pig told me as a positive fact that a few days before the Election he had three soverigns [sic] put in his hand to do as he thought proper with to get votes for Mr Shaw.' The letter continues with details of another man being offered four quarts (a gallon) of ale for his vote.

In response to this sort of activity – pigs for votes – a wave of reform swept the country.

An Electoral Reform Act in 1867 lowered the financial thresholds for voting to include 'respectable' working men renting lodgings at £10 a year, doubling voter numbers to around 2 million. A Ballot Act was passed in 1872 which for the first time introduced secret votes. This was followed by the Corrupt and Illegal Practices Act of 1883, which established what a candidate could spend on election expenses and exactly how the money could be used. Further reform in 1884 abolished the double system of electing both counties and boroughs, and enfranchised a further 2 million male farm labourers, giving up to 29 per cent of adults the vote.

And in the decades that followed, the push for true universal suffrage – votes for all adults, women and men – finally became irresistible.

Up to the middle of the nineteenth century, despite all the clamour for reform, there had been little mention of votes for women. Married women at the time were still treated by society as being part of a family unit led by the man, who took responsibility for important decisions such as voting. Voting had also long been linked to property: and most women did not own property.

When the 1867 Reform Act was passed, the MP and philosopher John Stuart Mill had unsuccessfully tried to include women householders. But the tide was beginning to turn. In 1869, unmarried and widowed female property owners were given the right to vote in elections for town councils, and for county councils from 1888. In 1894, the Local Government Act allowed married women who owned property that was not in their husband's name to vote in local elections. The same law allowed women to be councillors for the first time (though not in all councils – that came in 1907).

Still, the government held out against giving women the vote at national elections, as New Zealand had now done in 1893. With outrage growing, the National Union of Women's Suffrage Societies (NUWSS) led by Millicent Fawcett and the more militant Women's Social and Political Union (WSPU) led by Emmeline Pankhurst, which split away in 1903, together focused the forces for change.

At the heart of these campaigns was a burning belief not just in equal rights but in the fact that a democracy in which women had the vote would be one which passed better and more humane laws, particularly those affecting women and children.

As WSPU leader Emmeline Pankhurst wrote in her book *My Own Story*: 'I am convinced that the enfranchised woman will find many ways in which to lessen, at least, the curse of poverty. Women have more practical ideas about relief, and especially of prevention of dire poverty, than men display.' On her work as a registrar, she writes: 'I was shocked to be reminded over and over again of the little respect there was in the world for women and children. I have had little girls of thirteen come to my office to register the births of their babies . . . In many of these cases I found that the child's own father or some near male relative was responsible for her state.' Later she notes that the maximum prison sentence faced by men who sexually abused homeless underage girls was two years, while harsher sentences could be handed down for crimes committed against property by the Suffragettes.

These insights help to explain why the battle for democracy has always been fought so hard. If laws are made – or at least influenced – by everyone, then laws are likely to be fairer to everyone.

Opinion is still divided on how far it was necessary for the Suffragettes to break the law, damaging property or works of art, for example, and whether direct action might have actually harmed the cause of women's votes for some years. But the outcome was surely never in doubt. The story of Fawcett's Suffragists and Pankhurst's more militant Suffragettes is one of courage and determination. From unarmed crowds of women battling mounted police to more peaceful strategies of fighting by-elections – everything was tried, rethought, and tried again.

In the end, the First World War was the catalyst that finally brought the vote to all British people: with women working tirelessly to further the war effort, and young working men who were still not allowed the vote giving their lives to protect their nation, their rights could no longer be denied.

In 1918, all men over twenty-one and all women property-owners over thirty were given the vote, followed in 1928 by the Representation of the People Act, allowing all women over twenty-one, regardless of property, to vote. In 1970, the voting age was lowered for everyone to eighteen.

In this way, one major struggle that had been taking place for more than a millennium had ended, but the story of British democratic reform certainly had not. Throughout the twentieth century and at the opening of the twenty-first, our democratic system has continued to change deeply and rapidly.

The monarchy has been slimmed down; the House of Lords has seen its powers steadily reformed and reduced; local government has been changed many times; new rules to regulate the press are being created right now; and government departments have come and gone.

Across the UK, devolution since the late 1970s has redistributed to Scotland, Wales and Northern Ireland powers not seen for centuries, from building roads to running their own health services. Further afield, the birth of the European Union has created new institutions whose final role in our democratic system is still unclear, and the rise of the internet has called into question the deepest issues of international state-hood and the rule of law.

If anything, across all these areas the rate of upheaval seems to be gathering pace. For those who think of our political system as ancient, dusty and fixed in its ways, the rest of this book will show that is certainly not the case. Some principles might be solid, but a lot of the detail is changing, all the time. We need to understand this, and we need to get involved.

Where to begin? As a fitting tribute to everyone who fought so hard for the vote, we start our journey through the modern world of British democracy with a look at elections.

Chapter 2

Elections – the heartbeat of democracy

Could they? Would they? Might they? Should they? Up until the last general election, UK Prime Ministers were able, within a five-year limit, to pick their own re-election date to suit their own strategies.

The passing of the Fixed-term Parliaments Act 2011 changed all that. Now we know with reasonable certainty that general elections will take place on the first Thursday in May every five years, starting on 7 May 2015.

There are possible exceptions: a delay of up to two months can be used in times of national crisis, and the House of Commons could also vote for an earlier election. But it is most likely that early May, every five years, will now be hard-wired into Westminster as a time to switch Parliament off and on again to see if it works any better.

Clearly, the old system gave an unfair advantage to the party in power. But is five years the best length for a fixed term?

There will be a review of how the new system is working in 2020, but it is interesting that, although five years has been the maximum, most UK governments have been much shorter: in fact, the average length of a UK government since the Second World War has not even reached four years, but is three years and ten months.

Who is entitled to vote? Thanks to the hard-fought battles described in the previous chapter, most UK citizens aged eighteen and over, plus citizens of the Irish Republic and of more than seventy Commonwealth countries, British Overseas Territories and Crown Dependencies who are living in the UK. Other EU citizens living in the UK cannot vote in general elections, although they can vote in local, devolved and European elections.

Nobody, however, can vote unless they are on the electoral register.

It is easy to register, by filling out the cards that come through your letterbox or contacting your council (see www.aboutmyvote.co.uk). In fact, the electoral registration officer in every local authority in England, Scotland and Wales is required by law to carry out a check every year of the voters in each household – the annual 'canvass' – so no one will miss the chance. Despite this, research by the Electoral Commission – the official agency set up to ensure our elections run fairly – has found that about 6 million eligible people in England, Scotland and Wales were not registered to vote in 2010, up from about 4 million in 2000. What is even more amazing is that the survey found that some 44 per cent of those not registered to vote mistakenly believed they were registered.

The proportion of unregistered people averages around 15 per cent of the voting population, and is known to be far higher in some areas and within certain social groups: more than 40 per cent of people who rent their home from a private landlord are unregistered, for example. So huge numbers of people are completely invisible when it comes to choosing their representatives and their government.

What can be done about this? One action being taken is a UK-wide move from household registration – everyone in a household being registered on a single form – to individual registration, where every voter is responsible for their own registration. This change is happening over the next year or so, with the final switch being made after the 2015 election.

Part of the reason for the change is to reduce electoral fraud: in recent years, there have been several high-profile cases where large numbers of people have been registered to vote at rather small houses. This could be down to simple bureaucratic error, but it's not great either way.

Individual registration has already been implemented in Northern

Ireland since 2002 and has improved public confidence in the register. The system in Northern Ireland is not quite the same – it does not include an annual re-registration canvass, for example – and it is not yet clear whether the changes will lead to more people being registered to vote. But for voters everywhere, the situation is the same: you must make sure you are registered.

Some people do not sign up because they have heard that the electoral register is sold to advertisers, but this is not the case. Although there is a version of the electoral roll that companies can buy, when you register you are given the chance to opt out of this version. The exception to this are financial credit-checkers – from them, there is no escape.

Most people who are allowed to vote in an election are also allowed to stand as a candidate (though many people holding public jobs are disqualified, including members of the armed forces, police officers and civil servants, because they must work entirely separately from politics).

You can stand as a representative of a political party, or as an independent candidate. To discourage too many hopeless candidates from running, a £500 deposit is required when submitting Westminster nomination papers; this is returned if the candidate receives more than 5 per cent of the votes cast. The same deposit is required for Scottish Parliament and Welsh Assembly elections. For the Northern Ireland Assembly, the sum was reduced in 2001 to £150, though candidates have to receive at least 25 per cent of votes at some stage in the count to hang on to their cash (see later in this chapter for more on the Northern Ireland voting system). Candidates in local council elections are not required to pay a deposit, but in European elections they must stump up a whopping £5,000, returnable if more than 2.5 per cent of votes are polled across a region.

Candidates in all forms of election appoint an election agent, who becomes legally responsible for the proper conduct of the campaign – unless the candidate decides to act as his or her own agent, which is allowed. All pieces of campaign literature (including, these days, emails

– and questions have been asked about tweets) have the names and addresses of the relevant agents marked on them.

One of the main jobs of an agent is to make sure candidates file their election expenses properly and that campaign spending limits are not exceeded. The Electoral Commission website (www.electoralcommission. org.uk) is the best place to find out all the rules, and its fascinating Party and Election Finance (PEF) online registers are well worth a rummage. For any election, try taking a look at spending by your local candidates and their parties, loans given to them and the sources of their loans. Sometimes there is a curious lack of detail about who has given a donation or loan, and at other times their sources seem oddly related to their policy interests, including overseas interests: all worth a look, to see what questions might need to be asked.

How campaigns are organized varies from area to area, depending on funding. In a small constituency the election agent might also run the campaign, but in bigger constituencies or those where the race is close, more funding is channelled in from central party organizations and hordes of volunteers will work the phones.

Once a campaign is under way, however, it is a little-known fact that most doorstep activity is not about trying to persuade people to vote a certain way. If you open your door to a person wearing a rosette, they are unlikely to try to change your mind if you have already decided their party could not run a lively soirée in a brewery; they simply want to know how the people in your household plan to vote. With limited time, it is more productive for them to make sure that everyone who might vote for them actually does so than to persuade the ones who might not.

There are three stages to this activity: canvassing, telling, and knocking-up.

Canvassing is the door-to-door work, asking how people might vote. On the day of the election come the tellers: volunteers who sit outside a polling station and ask for your voter number. They don't ask you who you have voted for; they simply want to know who has voted.

Finally comes the knocking–up: in the afternoon, someone races over from campaign headquarters on a bicycle and works out which possible supporters have not yet voted. Then off campaigners will go to try to make sure they do vote.

But if they're not being persuaded on the doorstep, how do people make up their minds who to support?

An obvious place to start might be the manifestos. A manifesto is a public declaration of what an individual or party believes in, and what, if elected, they intend to do. They are not legally binding – more's the pity – but then again, events can mean a party in power faces a very different situation to the one they thought they would be facing, or they might become part of a coalition, which will mean compromise.

Nevertheless, a party in power needs to try to carry out as much of its manifesto as possible, or risk weakening its credibility for the next election.

The main party manifestos used to be on sale in newsagents and bookshops at hopeful prices such as £5.00; these days, however, they are more likely to be downloaded for free from the internet. It has to be admitted, though, that not many people look at the manifestos in much detail. So how *do* we make our choices?

The British Election Study, an analysis of voter data carried out for the past three general elections by the University of Essex with the University of Texas at Dallas, spends a lot of time looking at this issue.

The book *Performance Politics and the British Voter* by the professors leading this study – Harold D. Clarke, David Sanders, Marianne C. Stewart and Paul F. Whiteley – examines two of the main academic models for voting: the 'spatial model' and the 'valence model'.

The spatial model says that for at least some issues – such as the balance between tax and spending, or the privatization of public services – there is a political line running from left to right – left wing to right wing – on which we can place a party's policies and a voter's views. The nearer a voter's views are to the party, the more the voter might want to support that party, depending on the importance of that issue to them.

There are problems with this model, though. For a start, it is not always that easy to say where a policy comes on the line; and some issues have more than one dimension. Sometimes this model might work well, where there is a 'killer issue' that clearly divides the parties – but otherwise it can be hard to use.

The other major academic model for voting examined by the professors is the 'valence model'. 'Valence' means 'value to yourself and society' and is a measure of how competent voters think a party is at running or improving vital services.

With the valence model, it is assumed that most of the things that voters want to happen – economic growth, higher employment and better health services, for example – are quite similar for the majority of people. What varies is how well people think the parties can actually deliver in these areas. Other factors play a role too, such as party identification – the feeling of solidarity with one particular political party, often established from childhood – and leader image, a judgement of how competent, trustworthy and responsive a party leader seems. Personal experience of public services – good or bad – can also play a part, as can media reports and the views of friends and family.

All these factors can build up slowly, over years and years: they do not just come into play all of a sudden during an election campaign.

The professors suggest that valence judgements are the most important, but clearly a voting decision is quite complicated, however we do it. The way through this complexity is something the academics call 'heuristics', or decision-making shortcuts, and we might call gut feeling.

It seems we keep an unconscious record – a running tally – of the positive and negative messages associated with candidates or parties, and then draw on these to make a choice on polling day.

This feels true. The website of the last British Election Study (www. bes2009-10.org) has some fascinating graphs showing heuristics in action. In terms of ranking the issues, anything to do with money dominated hugely at the last election, as one might expect during times of intergalactic economic meltdown. Among topics rated as most important to voters, 'economy generally' rates 42 per cent, but if you add on government debt and unemployment, as both being issues affecting the money in people's pockets, you reach 61 per cent, with the next biggest issue being immigration – at 17 per cent.

So the biggest political issue at that time really was 'the economy, stupid'.

Another factor in some voters' decisions is the latest opinion polls. But how far can we trust the polls? And how accurate are they?

'Polls are usually accurate enough to inform people how the election is going,' says Dr Roger Mortimore, director of political analysis at pollsters Ipsos MORI. 'But they are not a form of magic – they certainly can't predict the election result to fractions of a percentage point, nor should anybody expect them to.

'They are sample surveys. We're trying to get a representative sample of people, but not everyone is prepared to take part, and if it happens that people who don't want to take part are more on one side than the other, it skews the poll. Even if they will take part, some people may be harder to contact, because of work, or kids – and again it could distort the results.'

It could also be that supporters of one party are less inclined to admit it, Mortimore says, and another big problem these days is knowing whether or not someone is actually going to vote at all.

'They may not even know themselves – we've got to guess which ones are going to vote and which ones are not. You've got to constantly keep an eye on these issues and be building corrections for them – it's a battle to keep up.' So while polls are rarely completely wrong about the outcome of an election, they are rarely completely right either.

So why bother with them at all? Apart from simple curiosity – 'the public wants to know what everyone else thinks. That desire for knowledge is not going to go away' – there is a strong democratic reason to publish polls, Mortimore says.

'With no polls, you would have to rely on what politicians claim

– and they would all say "we're massively ahead". It is essential for any proper democratic election that information is available to voters – they should have everything they want to know before they make a decision.'

It could also be argued that polls act to give voter feedback before it is too late, helping politicians know what people think of their plans and giving them a chance to change them before an election. So they could make politicians more responsive to voters' views even before they vote: a strongly democratic role.

When the day for making the decision finally arrives, not everyone is ready – or willing – to vote at all.

Here are the figures for the turnout at recent UK national and devolved elections.

UK Parliament

1997: 71.4 per cent

2001: 59.4 per cent

2005: 61.4 per cent

2010: 65.1 per cent

Scottish Parliament

1999: 58.2 per cent

2003: 49.4 per cent

2007: 51.7 per cent

2011: 50.4 per cent

Welsh Assembly

1999: 46.4 per cent

2003: 38.2 per cent

2007: 43.5 per cent

2011: 41.5 per cent

Northern Ireland Assembly
1998: 68.8 per cent
2003: 63.9 per cent
2007: 62.9 per cent
2011: 55.6 per cent

For a UK general election, we can see that the lowest turnout in recent years was in 2001, when less than two-thirds of all people entitled to vote – just 59.4 per cent – did vote.

This figure, in fact, was not just the lowest turnout in recent years but the lowest in a general election since 1918. The result was the election of a government which received 40.7 per cent of the vote, which translates as just 24.2 per cent of all people who could possibly have voted, once you take the low turnout into account.

In other words, less than fifteen years ago, a government was elected to run this country with positive votes of support from less than a quarter of voters. This hardly seems representative, which is why turn-out matters.

It's true that the turnout in elections since 2001 has been a bit higher – but not by that much, and so far it has still always remained below two-thirds of the UK's registered voters.

For the devolved bodies the picture is, on the whole, even worse. Even in Northern Ireland, where political passions run so high, turnout at the most recent election to the devolved Assembly in 2011 dropped to 55.6 per cent from a high of almost 70 per cent when elections were first held in 1998. The turnout figure for Scottish Parliament elections only just topped 50 per cent in 2001 and has been hovering around the 50 per cent mark for the last three votes; while Welsh Assembly turnout has never hit 50 per cent, reaching just 41.5 per cent in 2011 and in 2003 clocking in at not much more than a third of the electorate. Local and European elections also suffer from low turnouts (about 31 per cent for UK council elections in 2013 and about 35 per cent for the UK European elections in 2009).

Research suggests there are many factors why some people do not vote. Partly, it is linked to how close an election is – if the outcome seems clear, fewer people will vote, which makes a certain kind of sense. But turnout also varies by age, gender, ethnicity, earnings and education. In general, older, affluent and more educated people are more likely to register and to vote.

The fact that turnout is significantly lower among young people is a major concern. Although they may engage with their communities in other ways, many young people do not feel as strongly as older people that it is their civic duty to vote. The worry is that these habits may then be ingrained for the rest of their lives.

Another huge concern is that turnout may be lower in less affluent areas. According to Colin Rallings, politics professor at the University of Plymouth, this pattern has worsened in recent decades.

'If you go back 40 or 50 years, the general election turnout in poorer areas of cities like Liverpool would be much the same as in more affluent parts of areas like Surrey. Now the turnout in Liverpool is only half the level it is in Surrey. The social problems now are no different to what they were then, so why the spiral down in engagement?

'It seems to me that this is a classic function of decline of community, and anti-politics feeling – people thinking "what have they ever done for me, they're all the same?"'

These feelings are genuine, but as voting is linked to social influence – since the people in charge might sometimes pay more attention to the groups of people who vote – the result, ironically, could be a further blow to people's aspirations of building a fairer society.

At some English local elections new voting methods have been tested, such as electronic voting or all-postal voting, to see if turnout could be boosted that way, and other suggestions have included opening polling stations at the weekend.

On the whole, however, despite many non-voters in all parts of the UK previously saying they were 'too busy to vote', such trials have had mixed results and seem to show that new methods of voting mainly just make it easier for people who would have voted anyway. It seems it is already easy enough to vote, if you want to. The problem – which we will return to at the end of this book – is that too many of us do not want to.

For those of us who *have* made up our mind to vote, most will then visit a polling station. The location of these places – often a dusty church hall or school gym – is decided in each area by a Returning Officer, an official appointed by each local authority to run elections.

The Returning Officer post is often assigned to a council manager such as the chief executive – there is no standard national way of doing this – and any deputies or helpers they might appoint. In carrying out these roles the officers are not responsible to the council, they are part of a national system, accountable only through the courts. The result, says John Turner, chief executive of the Association of Electoral Administrators, is 'inordinately messy'. With council officials often having to wear two or three hats at once, it could even be that conflicts of interest arise, particularly given that the costs of local elections are funded by the councils.

'Because the local authority who has appointed these officers is re-sponsible for all the costs the officers say are necessary for electoral process, if it comes to priorities, with their council hat on, they might decide that filling up holes in the road or children's services are more important.'

Another issue for concern is the inaccessibility of many polling stations to wheelchair users and other disabled people. According to a report by the Equalities and Human Rights Commission, most polling stations at the last election presented at least one significant access barrier to disabled people.

The Electoral Commission offers guidance on all such issues, but the problem is it does not have strong enough powers to ensure that these guidelines are followed by each council, Turner says. All in all, he feels the whole system is long overdue for a check-up.

'I wouldn't want to pre-judge what would come out of it, but our electoral system needs examination and discussion. Most of these issues have not been addressed since 1872, so it's about time those responsible sit down and decide whether the system we have is still appropriate.'

However the vote is taken, at the close of polling comes the moment it has all been about: the count.

All ballot boxes are sealed and escorted to a big room at the local town hall where the counting staff are ready and waiting. The seals are cut, the papers tipped out and the counting can begin, overseen by another group of people clustered around the outside: the 'counting agents' – observers appointed by the candidates and parties to keep an eye on everything that happens.

First the counters sift the ballots into rough piles and then the detailed count will take place, with verified votes sorted into bundles of fifty and placed on a rack. Observers are not allowed to touch the ballots but can call out 'Stop' at any time if they see anything they don't like, and ask for checks to take place.

If it is unclear what the marks made on a particular ballot paper might mean, the Returning Officer will consult the candidates' agents to discuss which papers will be called 'spoiled' and discarded, and which can be accepted as a vote. When all papers have been counted, the Returning Officer tells the agents the result they would like to declare and asks if they are happy with it. At this stage, if it is close, the agents can ask for a full or partial recount, which the Returning Officer can accept or reject. Finally comes the moment we see on TV, where the candidates stand up and hear the results read out, pretending to be surprised – because by this stage, they mostly already know.

Once a result has been called, a candidate or a certain number of voters can challenge it in the High Court. The most usual reason for legal challenge is if the margin of victory is very small and there were a larger number of disputed ballots; but challenges can also be made on issues such as the legality of a campaign (if someone may have spent over their limit, for example).

The process of counting votes is different under different voting systems, and a range of systems is now used in the UK.

In general elections, the system used is 'first past the post' (FPTP), where the candidate who gains more votes than anyone else is the winner in each constituency. Nationally, the new government is then formed either by any party gaining a majority of parliamentary seats or, if no one has a majority, by any group of parties who can agree to share power, or by the biggest minority party, if the others agree to allow it.

Since it is so hard for smaller parties, even third parties, ever to win anything at all, FPTP tends to lead to a two-party system, and its supporters say to strong government – winner takes all. Others point out, however, that it leads to a lot of people in each constituency feeling their vote is wasted, and it often does not end up with the number of seats won by each party being closely connected to the proportion of votes it receives nationally. Instead, because it is made of many small individual races, it can reward parties who have support concentrated in certain areas and give nothing to parties who have low levels of support spread around many places.

In the 2010 general election, for example, the Conservative Party won a 36 per cent share of the votes, but 47 per cent of the seats; Labour won 29 per cent of votes, but about 40 per cent of seats; the Lib Dems won 23 per cent of votes, but 9 per cent of seats; and other parties won 12 per cent of votes, but 4 per cent of seats.

Council elections in England and Wales also use FPTP. However, council elections in Northern Ireland and Scotland, all the UK devolved bodies, the London assembly, votes for elected mayors in other cities, many political party leadership elections and the European Parliament elections all use other systems, such as alternative vote (AV) or single transferable vote (STV) – and many of these systems were set up or approved by the Westminster Parliament. (The Scottish system is actually a 'mixed member' system, combining FPTP for constituency members with additional members elected across larger regions by a party list system to make the composition of the Parliament more proportionate.

Each voter has two votes: one for the constituency and one for the region.) In fact, there are hundreds of voting systems possible, many designed to reflect closely the proportion of voters for each party in the number of seats – hence you might hear people speak about 'proportional representation' or PR.

Details of all the UK systems can be found on the Electoral Commission website, but let's have a closer look at one of them as an example: the system used for Northern Ireland Assembly elections, which is a type of PR known as the single transferable vote (STV).

For these elections, the same eighteen constituency areas are used as for Westminster elections in Northern Ireland, but with six Assembly members elected for each. Voters mark preferences for their candidates – first choice, second choice and so on to as many choices as they want.

Counting then happens in stages. In the first stage, a 'quota' is worked out according to an equation based on the number of votes cast and the number of seats to be won, and all candidates who receive enough first-preference votes to exceed the quota are elected. If there are fewer than six elected, all excess votes of the elected candidates are transferred to their second preferences. Once again, anyone over the quota is elected. In third and subsequent rounds, the candidates with the least numbers of votes are eliminated one by one, and their supporters' other preferences reallocated.

This is a complicated process – but the final results are much more proportionate to people's votes. If we look at the top four represented parties in the Northern Ireland Assembly from 2011, for example, we find the Democratic Unionist Party won 35.2 per cent of the seats on offer with 30.0 per cent of the vote; Sinn Féin won 26.9 per cent of the seats with 26.9 per cent of the vote; the Ulster Unionist Party won 14.8 per cent of the seats with 13.2 per cent of the votes; and the SDLP won 13.0 per cent of seats with 14.2 per cent of votes. Clearly, this is much more proportionate than the Westminster result listed above – though with such a complex system, the votes can take up to two days to count.

One argument often used against proportional representation is that it would make hung parliaments far more common. Coalition government could become the norm and, it is said, this tends to be weak, with minor parties potentially becoming all-powerful 'kingmakers'. Because the terms of a coalition are not known before an election either, opponents argue that 'no one voted for it'.

On the other hand, supporters of PR see these same features as strengths: coalition governments can be seen as representing a genuine majority and genuine negotiated compromise. They also point out that the UK's devolved bodies seem to be working fine.

But when the UK was offered a referendum on partial voting reform – a move to the 'alternative vote' (AV) system for Westminster elections – it was firmly rejected, by 68 per cent. Under AV, voters mark preferences in order, as many as they like. Any candidate winning more than 50 per cent of votes is elected straight away; otherwise, the candidate receiving the least votes is eliminated and their second preferences reallocated. The process continues until one person wins more than 50 per cent of votes. The AV system is not as proportionate as multi-member systems, because small parties are not given much more of a chance. It can also work in confusing ways, because after a while people's votes are counted only if they continue to express many preferences, but it can improve proportionality for bigger parties. Understanding the exact way the system works is not easy, and in the end voters decided to stick with what they have. But with other systems working well for so many UK elections outside Westminster, we have not heard the last of the calls for voting reform.

Voting in a democracy does not just relate to national, devolved or local elections. As we have just seen, there is another kind of vote which comes up from time to time and could begin to play an even larger role in UK democracy, especially locally – the referendum.

A referendum is a vote when everyone is asked to decide on a single issue. Nationally, across the UK, these have not taken place very often – surprisingly, in fact, just twice. The first time was in 1975, when a strong majority (67 per cent) voted in favour of Britain's membership of the then European Economic Community; and the second in May 2011, when voters rejected the alternative vote system. Two referendums each have also been held in Northern Ireland, Scotland and Wales on matters of peace, sovereignty and devolution and a third is set to be held in Scotland on independence – so again, they are quite rare at that level.

At local government level, however, such votes are on the increase: an Edinburgh-wide city referendum a few years ago rejected a city-centre congestion charge scheme; similar exercises in Croydon, Milton Keynes and Bristol invited all residents to vote for or against council-tax increases (two for, one against); and a vote in Aberdeen approved a city-centre redesign plan. In London and many other cities in England and Wales, referendums have also been held on whether or not to introduce directly elected mayors.

In England and Wales, referendums on whether to introduce a directly elected mayor can be triggered by gathering signatures on a petition (a power introduced by the Local Government Act 2000); the same process can also be used to trigger a referendum to remove the post. The Localism Act 2011 has also introduced a requirement for councils to hold referendums on council-tax increases where these are deemed to be 'excessive', and on citizen-led neighbourhood development plans.

Matt Qvortrup, senior politics lecturer at Cranfield University, says referendums can play a useful role on major issues.

'It is perfectly possible to be a Lib Dem but not be in favour of the euro, or a Conservative and in favour – so a referendum on a subject like that gives you an extra opportunity to have your cake and eat it. It's a corrective opportunity.'

For cost reasons alone, however, there is a limit to how often they can be held, Qvortrup says, so 'they are not a panacea. But they are a good idea to have on issues that are really contentious, like a political safety valve.'

In the end, whatever the kind of election being fought, non-voters run the risk of making themselves invisible: they write themselves out of the scene.

And anyone who does not vote in any election should consider another point, too. How would you feel if someone came along tomorrow and said you were no longer allowed to vote, even if you wanted to? Would your vote seem more precious then? The truth is, it is just as precious now.

Chapter 3

Party time

With the election getting tight, everyone
was chasing the looney vote.

Government in Britain is party government. The leaders of parties – elected by members of those parties, not by the public – become the UK's Prime Ministers and First Ministers. Party policies set the programme for government, and party loyalties help to hold a government together.

But what is a party?

It is not a charity. It is not a company. In fact, it is not a legally incorporated body of any kind. It is simply a group of people working together voluntarily, with rules they draw up on how they decide their policies, how they pick their officials and leaders, and how any local branches relate to the national organization.

If a party wants to run for election, however – and hard as it can be to believe, that is the point of most of them – they must register with the Electoral Commission according to rules set out in the Political Parties, Elections and Referendums Act 2000. And once they are registered, parties must follow strict rules for financial management, funding and campaigning.

So a political party is any group which registers itself as such.

Anyone can become a member of any party as well, subject to each party's particular rules for membership (for example, most parties do not like it if you join another party as well, though this is not illegal). Once you are a member, you have the same rights as any other member.

A 'first past the post' election system such as the one used for the UK

Parliament tends to lead to two parties becoming bigger than the others, as smaller ones have a disproportionately small chance of winning any seats at all. That has been the case in the House of Commons for some time: from the late seventeenth century to the mid-nineteenth century, the Tories swapped places in and out of power with the more reforming Whigs; then the Tories became the Conservative Party and the Whigs became the Liberal Party, but they carried on swapping places. In the early twentieth century, the rise of the Labour movement led to the Conservatives and Labour becoming the two parties of alternating power, with the Liberal Party, now the Liberal Democrats, occupying a distant third place. At the time of writing, the UK has a rare Coalition government formed of the Conservatives and the Liberal Democrats, though the Liberal Democrats remain much smaller nationally in terms of Westminster seats than the main two parties. A fourth party, the UK Independence Party, is also now on the rise but while it may rise high in some areas, third or fourth place seems the highest it can hope for overall, nationally.

In the parliaments and assemblies of Scotland and Wales, devolved groups of the main UK national parties still play a major role. But the drive for ever greater devolution or independence since the early twentieth century has also seen the rise to power of the centre-left Scottish National Party (founded 1934) and Plaid Cymru, the Party of Wales (founded 1925).

As for Northern Ireland, its political parties have evolved out of the region's own unique, disputed place in the UK, balanced between the nationalist community, which views any partitioning of Ireland as illegitimate, and the unionist community, which wants just as passionately to stay part of the UK.

The main unionist parties are the Democratic Unionist Party and the Ulster Unionist Party; the main nationalist parties are Sinn Féin and the Social Democratic and Labour Party. The Alliance Party is a non-sectarian party spanning both camps. Traditionally, the UUP has had links with the Conservative Party, the SDLP with the

Labour Party, and the Alliance with the Liberal Democrats, though all remained as separate parties. In recent years, however, there have been moves to strengthen the devolved arm of the national UK-wide Conservative Party – separate from the UUP – and to create a devolved arm of the UK-wide Labour Party in Northern Ireland for the first time separately from the SDLP, at least to fight local government and Northern Ireland Assembly elections. But the political map remains much more complex and sensitive in Northern Ireland than in the rest of the UK.

Several other smaller parties have enjoyed at least some electoral success across the UK in recent years, including the various devolved arms of the Green Party.

As we have already noted, another party which appears to be on the rise is the UK Independence Party (UKIP), which describes itself as a 'libertarian, non-racist party seeking Britain's withdrawal from the European Union'. Until recently, UKIP had paradoxically achieved most of its electoral success in the European Parliament. However, the party has now also begun to make major breakthroughs in local government, and may continue to grow while the development of the European Union remains such a contentious issue in the UK – an issue we will come back to later in this book.

Overall, at the time of writing there were seventeen parties with at least some representation in the House of Commons or a UK devolved body, and about 450 parties in total on the Electoral Commission register, including all the minor, fringe, protest and independent parties.

Most people who have stayed up late to watch election results have been grateful to some of these fringe parties for livening up a long night. Believe it or not, however, although we do have both Citizens for Undead Rights and Equality and the New Millennium Bean Party, there are a few restrictions on what parties can call themselves. Names are not allowed to mislead voters by being too similar to an existing party; and they can't be obscene, or (since 2000) longer than six words – so it would no longer be possible to register 1987's 'I Want to Drop a Blancmange

Down Terry Wogan's Y-Fronts Party', the name of which doubled as its only policy.

You don't have to be in a party to run for election, but without party registration people can only run either as independent candidates, or as candidates without any description or party emblem on the ballot paper at all – just their own name.

An important reason for party registration is that it helps to track how money – and whose money – is spent in politics, especially on campaigning. The law sets limits on campaign spending by registered parties and rules about donations; and it requires all parties to submit accounts.

The Electoral Commission website holds details of every party that has fielded a candidate for the past ten years or so, along with their accounts.

Accounts hold a lot more interesting information than simply profit and loss – they can also be used to gather clues about important facts, such as size of party membership, its structure and election record. Accounts filed after the last general election for the Fancy Dress Party, for example, show it stood one candidate, in Dartford. The party boasts a proud history dating back to 1979, when it came up with the idea of reducing unemployment figures by using a smaller font size. This policy proved so popular it was later transferred to crime figures, and its potential application seems very wide indeed.

The accounts pick up the story: 'At the election of 6 May we polled fewer votes than expected [207] and came last of all six contenders at Dartford. The rest of the year was spent fundraising to re-fill the Partys [sic] depleted Purse. At Christmas Alan Munro was voted best Dame for the second year. Total funds remaining: £72.73.'

Accounts of larger parties hold details that are almost as fascinating.

For example, the accounts filed after the last election (for the year ended 2010) by Plaid Cymru detail what campaigning activity was undertaken at all levels – local, Welsh Assembly and Westminster, with income and spending broken down into accounting units by geographical area, as they are for all the major parties.

This leads the party to speculate why local party groupings in some areas seem so much more efficient than others. In a report attached to the accounts, it says: 'we must be in a position to understand why constituencies with similar memberships have such widely varying financial performance. Some contribute generously to the national party and can maintain effective local year-round campaigning. Others, in areas of electoral strength, do not have the financial capacity to fight effective electoral campaigns'.

So the accounts hold a lot of interesting detail, including some on membership. Parties are not required to publish membership numbers, although many do. Membership figures published are not checked, however, and are notoriously unreliable. But parties do publish exactly how much money is raised from membership fees and subscriptions, so better estimates can be made.

More on party membership levels – and how they are plummeting – in a little while. But first – why do people join a political party?

Many people sign up because they want to support a party in its battle to win elections, to help them stay in power or – more often – to help get them into power. Most often, therefore, party activity is local activity: door to door, street to street.

Often people start to help a party informally, delivering leaflets or stuffing envelopes to help a friend without actually joining up; after that, they might be asked to join.

'Parties always need people, and you never get paid, so they are always desperately pleased to see anyone who volunteers to help,' says one local activist. 'It gives you a local community to join, which isn't a niche interest group because politics gives you everything to talk about. It's a place to meet other people, and do something useful. So it can be a bit of a refuge for the lonely. But it becomes a vocation.'

Though it is a very important part of what they do, parties are not just about fighting elections – they also support their councillors and national politicians once they are elected, and they support the national or devolved government or opposition. Between elections, parties also campaign on particular issues: the health service, for example, or clean energy.

The fact that parties are staffed largely by volunteers is both a strength and a weakness. It gives them a democratic legitimacy, connecting them to ordinary people – anyone can join in. But it also means a lot of hard work must be done by people who are not being paid. And when there are local council elections, campaigns are fought in every ward – a huge amount of work. 'The fact we are driven by volunteers causes a lot of problems because in an election, people who contact the local party expect us to reply quickly,' one local campaigner says. The larger parties can sometimes afford to hire people for certain key jobs, such as designing leaflets or building websites, but all are over-stretched. More volunteers are always needed.

Apart from campaigning, local branches play an important role within parties in connecting national representatives with their local grassroots – and hence with their voters. When a national, regional or devolved party makes policy, it will consult with local branches. These days, the web is an important tool for party consultation, with local and national activists swapping ideas through huge networks of websites and blogs that have no central party control but are vital communication tools.

Lord Toby Harris, a past holder of many local and national posts within the Labour Party, including its National Policy Forum, says officials at the centre do try to pay attention to messages from local branches, but there is a limit to how far they can respond.

'It is certainly true that if many constituencies are saying "x" is important, the chances are that will be recognized somewhere in the next policy document. Any party leader – or potential future leader – is always going to try to take local views into account.

'On the other hand, it would be naive to say that eight pages of closely typed script from a remote outpost of the party with five members is going to be examined carefully by the Cabinet.'

One problem that often gives rise to tensions is the need for elected representatives at the centre to respond fast to situations which are the subject of complex negotiation on all sides, while local party members may see matters differently, Lord Harris says. There is rarely time for extensive consultation. But if rifts become too large between the centre and branches, as with any rifts within a party, the result is likely to be lost votes. 'Bitter experience has shown if you have a party constantly fighting with itself – and this is the same for all parties – voters don't like it, and assume you don't know what you're doing.'

With ever greater devolution within the UK, there is growing potential for internal party rifts along these lines, as devolved arms of national parties display their independence by taking different policy positions to their leaders, including on issues that are not supposed to be devolved, such as defence.

These tensions are not helped by the fact that many working in devolved branches of national parties feel the centre sometimes treats them as a bunch of 'glorified councillors'. As devolution beds in to central party machinery, however, and the national parties themselves devolve policymaking to each part of the UK, the situation is likely to improve.

All levels of a party come together – or collide – at their annual conference, usually held in the autumn, and most major parties now hold a smaller spring conference as well.

Local parties usually have an allocation of voting places – for delegates who will be allowed to vote on new policies or statements – and other members can attend at special rates. Non-members can sometimes attend as observers for a higher fee.

At conferences, party policy is debated, and sometimes it is made. On the whole, though, the larger the party and the closer to power, the less meaningful an arena their conferences become for creating or scrapping policies.

The Liberal Democrats are one party which has developed a system whereby all policy is decided by the party's members, linked to their conference. Any local party or ten voting representatives can propose a policy motion to conference, and most of the motions at party conference come by this route. A consultation is held at conference, and a policy working group set up which will work for a year or two to develop a policy paper to be voted on at a future conference. If approved, it goes into the party's manifesto.

After the party's rise to national power as part of a Coalition government, however, the principle of member policy-creation was severely tested by the need for the party's leadership to negotiate a Coalition Agreement with the Conservatives in a relatively short space of time.

'Being in government means several things,' says Mary Reid, the former Liberal Democrat mayor of a London borough who has sat on national policy committees for the party. 'Ministers are bound by collective responsibility in Cabinet, and the government also has to develop responses to things on the hoof. So there has been some pretty robust debate about what is the role of members now in policymaking.' For the moment, this problem has been tackled by inviting party representatives to vote to approve the Coalition Agreement, which they did.

Whether or not policy can be made, however, party members at conference can find ways of making their views known on issues they feel strongly about, and the events bring together activists at all levels of the party from all areas.

The big party conferences last several days, and they are long days, packed with sessions and meetings from breakfast until late at night. You have to like politics to survive them, but for those that do they represent a fantastic opportunity to talk to activists, hear top politicians make speeches live, and get wildly drunk, sometimes all at the same time.

Local party activism is also often the first step in a political career. Many councillors, MPs and members of devolved bodies have started out on the front line, practising their trade by making speeches in the running for local party chair, secretary or treasurer.

Local party positions might be uncontested; or they might require people to be nominated, submit statements and make speeches to local members as part of an election process. Prospective candidates to be local councillors are usually interviewed for suitability by an appointments panel, often with some oversight or participation by the national party. For national MP or devolved body candidates, the process will be even tougher, with larger selection committees, and the wider party machinery will definitely be keen to have a say: while local parties are fiercely protective of their right to choose the candidates they want, the centre may want to approve shortlists, suggest their own potential candidates, and check that the election processes are in line with national policy. In the end, however, ownership of the process will be local, as it should be in picking a local representative.

The ultimate internal party elections come when a new party leader is elected. The process for doing this varies from party to party, but mostly ranges from a vote of the whole party membership to some combination of vote by a party's elected politicians and its members. Ordinary party members do always have an important say in the choice of party leader, if not always a complete say, and this is another reason why many people join a party in the first place.

Local party members also play a role in holding their politicians to account once they have been deserving, skilful or lucky enough to be elected to power. Traditionally, UK constituency branches will hold meetings once a month and if the party has an MP elected at that time, they will usually come along to report on their recent activities and be quizzed on party policy, and whether or not they support it. When national policies are unpopular, these can be lively sessions.

One recurring way that political parties make the news in a negative way is through rows about funding. As organizations which need to raise large amounts for campaigning and advertising, money is always desperately needed.

By law, people must be on the electoral register to make a donation or subscription payment to a UK political party of more than £500, and any donation of more than £7,500 must be reported to the Electoral Commission, which publishes the details.

Scandals break regularly, however, usually after party fundraisers are secretly taped by journalists promising all sorts of access to top politicians for cash. They are not supposed to promise this access, but some people will always hope for it, so the temptation to promise it is strong as parties fight to secure donations. Some donors might just want to feel they are hobnobbing with powerful people; others might have more shadowy motives and hope directly to pressure politicians to alter policies in ways that could benefit them. But as money is always short, those seeking funding for their parties may not ask too many questions about why people are donating.

Although all parties have long agreed this area needs reform, the process has understandably been slow since no-one wants to turn down money while their political opponents carry on spending. In 2014, however, major changes are underway after the Labour Party approved reforms of funding links with the trade unions. This move caught many observers by surprise as there is a real funding risk for Labour. Since its inception, the Labour Party has drawn large amounts of funding – more than £10 million a year in recent years – from the trade unions. Some fifteen trade unions have been affiliated to Labour 'en masse' by their leadership, bringing about 3 million people into the Labour Party as affiliated members. Affiliated unions have a special relationship with the party, receiving seats on its national executive and some other voting powers.

Although individual members of any union had already been able to opt out of donating to the union's political fund – the pot of money out of which party donations have to come – most did not. Unions are also free to donate to any party they like and to undertake other political activity, as long as their members can opt out. In practice, however, almost all union party funding flows to Labour.

In reforms announced in 2014 and being phased in over five years, however, every union member will now have to opt in both to the union's general political fund – which can still be used however the leadership wants – and to a separate paying affiliation with Labour, which would give them affiliated membership and an individual vote in party leadership races.

Some party members fear that this could lead to Labour losing more than 10% of its annual funding, though the eventual results are hard to predict as unions might continue to back Labour strongly from their central funds; and other sources might be found.

The Conservative Party, by contrast, receives the biggest chunk of its donations from corporate sources, particularly from the financial sector – more than £10 million in 2010, comparable to Labour's union funding. This source could also be under threat however, with Labour pushing for limits on donations from individual organisations which would hit the Conservatives hardest.

Further reform is likely to be a trade-off between limiting the size of individual donations, more reforms to the rules on trade-union support and possibly using more public money to fund political parties.

But whatever happens, these problems will never go away completely. Parties will always need funding, and will work to maximize funds within whatever boundaries are in place. This means rules will always be stretched, and controversy will never disappear.

One thing that would make it easier for all parties, however, would be if their memberships were bigger, so they could gain more money from ordinary members paying their subscriptions every year. Despite the fact these are not that large – typically somewhere between £15 and £40 a year, or roughly the price of one pint of beer a month – this is not looking likely at the moment.

With the significant exception in recent years of the Scottish National Party and Plaid Cymru, most of the larger UK political parties have watched their members steadily drop away for the past fifty years or more.

In the late 1950s and early 1960s, more than 3 million people across the UK (more than 9 per cent of the electorate) were members of a political party. By the late 1980s, membership levels had fallen to around half that number and by 2013 they had dropped to about half a million in total, excluding affiliated memberships through the trade unions. For both the largest two parties, Labour and the Conservatives, membership (again excluding affiliates) has dropped below 200,000 – still enough to raise a few million pounds each, but less than a sixth of their total funding. Labour's trade union reforms might boost its numbers of individual members, but they will still just be 'affiliates', paying much less than full members.

So total UK party membership today represents a little over 1 per cent of the electorate – and falling. As BBC reporter Brian Wheeler wrote in 2011, there were by then already 'more members of the Caravan Club . . . than of all Britain's political parties put together.'

There have been blips in the long-term trend: often when a party is in opposition, membership figures rise as its supporters feel they need to do more to bring their party back into power; but generally they fall away again. Smaller parties such as the UK Independence Party and the Green Party often show a surge as well when a key issue is in the news, but in general membership of political parties does not seem to be considered important by most people in modern Britain.

The UK is not unusual in this: most European democracies have experienced a drop in party membership along a similar timescale. The UK situation does seem to be worse than in most other countries, however. According to a 2011 paper 'Going, going . . . gone? The decline of party membership in contemporary Europe', published by Ingrid van Biezen, Peter Mair and Thomas Poguntke in the *European Journal of Political Research*, the UK was placed 25th out of 27 for party-membership levels as a percentage of electorate, at 1.21 per cent. The only two countries with lower party-membership levels were Poland and Latvia, both relatively new democracies.

Does this matter? Other reports have shown that, despite falling memberships, the bigger parties have been able to hold their revenues steady by raising membership fees, changing membership structures or raising money in other ways – though this again poses the question of what is the best way of funding political parties.

It might be, too, that fewer people have strong lifelong links with parties these days – they vote for different parties at different elections, so why should they join one? And why is that a problem? On the other hand, the core vote for all parties is surely still much larger than their membership – and it could be made easier for people to join one party and then switch to another, in the same way that we might switch gas or electricity providers.

Of course, people can be politically active in many other ways, and can also support and help a party without joining. But overall, it cannot be a good thing for political parties in a major democracy to have small memberships. As parties make the policies we all have to live by, and elect the representatives and the leaders who lead us all, it must be the case that the bigger the membership of any party, and the more active that membership is, the healthier the party and the better our politicians will be.

It is members, not just votes, that provide parties with democratic strength, creating broad-based organizations that can govern everyone, not small special-interest groups that are pushing for narrow goals.

If people are not joining, it must be the case that they simply can't see the value in paying even a small sum to support any party.

Could anything change their minds?

The academics Patrick Seyd and Paul Whiteley have published research which suggests that, with the right incentives to join, the decline in membership could be turned around. Clearly for this to happen, however, people would need to feel they were gaining valuable benefits from joining.

Parties must now consider how to make this value clear. Could local meetings be made more interesting, for example? (At the moment, most people would probably prefer to go to the pub – or anywhere else for that matter.) Could other membership benefits be better? Online networks? News services?

Political parties are a key part of democracy in the UK, but if they are ever to be mass movements once more, plugged into the hopes and energies of large numbers of ordinary people, they need to continue to listen, and to change.

Chapter 4

The House of Commons – into the bear pit

Once the candidates are chosen and the people have voted, the day of reckoning arrives: the successful candidates are elected, and overnight they become MPs.

New MPs have a lot to learn about the House of Commons and very little time in which to learn it. They are elected (often unexpectedly) on a Thursday and walk in wide-eyed the following Monday morning. At the last election, 227 of the 650 MPs elected – or just over a third of them – had not been elected before. And their work as a representative and supporter of everyone in their constituency starts on day one.

'When I was elected, I was given a laptop already set up with a log-in and official MP's email address – it all worked straight away,' says Stratford-on-Avon MP Nadhim Zahawi.

'Then you open the email box and there are already 800 emails sitting there saying: "I've been waiting for you to be elected – I need your help." You are also handed a big bag of post, and you realize you need to get your team together, quickly.'

There is no set structure to the life of an MP – every individual must work out a balance between constituency work and work in the House of Commons. New MPs will be briefed by more experienced colleagues and there is a learning centre for MPs' assistants and researchers to help them carry out urgent tasks such as running constituency surgeries. Nevertheless, some MPs feel more training could be offered to help them become more effective more quickly. In many areas of their work, it is sink or swim.

One major chunk of that work is examining and debating new laws the government wants to pass.

A proposal for a new law is called a Bill and once it is passed it becomes an Act of Parliament. A Bill can start its journey in either the House of Commons or the House of Lords, but either way it must usually be agreed on by both Houses before it is sent to the monarch for Royal Assent (a formality these days – see Chapter 8).

Bills pass through a few stages in each House, including a committee stage, where a group of particularly interested MPs or peers – or sometimes, in a committee of the whole House, all of them – debate and vote on possible amendments.

After all stages are complete, if the Bill started in the Commons it goes to the Lords for a similar process; and if it started in the Lords it goes to the Commons. If new amendments are passed, the Bill will go back to the House where it began, and can continue backwards and forwards in what is known as parliamentary 'ping-pong'.

As the elected chamber, the Commons does have powers to push its laws through Parliament whether the Lords like it or not, but most often politicians are keen to avoid a head-on battle and disagreements are sorted out by negotiation and compromise – unlike in ordinary ping-pong (we will look at this more closely in the next chapter).

In fact, any government's biggest enemy is time. With a huge amount to do and a limited amount of time in which to do it, it falls to one Cabinet minister – the Leader of the House of Commons – to draw up the business timetable.

Before the start of each annual parliamentary session, government departments put in bids for time to debate laws in their own areas, such as education or health. The government prioritizes the bids and creates a workable programme for the year ahead, to be written into the Queen's Speech – the programme read out word for word by the monarch ('My government will . . .'). Monarchs have long made this kind of speech – though in times gone by they used to write it as well.

Other days are set aside for government debates on key topical issues; Opposition debates; and debates on Private Members' Bills – proposals for laws brought in by randomly picked backbenchers (ordinary rank-and-file MPs who are not government ministers or Opposition spokespeople). Private Members' Bills usually peter out through lack of time, although they are sometimes passed with government support, and the Commons Procedure Committee has now recommended giving them more time and allocating them priority by level of support, rather than at random.

Typical enquiries can be put by MPs to the government every week in questions to ministers and to the Prime Minister – both in regular scheduled sessions and as 'Urgent Questions', which the Speaker can allow as necessary. These did not used to be granted more than a few times a year, but the current Speaker John Bercow has greatly increased the use of Urgent Questions as a way for Parliament to keep the government on its toes.

For many people, however, it is the Wednesday afternoon Prime Minister's Questions (PMQs) – as seen on the news – which forms their image of the Commons. MPs jeer and bellow across the wood-panelled chamber. The Speaker's chair is the focal point at the far end, with the Prime Minister (to the left) and leader of the Opposition (to the right) shouting to make themselves heard over a disembodied roar like a jumbo jet crash-landing in a safari park. The Speaker tries to calm everyone down: 'Order, order. Order!' Sometimes the exchange is worth hearing over the din, sometimes not – but PMQs serves the purpose of putting the Prime Minister on the spot and giving the leader of the Opposition a chance to make strong attacks.

Most government Bills do eventually pass, partly because the Opposition – while sometimes trying to force concessions – accepts it is basically right to let an elected government govern.

But it is always vital for the Opposition to criticize, attack, expose weak arguments and say what it would do differently, because it is always creating the basis for a possible alternative government for people to choose in future. We might sometimes be irritated by what seems like automatic criticism of everything the government does by the party which lost the election – but that is its job.

The constitutional expert Sir Ivor Jennings once wrote: 'If there be no Opposition, there is no democracy'. Tyrants understand this, which is why they spend so much time persecuting their critics. Argument for the sake of it is an absolute necessity, because it is never just for the sake of it. Disagreement and argument, happening in a controlled way, are essential to democracy. Democracy could be partly defined as a way of handling disagreement. We must never look at a row or disagreement as a sign that democracy is not working. It is the opposite: a sign of health, a sign of life.

Trying to referee all this is the Speaker, the highest authority in the House of Commons. In a debate, the Speaker is in absolute charge. When he or she stands up, the MP speaking must immediately sit down.

In addition, there are strict limits to parliamentary language and conduct. If an MP implies that a colleague is dishonourable or drunk, he or she may be thrown out – the MP who made the observation, that is, not the one accused. Debating rules enforced by the Speaker include ensuring all contributions are relevant and the proper use of 'Hear, hear' (when someone has finished a sentence, and not before). The rules are all covered in the Speaker's bible, 'Erskine May', named after its original author, nineteenth-century House of Commons clerk Thomas Erskine May. It is kept updated under the title *Parliamentary Practice*. Versions can be bought online, though the new ones are expensive.

MPs (and Lords) are not subject to various laws such as slander when they speak in Parliament – an important rule, known as Parliamentary Privilege, to ensure they are not restricted in their debates. But it is important for the reputation of Parliament that this 'super freedom of speech' is used for a purpose. The naming in 2011 by MP John Hemming of the footballer Ryan Giggs as the holder of a court injunction banning mention of his private life, for example, led to widespread bafflement as to why the case could not have been discussed in general terms – without naming Giggs. Perhaps Hemming did it simply because he could: it's why some people climb Everest.

As the two most powerful forces in the Commons, the Speaker and the government (or its ministers) are often at loggerheads with each other, though the Speaker has the upper hand. If ordered to sit down, even the Prime Minister can do little about it beyond glaring at his tormentor with what have been described as 'Paddington Bear hard stares'.

The Speaker's office will also decide who will be able to speak in any particular debate, and for how long – as well as trying to make sure people stick to their time slots, often an extremely hard task.

Experienced MPs learn to make some of the points they want to make not through their own speeches but by intervening during ministers' speeches, says the former Labour MP Derek Wyatt. Wyatt welcomed the introduction in 2001 of short debates initiated by backbenchers in the separate chamber of Westminster Hall, though he says these are too short (up to an hour and a half) and too easily ignored by ministers. 'Have there been more than a couple of Westminster Hall debates that have made news?'

The introduction of Westminster Hall debates, however, as well as backbench debate days whose topics are decided on by a new Backbench Business Committee, show that changes can and are made to the way Parliament works. Despite the impression that much around Parliament is set in stone, reform is constantly taking place, chip by chip.

One feature of Parliament that is constant, however, is that it is a place for debate. Proposals for new laws are debated for their general principles and their detail by MPs, who suggest their own ways of making the new law better by proposing amendments to it. It is by debating possible amendments to the laws – possible changes and improvements – that MPs can examine in detail exactly how good the laws are in the first place.

For each Bill, a public Bill committee is set up, whose members are all backbench MPs. The committee can interview people or organizations to discuss the implications of the Bill before debating possible amendments. This is the 'committee stage' of the Bill.

Often, debates will end with general agreement, but where an amendment to a Bill is disputed, or in other cases where there is disagreement and a vote is needed, the Speaker first asks those in favour to say 'Aye', those against 'No'. If the result is not a clear 'Aye' (in which case 'the Ayes have it'), or 'No' ('the Noes have it'), then a vote – or 'division' – is called.

A division is so called because MPs must physically divide into two groups and walk into two small rooms on either side of a door hidden behind the Speaker's chair – the Aye lobby and the No lobby. They must do this in person, so when a division is called, bells ring in all rooms in Parliament, nearby parliamentary office buildings and even some local restaurants and pubs, informing members they have eight minutes to dash to the chamber before the doors are locked. Occasionally the bells malfunction, forcing clerks to stick their heads round the doors of meeting rooms and yell 'Division!'

One quirk of the parliamentary division system is that it does not allow for abstention. Everybody must vote yes or no – or not turn up to vote, in which case it is not clear if they have abstained or are simply unwell, or have strayed out of running distance.

The voting system itself has caused much debate. When Britain's first Green MP Caroline Lucas was elected in 2010, for example, she was surprised at the amount of time spent on voting, working out that it eats up about six weeks of each MP's time over a five-year Parliament. She suggested it would be better to use an electronic system – such as the ones used in the Scottish Parliament, the Welsh Assembly or the European Parliament. MPs would still have to be present to vote electronically, but votes would be quicker and perhaps taken in groups.

'My office is six or seven minutes away from the chamber, and I am often in meetings when the division bell rings,' Lucas says. 'It is disrespectful to the people in your meeting and an enormous waste of time that you have to dash out for 15 minutes with no warning. Six votes in the current system take an hour and a half – but six votes electronically take a minute and a half.'

Many MPs disagree, however, saying the division process, where members of all kinds can meet and mingle, are valuable opportunities to chat with ministers – who (they say) can be almost impossible to get hold of in any other way.

Whatever the process, voting on most issues in Parliament, including to pass or to amend laws, is not usually the subject of MPs' personal choice: more often than not there is a party line along which they will vote. They know what the party line is on each vote, and how strongly their party would like them to follow it, through the process known as 'whipping'.

Before each session, MPs in the main parties will receive a letter from their whips' office with voting instructions underlined once, twice or three times: known as a one-, two- or three-line whip. The more lines there are, the more a party wants their MPs to vote that way.

Career punishments are sometimes handed out to MPs who defy the whip, and MPs who want to become ministers one day are advised not to rebel too often, if at all. But party whipping – which also exists at devolved and even local government levels – does serve a democratic purpose, and arguably one which champions the rights of citizens. Because while people do like strong-minded MPs to fight their corner, they do not like splits within parties. If a party is split, what is its policy, and how can you vote for it? And if you have already voted for a government, is it not fair that the government can vote through what it wants – most of the time?

Sometimes, though, the rebels do win. If enough MPs feel very strongly that their own party has got it wrong, there is little the whips can do. Most governments experience a series of backbench rebellions in their lifetimes. When one is threatened, it is another part of the whips' job to convey messages from backbenchers back to the party leadership about ways they may have to compromise to restore calm.

Whips from different parties also talk to each other to help plan the parliamentary timetable. The idea most of the time is to try to agree a timetable which will allow the government to get its Bill and the Opposition to have enough time to debate key problem areas.

Another controversial area of Commons procedure is that of MPs' working hours.

Some say the need to work long hours is one reason why MPs are unrepresentative of the UK population. They certainly are unrepresentative, in gender terms, though matters have improved drastically since Westminster's first female MP was elected in 1918. Between the 1940s and the 1980s, the number of female MPs hovered around the 25–30 mark, climbing to 60 in 1992 and doubling to 120 in 1997. At the 2012 election, 145 female MPs were elected out of 650: but this is still only about 22 per cent, in a country where there are more women than men.

Late hours are often cited as deterring women with families, and also disabled people, from becoming MPs: although some mornings are free, and Fridays are usually set aside for MPs to work back in their constituencies, the Commons sits till 10.30 p.m. on Mondays, and sometimes even later.

On the other hand, there are many parliamentary breaks or 'recesses', when MPs can base themselves far more in their constituencies. In a typical session of a year, these can add up to twenty-one weeks, namely Whitsun (one week), Summer (six weeks), Conference Recess (four weeks), Christmas (four weeks), Half term (two weeks) and Easter (three weeks).

Supporters of the current system point out, too, that MPs who live a long way from London cannot get back to their families even after normal working hours, so they might as well work late and have long weekends in their constituencies.

Apart from debating new laws, the House of Commons plays a vital role in examining what the government – and any other part of UK society – is doing from day to day through 'select committees'.

There are currently about forty Commons select committees, made up of backbench MPs with an interest in a particular area. About half of them are set up to shadow and scrutinize the work of particular government departments, such as the Business, Innovation and Skills Committee, which shadows the department with the same name. Others cut across all departments, such as the Environmental Audit Committee, which considers how well government policies contribute to environmental protection; and the dreaded (by civil servants) Public Accounts Committee, which looks at how well government departments and other public bodies have been spending their money. There are House of Lords select committees as well, and a few joint Commons and Lords committees, such as one on human rights. The way committees are set up, and how they run, is managed by the House of Commons (and Lords) separately from the government: the Commons has a procedure committee, with its own standing orders, and changes to the way it works are often voted on by all MPs. It keeps itself fiercely independent from any one party or government.

So who decides who will sit on the committees? Membership of select committees used to be handed out by the party whips, as another tool of 'persuasion' for MPs to vote with their party. But this power – which was seen to cloud the proud independence of Parliament from government – has been taken away, and backbench MPs can now stand for membership of committees and be elected on to them by their colleagues. The governing party has a majority of members, but representatives are elected from other parties too.

Select committees can decide to hold inquiries into key topics, and publish reports, to which the government must respond. Some reports are debated in the Commons. The committees undertake scrutiny of all sorts of issues as they see fit. While the fact that they are dominated by MPs from the party in government will usually soften the tone of their final reports, their overall mixed membership does often lead to criticism of the government.

The requirement for a government to respond to select committee reports, the media attention they generate and the fact that they are nowadays viewable live on TV or online, all adds to their power. It makes good TV to see celebrities, bankers or media moguls cross-questioned, as sometimes happens. For some, the appearance of Rupert Murdoch before the Culture, Media and Sport Select Committee to give his views on phone hacking, for example, was the first time they realized you could watch committee proceedings live – and it made for riveting viewing. For others, the sight of comedian Russell Brand appearing before the Home Affairs Select Committee in a vest to discuss the decriminalization of drugs will live longer in the memory, for a variety of reasons (just search for it on YouTube). Committees might not always be so watchable, but their role is well publicized by such events.

Part of the power of select committee reports is that they become 'a matter of record', just like debates in the Commons chamber. When the government says in Parliament it plans to do something, every word is recorded, and examples of a minister saying one thing and doing another will be jumped on by the Opposition.

The official report of UK parliamentary debates is entitled (wait for it) *The Official Report*. It is also known as 'Hansard', after its first publisher Thomas Hansard. The 1947 debate quoted in this book's introduction, featuring Churchill's famous comment on democracy, and most other debates stretching back to 1802, can be read online thanks to the Hansard Digitisation Project (http://hansard.millbanksystems.com). More recent reports can be found (and searched) on the main Parliament website. It is all a matter of record: and now we all have access to it for free, unlike in the fairly recent days before the web when expensive printed copies of Hansard were all that existed.

As well as lawmaking, MPs have another vital democratic role: representing and helping everyone who lives in their constituencies, however they voted.

A 2011 report by Tobias Escher at the Oxford Internet Institute found email has become the most common way for people to contact their MPs, with each receiving on average 360 emails, 230 letters and 180 phone calls a week (and sometimes many more).

Though many do a lot of responding in person, MPs do not handle this work alone, with staff (usually different from their Westminster staff) to help them with constituency work. Fridays are MPs' main constituency days. So on Thursday evening MPs make the journey back to their constituencies, and on Fridays and over the weekend hold their open meetings or 'surgeries', visit local businesses or hospitals and do other constituency work.

MPs' surgeries are not for the faint-hearted. Often they are difficult and distressing and sometimes even dangerous, as people in all stages of desperation bring their problems to be solved. Sometimes they will have severe health problems and will bare their symptoms directly as to a doctor; at other times they may have just been made homeless and the housing office is closed for the weekend. Occasionally they might want to talk about national politics, but usually about local issues – planning, parking tickets, street-cleaning.

None of these issues is the direct responsibility of an MP, but the MP's office will over time build up a list of numbers of local officials, government ministers and civil servants in the departments handling health, education, benefits. They will phone these numbers and action will often then be taken, just because they are an MP. This is not a perfect way to run public services: but MPs do act as a valuable last resort for many people facing desperate struggles.

MPs will also try to represent the general interests of the people in their area in national debates and champion particular issues of importance to groups in their constituencies, such as soldiers or single families. Exactly how they do this is up to individual MPs. Some find the best way is not through parliamentary debates but by gaining publicity outside the House of Commons by working with charities or interest groups. Others prioritize their work with All-Party Parliamentary Groups (APPGs) – small groups led by MPs and peers of all political parties which have no official powers or funding but seek 'soft' influence on specific topics.

It sometimes seems that there is an all-party group for every topic in the known universe, and a few yet to be discovered: more than 600 in all, of which around 140 are country groups for links with other nations and the rest are subject groups, such as Beer, Bingo, Biomass, Boarding Schools, Body Image and Brass Bands – to name just a few of the Bs.

APPGs often provide MPs with briefings on key issues to help them take part in relevant debates. Many of the groups do valuable work to a high standard, filling in gaps that parliamentary researchers cannot reach; others overlap, however, with fifty or so in the area of health and care alone, for example.

Groups are often given free admin support by a charity, trade association or professional body, but sometimes there is involvement from a PR or lobbying company which might also be working for private clients. APPGs must declare donations they receive above £1,500 and state who provides support. So these links should be clear enough, but the accounts do not receive much scrutiny and this is an area where more light could usefully be shone.

MPs' own sources of support are declared in the Register of Members' Financial Interests, listing everything from jobs to newspaper columns, properties owned and sources of sponsorship. The register is a central part of a wider MPs' code of conduct, covering standards of honesty and integrity expected of members. As well as registering interests, MPs must declare them again when debating any relevant issue (for example if they rent out a property and are debating landlord behaviour).

When it comes to MPs' honesty, however, the biggest talking point of recent times – and one still bubbling on – is that of MPs' expenses. At a time when many people's views of politicians' motives and morals was already dim, the MPs' expenses scandal of 2009 triggered a frenzy of outrage from the public and the media.

Was this deserved?

MPs do need support with office, staff, travel and living expenses away from their constituencies, which will vary greatly: they could not simply be asked to pay all these costs out of their salaries, for example, since while a few do already live in London, others live as far away as the Scottish Highlands.

The old expenses system, however, had developed as a closed, hidden process under which all sorts of dubious claims were waved through in an unspoken pact between MPs (or some MPs), political parties, governments and the House of Commons authorities. Many members appear to have been encouraged to view the expenses system as a sort of 'salary top-up': all sorts of things could be claimed for, and it was all fair because it was all in a good cause – or so the thinking went. It had also become hard for MPs to raise their own salaries – understandably, this never looks good – so the expenses system was seen by some MPs as a way to survive.

While most MPs remained honest despite all this, a significant number of claims were questionable, and a few were downright criminal. But all this came about largely because the system was closed and claims were authorized with no outside scrutiny. Would a closed and secret system of expenses work well for people in any walk of life – for builders, teachers or priests, for example? Were questions ever raised with ministers before the scandal broke, but they refused to act? It is not clear. But in the end, all MPs took the blame for a bad system.

Dan Mount, head of policy at consultancy Civic Agenda, says disaster was inevitable sooner or later. 'An expenses system shouldn't depend on the absolute moral integrity of the people it regulates, it needs to just regulate. While the old system would have worked very well for the most virtuous MPs, for anyone with a slight inclination towards taking advantage, it wouldn't.'

Following the scandal, however, a new expenses system has been put in place that – understandably – could be seen as over-compensating, according to Mount, forcing 'relentless chronicling by MPs and their staff of every micro-expenditure relating to their job.' This, he says, 'has the undesirable consequence of reducing the amount of time they can spend doing their real job – representing and responding to their con-stituents and holding the government to account'.

In time, however, Mount anticipates the new system will become 'something more flexible which strikes the right balance by imposing the necessary amount of bureaucracy to hold MPs to account without significantly undermining their ability to carry out their responsibilities to their constituents.'

Of course, if one reason for all this is that MPs are underpaid, then there would be another solution: raise their pay.

At the time of writing, an MP's basic salary was £66,396, with higher rates for ministers, select committee chairs and some others. Supplemented as it is by other benefits such as pensions, this seems like a good wage, even to attract the best and brightest of people. Job security, however, is not good for an MP and, in the absence of standard support budgets, some MPs are stretched to fund their Westminster and constituency offices and have to dip into their salaries to pay some costs.

'If you are doing an MP's job well, it is a massive undertaking,' says Dan Mount. 'It is an incredibly intensive, all-consuming job which I think a lot of people wouldn't want to do, and for that, the benefits and compensations are not particularly impressive – less than most head teachers or chief police officers.'

MPs used to vote on their own pay levels, but not any more: a new Independent Parliamentary Standards Authority has been tasked with reviewing their pay and allowances. At the time of writing, MPs' pay had been frozen for 2013; but a survey carried out by the new authority found that 69 per cent of MPs feel they are currently underpaid.

The new body will try to address this issue – but it is not going to be easy. For now, the chance of a significant rise in MPs' pay being acceptable to the public seems about as likely as a dead llama winning the Grand National. Twice. But the issues of pay and expenses and working hours must not be glossed over if we want to have MPs who represent the whole of UK society. Pay too little, and only people with other income will be able to take the job; work too late, and others might be excluded. MPs represent the public, and the public deserves good representatives.

Chapter 5

Another place – the House of Lords

People used to believe that elephants all instinctively amble towards the same quiet spot to die, and in the minds of some the Lords offers a rough political equivalent – a pleasant place for elder statespeople to round off a life of public service with stimulating chats and mind-bending crumpets. If this were ever true, however, the House of Lords in the twenty-first century is a very different place, following several waves of reform and modernization that have transformed the way it works. It is still a richly historical place, but it is also a place which is, for example, more ethnically diverse than the House of Commons, and where many members blog and tweet far more freely than their colleagues down the corridor.

The House of Lords – traditionally referred to in the House of Commons as 'another place' (and vice versa) – forms a fascinating part of the UK's democratic structure.

Sometimes it is controversial – though not because most people do not think it should exist. Opinion surveys show that most people think it is a good idea to have a more independent-minded second chamber of Parliament in which a wide range of experts and wise heads can take time to examine carefully new laws that are proposed, suggest improvements or sound warnings about where they could go wrong.

Much of the controversy stems from disagreement about how people should become members of the second House in the modern world. Should all its members now be elected? All appointed, so we can guarantee a balance of expertise, experience and wisdom? Some of each? To examine these questions, we need to look more closely at the current position.

The past is certainly still in evidence. The opulent Lords debating chamber was designed by Charles Barry and Augustus Pugin to be the most impressive room in Parliament, reflecting its position in the power chain above the House of Commons, as it still was then in the late nineteenth century. The chamber is decked with stained glass, red leather and gilded woodwork, presided over at one end by a dazzling golden throne plucked straight out of a fairy tale. Here it is that the Queen sits to deliver the gently paced speech about new laws that is written for her each year by the government in the lower chamber. So while this theatrical scene still has the appearance of awesome power, the Commoners now write the script.

The chairperson of the Lords, the Lord Speaker, sits on a large red cushion known as the Woolsack. This is really more of a seat or bench made out of a bale of wool, which might seem lowly but dates from a time when wool represented wealth – fourteenth-century bling. Like the Commons, this chamber is definitely worth visiting – contact any member of the House for a ticket, or queue up for a debate.

Another ceremonial aspect of the Lords is the wearing of furry robes at the annual State Opening of Parliament – when the Queen reads her speech. They are also worn when a Lord is first introduced to the House, when there is a procession into the chamber in which Black Rod (a person) and the Garter King of Arms (also a person) lead the way. Peers' red robes are decorated with black and golden trim and bands of white fur referred to as 'ermine' – or winter stoat – but most often these days made from cheaper white rabbit fur with black spots painted on to it (true ermine has dark spots where the animals' tails used to be). One peer – Lord Alli – has commissioned a synthetic version made from knitted nylon.

But apart from the State Opening and when peers first arrive, the robes are not worn much any more. In fact, in these times of internet image search, peers have found it is not always a good idea for their official introduction portraits – in full furry splendour – to be released to the public. They can seem so – out of date. Colleagues advise them when they arrive: 'Be careful what happens to that photo – keep it for your family.'

Historically, there have been five grades of peer. These are, in order of seniority (highest first): Duke and Duchess; Marquess and Marchioness; Earl and Countess; Viscount and Viscountess; and Baron and Baroness. Since 1958, however, and the creation of life peers, all new peers created have been Barons and Baronesses.

The welcome truth, though, is that in the modern world few people know or care much about ranks, titles or 'orders of precedence'; but they do care about appointment or election to – or inheritance of – a seat in Parliament.

There is still a small proportion of peers (roughly 90 in 800, or 11 per cent) who have gained their seats simply by managing to be someone's eldest male child.

Up to 1999, there were more than 700 hereditary peers with the right to sit in the House of Lords. With the passage of the House of Lords Act 1999, this number was cut to ninety-two, of whom ninety are chosen by internal election and two are 'officers of state' (the Earl Marshal and the Lord Great Chamberlain, who are born into jobs such as organizing state funerals).

Pending further reforms, the number is being held at ninety-two, so as and when a hereditary member dies a by-election among the remaining hereditary peers or sometimes just among party groups of hereditary peers is held (under the alternative vote system) to fill the vacancy. For the moment, this means the hereditaries that win seats can (and do) declare triumphantly from time to time that they are the only peers currently elected in any way, as everyone else is appointed.

Another controversial category of peers is that of the twenty-six 'Lords Spiritual' – archbishops and selected bishops of the Church of

England with seats in the Lords. As part of the failed reform proposals of 2012 (of which more shortly), their number was going to be cut to twelve. Even so, the UK would have remained the only Western state outside the Vatican with so many theocrats, and polls show that for most people this would still be twelve too many.

All these issues are of much less significance these days than they used to be, however, since the great majority of peers are now 'life peers' – people appointed to the House of Lords on the basis of their wide-ranging achievements, knowledge or expertise, for the rest of their life. This form of Baron and – for the first time – Baroness was established by the Life Peerages Act 1958 (before then only men were allowed to take seats in the House of Lords). Since then, more than 700 life peers have been created, still mostly men, but now with 181 female peers within the current total of around 825 of all types of peers (so the House as a whole has about 22 per cent female members).

Life peers include former politicians, businesspeople, voluntary workers, sportspeople, environmentalists, academics, public service managers, TV presenters, scientists and playwrights.

It is true that even pre-reform, many peerages had been awarded to people for their achievements, and from all walks of life, though because it had been possible to create only hereditary peers, their children – whatever they were like – had been rewarded as well. Now, life peerages are for the individual only.

Life peers are appointed either within a political party group, or – if they are non-political people by nature or choice – as 'crossbench' peers. Crossbench peers, or crossbenchers, form a key part of what gives the House of Lords its distinctive character and value. There are currently about 180 of them, a significant chunk of seats to be given up to political independents and an important part of the Lords' more independent nature.

Since 2000, the crossbenchers have become even more independent with the creation of the House of Lords Appointments Commission, an independent body which recommends crossbench appointments. To qualify, as well as demonstrating 'a record of significant achievement within their chosen way of life', crossbenchers must be people 'who are and intend to remain independent of any political party'.

Overall, party politics plays a lesser role in the House of Lords than in the Commons, says the Labour peer Lord Toby Harris.

'If you are trying to win an argument here, being overtly political is not a good way to do it,' Lord Harris says. 'Crossbenchers tend to see it as a political row and think, "This is not for us."'

'Even among those who do have party allegiance, most are here at the end of a career, and they no longer feel they have to always vote exactly as their party would expect. They do need to be persuaded.'

Although party whips will try to persuade all their peers to vote in a certain way in Lords debates, there is little they can do to enforce it, since 'withdrawing the whip' – expelling someone from a party – does not have the same consequence for a peer, Lord Harris says.

'I do get text messages and emails, but what can they do? If they threatened to withdraw the whip it doesn't mean I can't be a party's candidate in the next election, as with MPs, because there is no election. It would just mean I stop receiving their text messages – which might be nice.'

With crossbenchers limited in numbers, however, party voting does still play a major role in the Lords.

Party political candidates for life peerages are proposed by the various parties themselves, with the Prime Minister ultimately deciding who and how many should be appointed, subject to checks by the Appointments Commission on their character and suitability.

In recent years, Prime Ministers have looked to create large numbers of new peers from their own party, to align the political balance of the second chamber more closely with the Commons. The current government, for example, created more than a hundred new peers – mostly former MPs – in its first year, in line with a stated Conservative/Liberal Democrat Coalition government agreement that 'Lords appointments will be made with the objective of creating a second chamber that is reflective of the share of the vote secured by the political parties in the last general election.'

This is not a new strategy, but it is not sustainable either: if every new government has to create so many new peers to change the balance, the number of peers will soon swell to a thousand and beyond.

Already, with more active peers than ever before, debates are harder to manage. And if a peer wants to table a written question to the government – as in the Commons, a valuable way members can ask for detailed information about policies from government departments, for their research – they have to turn up an hour and a half before the deadline to beat the queues.

This alone means that further reform of the Lords cannot be put off for ever – or even for much longer. But we will come back to the subject of reform, which has not been proving easy.

First, more about what all these people do.

As we saw in the previous chapter, the main role of the Lords is to look carefully at proposed new laws and suggest ways of changing them to improve their effectiveness, called 'amendments'.

Often, if the Lords feel strongly enough to vote through a proposal, the government in the Commons accepts their amendments, or makes other similar changes as a compromise. At other times, ministers will stick to their guns and Lords amendments are rejected. When the law then comes back to the Lords for a second look, they may decide not to press their case, accepting that the Commons has 'primacy' because its members have been elected.

Sometimes, however, often on issues of fundamental constitutional importance such as civil liberties, feelings run high and the Lords press again for changes to be made.

If it really comes to it, there are legal limits to the defiance of the Lords, as set out in the Parliament Act 1949 – the law about which Churchill made his famous remarks on democracy. This asserts that in most cases the Lords can delay a Bill by only up to a year, after which the Commons can pass it anyway. When it comes to 'money Bills' – laws or measures relating to tax or public spending – the Lords have even weaker powers and cannot delay them for more than a month.

There is also an understanding known as the Salisbury Convention, under which the Lords agree not to vote down government Bills that were promised in an election manifesto.

In practice, however, when the Lords do object strongly to a new proposal or a part of it, the best way through for all sides is usually negotiation.

For a start, with governments always running on limited time and keen to push through their legislation as quickly as possible, the power of delay is a bigger threat than it might sound. If the Lords do reject a government Bill, sending it back to the Commons in the 'ping-pong' described in the previous chapter, it forces the government to decide whether to carry on fighting, losing more precious time for other Bills, or to give way.

But it is not just about time; it is also about the wider political battle, and public opinion. Often, if the Lords feel strongly enough about something to reject it, a wider debate will already be raging in the Commons and in the media. A Lords rebellion can fuel a Commons rebellion, or a potential Commons rebellion, and cause the government to seem stubborn and inflexible. In the end, in the face of all these pressures, ministers will often accept a change of plan.

For this reason, the Parliament Act and other powers the Commons has to throw its weight around are very rarely used – most often, a compromise is found.

There are some areas where the powers of the Lords are stronger: it has the power to reject any attempt by the Commons to pass a law extending the lifetime of a government beyond its legal limit, for example, and can also, if it wishes, block secondary legislation – regulations drawn up by the government under existing laws without new laws needing to be passed. In theory, too, it has power to veto any laws that begin their passage through Parliament in the House of Lords – about a third of them do – though in practice this does not happen, not least because controversial Bills are usually started in the Commons.

Overall, like all the best parts of democracy, the system works by negotiation and compromise. The House of Lords plays a genuinely influential part in the lawmaking process without ever actually being in charge. And the result is – or it should be – that the UK ends up with better laws.

'Without a second chamber, the danger is that you would get much poorer legislation – bill after bill would have all sorts of unforeseen consequences which would still be reaching the courts, many years on,' says Lynda Chalker, Baroness Chalker of Wallasey, a Conservative peer and former MP who has served as a government minister in both Houses.

The secret to the second chamber's effectiveness is the wider life experience of its members, Baroness Chalker believes. 'Fifty years ago, Members of Parliament had wider non-political experience than they do today. But nowadays, people in politics tend to go to university, study politics, become political researchers or assistants and end up standing as candidates without doing any jobs outside politics like business or teaching. In the Lords, we have many more people with much wider experience – academics, people from professional backgrounds, and from the voluntary sector.'

As an example, she cites a debate on Antarctica in the Lords last year: participants included 'two geologists, one climate change expert and a specialist in mammals of the Antarctic region. You just don't tend to have that level of expertise in the Commons.'

The Antarctica debate was broad: discussion ranged from the future of British science in the region to the 'depraved sexual appetite of penguins', which are (according to Lord Giddens) 'far more racy than *Fifty Shades of Grey* . . . like fifty shades of black and white'.

The debate had taken place on a type of motion exclusive to the Lords: a motion to 'take note of' something – in this case 'that this House takes note of the centenary of the Scott expedition to Antarctica and of the United Kingdom's enduring scientific legacy and ongoing presence there.' The format allows peers to debate a subject without taking a specific decision. In this case, it might well have had an effect: plans to merge the British Antarctic Survey and the National Oceanography Centre (NOC), the UK's two main scientific bodies in the Antarctic, were ruled out later that same year following harsh criticism by peers.

The government appoints ministers in the House of Lords, though far fewer than in the Commons: most of the main government departments have just one minister in the Lords, whose job it is to guide through new laws and respond to debates on behalf of the government across the whole range of subjects covered by that department.

In 2012, for example, the Foreign Office had seven ministers, of which two were peers and five were MPs. But just one of those peers, Baroness Warsi, had responsibility for leading all Foreign Office business in the Lords, from trade to Europe, and Afghanistan to Antarctica. Being a government minister in the Lords is hard work – though at least there is no constituency caseload to consider.

There are select committees in the Lords as well and, because of peers' expertise and independence, their reports are usually highly regarded. They do not simply mirror Commons committees, however, which would be pointless and a recipe for conflict; instead, they focus on areas that cut across the lawmaking process, such as Europe, science and technology, and the UK constitution.

There are various bits and pieces, therefore, to the peers' workload and, as many of them still have part-time work elsewhere – regarded as essential to keep up the House's depth of experience and expertise – only a few of them (such as the Lord Speaker) receive a full-time salary. Instead, peers can claim an allowance for days they attend, and some other limited expenses – though again, much less than for MPs.

Most are entitled to claim a flat rate of £300 a day tax-free, plus travel expenses (Lords who are government ministers and some others with certain jobs have a salary instead and cannot claim the allowance). As Parliament (both Lords and Commons) sits on average about

150 days a year, peers can claim for a maximum of about £45,000 in allowances.

Although the sums involved are lower, and the issue of Lords' expenses has not been as incendiary as it became for MPs, in the parliamentary expenses scandal of 2009 several peers were exposed as having misused the system, with two ending up in prison. Now, as for MPs, the claims system is more open.

There is sometimes controversy over the fact that no peer has to turn up for work at all. Such concerns need to be set in the context of peers being encouraged to keep outside interests, however – often, in fact, being chosen to represent those interests in the first place. Also, if they do not turn up, they cannot claim any money.

There are also complaints that some peers do not seem to vote very often. In 2012, the campaign group Unlock Democracy published figures showing thirty peers (about 4 per cent) had claimed more than £20,000 in allowances the previous year despite taking part in fewer than one in four votes (they just have to turn up to work in their office to claim their fee, not vote in the chamber).

On the other hand, voting in many cases is not seen as an important duty if an issue is not contentious – the real work of the Lords is in discussing the detail of proposed new laws. Crossbench peers in particular often choose to abstain from voting to remain independent, so whether or not someone votes is not always a strong measure of their quality and influence.

So should peers be paid differently, or salaried?

In fact, allowances are just one minor aspect of two little words that have given politicians one massive headache in recent years: Lords reform.

When it comes to reform, everyone agrees on one thing: despite the major positive changes that have already taken place over the past hundred years, more change is needed, and soon. The problem is that no two people want the same reform, from appointment to powers, composition and pay.

In the end, this lack of agreement was what caused the most recent major attempt at reform – in 2012 – to founder: faced with a backbench rebellion in the Commons, the Coalition government admitted defeat, withdrawing its plans for an 80 per cent elected house with no word of what might happen next.

Astonishingly, the reform attempt was the third in the space of just ten years. In both 2003 and 2007 the government offered MPs and peers a vote on all sorts of options, from fully appointed to fully elected. No option gained general approval and most were massively rejected.

Among MPs, the 'least disliked' option in 2003 was a House of Lords that would be 80 per cent elected and 20 per cent appointed – with MPs voting against it by only 284 to 281. The next least popular was for a wholly elected upper house, with the others thrown out even more convincingly.

For their part, the House of Lords rejected by huge margins all proposals that involved election, in any amounts. Instead, by an overwhelming 335 to 110, they backed the option of an all-appointed chamber – the option that had gained the least support in MPs' votes.

In 2007, MPs caught everyone by surprise by changing their position and voting (by 337 to 224) to support a fully elected House of Lords, with narrower majority support now for an 80 per cent elected house and rejection for all the other options; the Lords, however, stuck to their guns, with massive support for an all-appointed house and massive rejection for any level of election.

This deadlock remains today.

The 2012 plan had hoped to build on the 'least disliked' option from 2003 and one of the options backed by MPs in 2007: the 80 per cent elected, 20 per cent appointed model – but it found that, while it may be the least disliked, it is still too disliked by too many people. With uproar in both Houses, it was booted out and no new agreement seems possible any time soon.

Why can people not agree?

The major sticking point is that of 'primacy'. It seems that some form of election to the House of Lords is favoured by most people – the version proposed in the 2012 reforms included election terms of fifteen years, with a third coming up for re-election every five years. The voting method would have varied across the UK, but included a regional party list element. But once peers are elected, even though their election terms and the voting method might be very different from House of Commons election, there are two big fears.

First, the House of Lords would almost certainly become more politicized, so debates would lose some of their independent flavour which is so highly valued.

But second, and strongest, there is a view among many politicians and lawyers that if you elect any Lords at all, the delicate balance between the two Houses of Parliament would be disrupted. Whatever legal safeguards were put in place, or restrictions such as once-only fifteen-year terms for elected peers, the Commons could no longer say it was the only home of elected representation, and the fear is that open warfare and even messy legal battles could rumble on for ever after. At the very least, elected Lords could feel more justified in using their powers of delay right up to the maximum far more often, slowing down our political system.

In many ways it is not surprising that the House of Lords is proving so hard to reform because it is such a delicately balanced, paradoxical construction that has evolved over many years as a counterweight to the power of an elected government. And like anything that is finely balanced, if shoved in the wrong direction it might fall apart.

This paradox is summarized by Meg Russell, deputy director of the Constitution Unit at University College London: 'If the two chambers are controlled by the same party, there is a danger the system becomes ineffective, but if they are controlled by different parties, there is a danger of too much conflict.

'This and other potentially explosive issues – such as how can you create two chambers that are sufficiently different from each other, but both of which enjoy legitimacy? – make bicameralism [government with two chambers] fundamentally controversial, not only in Britain but all over the world.

'Second chambers exist to get in the way of first chambers, which are themselves elected by the people. Hence even when these second chambers are elected themselves, they will often cause controversy. Nonetheless, there are many potential benefits from "second thought".'

What is the answer?

As the dust settles on the government's 2012 failure, various new ideas about reform are taking shape. Some favour the beefing up of the House of Lords Appointment Commission, with powers to make sure various professions – doctors, nurses, builders, bankers, professors, spies, musicians, artists – are represented in certain proportions.

Others – including Baroness Chalker – say more geographical balance should be built into the appointments system: 'We need to have the different parts of the country better represented from all party viewpoints'.

Whatever happens, the special role and characteristics of the second chamber of Parliament – an ability to think long term, its independence and its collaborative nature – must not be lost. The House of Lords must continue to be allowed to improve new laws; and it could have a greater role looking at possible new laws before they are even drawn up, or examining what happens to laws once they are passed.

There is even scope for innovation with technology: despite its slow-changing image, in the era of life peers the House of Lords has shown itself to be more than ready to embrace change in many areas, leading the way on use of tablet computers in the chamber. Free of party restraints, many peers are refreshingly idiosyncratic and free with what they blog and tweet – for examples, see the award-winning 'Lords of the blog' project run by democracy charity the Hansard Society (http://lordsoftheblog.net).

Any reforms must look to strengthen these characteristics, and make sure the 'other place' becomes another part of the solution of engaging more people with democracy – not a new part of the problem.

Chapter 6

Devolution – a patchwork in progress

When it comes to democracy, the UK is covered not by a single blanket but by a patchwork quilt.

Over the past fourteen years, more and more powers have been devolved from the UK national Parliament in Westminster to the Northern Ireland Assembly, the Scottish Parliament and the Welsh Assembly.

These devolved bodies have come a long way in a short time. Their foundations were laid between 1997 and 1999 with referendums leading to the creation of a Parliament in Scotland and an Assembly in Wales. The Northern Ireland Assembly was established as the result of the Good Friday Agreement of 1998.

With their members chosen using a variety of proportional representation voting systems, sometimes in combination with 'first past the post', political representation has become broader, with party patterns that had been fixed for some time giving way to diversity, variation and – whisper the word – coalition.

At the time of writing, there are no fewer than nine political parties in government and devolved government across the UK: the Conservatives and Lib Dems in Westminster; the SNP in Scotland; Labour in Wales; and a compulsory coalition of five other parties in Northern Ireland. And yet, just fifteen years ago, one party held sway everywhere.

No devolved parliament or assembly has total control over its area, even within the subject areas where it is allowed to make law: unless and until a part of the UK should actually assume full independence, the UK Parliament in Westminster retains the ability to overturn devolved laws or suspend devolved bodies (as it has done several times in Northern Ireland).

In practice, however, day-to-day creation and control of a huge number of policies has been devolved, and so has power, effectively – if the UK Parliament or government were to interfere in devolved matters, the system would be pointless and there would be political uproar. In fact, there is a written understanding between the UK and Scottish governments – the Sewel Convention – which accepts that Westminster 'would not normally legislate with regard to devolved matters except with the agreement of the devolved legislature'. Similar understandings apply to Wales and Northern Ireland.

Nevertheless, despite ongoing general support for the process of devolution so far, citizens across the UK are often confused about who is in charge of what issue these days.

This confusion may partly be caused by the fact that the amount and type of power devolved varies in each area, and the process is still developing: further powers are steadily being devolved to all regions of the UK, and the Scottish National Party and Plaid Cymru are still calling for full independence for their nations, with a referendum on the issue set for Scotland in 2014.

Where does all this leave the Westminster Parliament, making laws for the whole of the UK some of the time and only parts of it at other times? And where does it leave England, without a separate parliament or assembly of its own?

We will come back to these questions. But first, let's take a closer look at the new lawmaking bodies of Belfast, Edinburgh and Cardiff.

The Northern Ireland Assembly

The Northern Ireland Assembly is housed in Parliament Buildings on the Stormont Estate, about five miles east of Belfast city centre, a large public park featuring woodland walks – the greenest and leafiest outpost of the UK's devolved democracy.

The buildings, with their grand, neo-classical façade, were opened in 1932 to house the former two-chamber Parliament of Northern Ireland – with its own House of Commons and a Senate – which was closed in 1972 after Westminster imposed Direct Rule in a deteriorating security situation. The modern single-chamber Northern Ireland Assembly was established by the Good Friday Agreement of 1998, re-establishing more stable multi-party government after three decades of violent conflict between elements of the region's unionist and nationalist communities.

Since then the Assembly has been suspended four times in periods when political cooperation has broken down, and its birth out of struggle and loss on both sides of the community means it works very differently to the other two UK devolved legislatures.

The 108 Members of the Legislative Assembly (MLAs) are elected under the single transferable vote system, a proportional system with multi-member constituencies which leads to a pattern of party representation which matches quite closely how people vote (as described in more detail in Chapter 2).

Of the three devolved bodies, Stormont is the most Westminster-like in appearance, with its wooden panels, leather-upholstered benches (in sky blue) and two rows of desks in front with solid wooden chairs – the computer age (also as in Westminster) not much in evidence.

The Assembly has general legislative powers except for specific reserved or excepted topics remaining under Westminster control. These exceptions range from major areas such as defence, national security and taxation (a real point of friction) to lesser areas such as human fertilization and embryology. Devolved policy areas include agriculture; culture, arts and leisure; business and trade; education; employment; environment; health and social services; justice and policing; and regional and social development.

After the election, most government jobs and committee positions are given out according to parties' share of the votes, leading to a situation where all the five main parties – the Democratic Unionist Party (DUP), Sinn Féin, the Ulster Unionist Party (UUP), the Social Democratic and Labour Party (SDLP), and the cross-community Alliance Party of Northern Ireland – are in compulsory coalition, or power-sharing. The First Minister and Deputy First Minister are drawn from the largest parties, but because the coalition is compulsory they cannot sack the other ministers, who can be removed only by their own party group: so there are no Westminster-style reshuffles.

Also, because the five main parties are in government, hardly anyone is in opposition: the most opposition there has ever been is fifteen members, and the number has dropped as low as two; at the time of writing, it was four (Traditional Unionist Voice and the Green Party, at one seat each, plus two independents).

This unusual situation has obvious drawbacks.

'To have 104 out of 108 members in government is a bigger majority than Saddam Hussein used to have,' says Quintin Oliver of political consultancy Stratagem. 'It's rotten for decision-making, because it moves at the pace of the slowest, and if one party is unhappy it can veto developments. But it is good for peace, since once there is agreement, it has extraordinary validity: the development of democratic politics is hand in hand with the peace process.'

Other systems are in place to ensure consensus. Every MLA is invited to designate themselves as 'nationalist', 'unionist' or 'other', and some decisions such as changes to the way the Assembly works must receive a minimum level of support from both communities. In addition, any decision can be made to rely on support across the designations if thirty or more MLAs present a 'petition of concern'.

These measures create real unity of purpose where there is agreement, for example on the region's economic strategy, or its settlement on student fees, Oliver says. Or on certain transport campaigns: 'Our one flight out of Belfast to the US, to New York, was threatened with closure recently because our air passenger tax was much higher than on the US flight from Dublin – £60 compared with three euros. After lobbying from all Northern Ireland politicians to the Chancellor, devolution of air passenger duty was achieved so we could subsidize this flight, and it was saved.'

Where there is not unanimity, on the other hand, stalemate tends to follow.

Despite its relatively small population – about 1.8 million, compared with about 3 million in Wales and 5 million in Scotland – Northern Ireland's parties have made their presence strongly felt in Westminster. The DUP is the fourth largest party in Westminster, with more seats there than Plaid Cymru and the Scottish National Party. Sinn Féin members of the House of Commons are active behind the scenes. Though they decline to take their Westminster seats since they do not see Northern Ireland as part of the UK, Sinn Féin MPs do communicate with and lobby UK ministers, hold meetings outside the Commons and visit Downing Street.

There are strong lines of communication, too, with the Republic of Ireland: as part of a delicate balancing act, the Good Friday Agreement set up a series of cross-border consultative bodies, including a North–South ministerial council and a British–Irish inter-governmental conference on non-devolved matters relating to Northern Ireland.

'Because we share a land border with another country, we tend to look both east to Britain and south to Ireland,' says Oliver. In a European context in particular, perspectives change, he says, since European projects tend to be regional, and regional characteristics in areas such as farming may be more similar between Northern Ireland and bordering areas of the Republic of Ireland, for example, than between Northern Ireland and remoter parts of the UK.

'We have always been much more pro-European in both parts of the island – leapfrogging over Britain to get to Brussels and Strasbourg. Even unionists sometimes describe themselves as Irish in a European context. On agriculture interests, we are much closer to the Republic of Ireland than to big English farms, so it makes much more practical sense.'

With such a finely nuanced pattern of views, both the Assembly and all the agencies that provide public services in Northern Ireland have had to become closely tuned to public opinion, building on a strong public-engagement philosophy developed in the years of conflict.

With local government stripped of powers in the years before the Good Friday Agreement, the community and voluntary sector reached out to fill the gap in community consultation, guided by some of the world's leading academics in the field.

Dr David Newman, an academic formerly leading research into community engagement at Queen's University, Belfast, says that even in the darkest years of the Troubles, many people were experimenting with consultation techniques. Examples range from encounter groups to a voting system known as the 'preferendum', which Newman himself helped to demonstrate on the web in the mid-1990s, working with Peter Emerson, director of the de Borda Institute.

The preferendum is a decision-making process which involves a debate, followed by the awarding of preference points to a list of options by the people who took part. Finally, results are analysed to reach the best possible compromise on a contentious issue.

'Instead of people arguing they split into groups, work out their positions, present them calmly, challenge errors and find out what people will settle for if they can't get their ideal outcome,' Newman says.

Such experiments played a vital part in paving the way for the Good Friday Agreement of 1998. 'The overall impact was sufficient pressure for politicians to take part in negotiations and not continue things as they were'.

The task is by no means over: devolved Northern Ireland government departments are required to consult widely on their work, and for many this is a big culture change to the former centralized civil service culture which simply obeyed orders from Westminster. The departments must also follow tougher anti-discrimination rules in areas like job interviews than anywhere else in the UK.

The combination has created a very open, accessible atmosphere around the Assembly itself, with free public access allowed to the buildings, plenary sessions and many committee meetings without appointment. Assembly committees gather evidence from a very wide range of people and groups as they examine proposed new laws or carry out inquiries into topics of general interest, from transport in Northern Ireland to flexible working in the public sector.

Young people often take a lead role, as seen for instance in 'WIMPS' – 'Where Is My Public Servant?' – an internet TV channel run by and for young people. The channel helps engage teenagers with politics and presents their views directly to politicians and heads of public services, such as the Chief Constable or the Children's Commissioner – and builds their employment skills in the process. `

WIMPS' approach – a powerful mix of campaigning and serious coverage of democracy and human rights issues that would put much of the 'adult' press to shame – has cut through some tough barriers. 'If there is one TV organization that always gets ministers and assembly members to come along, it's WIMPS.tv, run by these 16-year-olds,' says David Newman.

The channel combines well-constructed films, including more traditional interviews with politicians in suits, with films that are part report, part art installation. In one memorable clip – 'a public achieve-ment production' entitled 'Moe is angry' – a sixteen-year-old addresses the camera, fighting to contain his rage at the slowness of politicians to help young people. He has been involved in five cross-community projects in Portadown and feels they are all leading nowhere.

'What makes me angry?' he says, looking straight at the camera. 'People like you make me angry.' It is a powerful and uncomfortable message.

The channel forms part of a colourful and varied local, UK and Irish media family with print and TV covering all angles of daily life. Politics in particular is abuzz with reportage, discussion programmes and satirical comedies unknown in the rest of the UK. This is just as well, says David Newman, since the rest of the UK's media tends to overlook Northern Ireland, apart from reporting on flare-ups of violence.

This is a great shame, since all parts of the UK could learn a great deal from Northern Ireland's innovation in community engagement and consultation.

The Scottish Parliament

The Scottish Parliament Building in the Holyrood area of Edinburgh – a short walk from the town centre – is architecturally stunning: a jagged, surreal construction that manages to combine solidity and grandeur with crazy angles and teetering corners that baffle and amaze. The cost of its construction – £400 million by the time it opened in 2004 – evoked a similar response, as did the near-decapitation of two or three of its members from a collapsing beam in 2006. However, the place now manages to feel both modern and established, woven into the city around it.

There are 129 Members of the Scottish Parliament – MSPs – elected under a type of proportional representation with one member each from seventy-three constituencies, plus an extra seven from each of eight regions. All members – constituency and regional – have equal status, so everyone in Scotland is represented by eight MSPs and can contact any of them about any issue. Elections were initially held every four years, but the next has been postponed until May 2016 – a five year term – to avoid a clash with the 2015 UK elections. At the time of writing we are also heading towards an independence referendum in the autumn of 2014, on which the future of Scotland hinges.

If the people of Scotland were to vote for full independence, it is likely that the Scottish Parliament would expand to take in new members as it takes on new powers, but the detail of this – as with much else about independence – is impossible to predict in advance. In any case; for now, the Parliament continues to strengthen and develop.

The modern, computerized Parliament chamber is formed in the shape of a large horseshoe – intended, like the circular Welsh Assembly chamber, to be less confrontational than the Westminster model.

As with the Northern Ireland Assembly, power is devolved to the Scottish Parliament except for 'reserved matters' – powers retained by Westminster. In practice, this means Holyrood has the power to pass laws in many policy areas, including agriculture, the arts, civil and criminal justice, education, the environment, health, housing, local government, planning, police and fire services, social work, sport and transport.

In fact, Scotland has always had strong separate systems in many areas of society – completely separate legal and school systems, for example. And with steady devolution of more powers than any other part of the UK, it is now striking out in its own direction in more and more key areas, such as local government (no elected mayors or police commissioners, for example), health (minimum pricing for alcohol, minimal role for the private sector) and education (higher funding for university places).

All this, despite a number of different types of government being in power since the new arrangements began.

'Since 1999, there has been coalition government in the first eight years, then a minority government, then a majority government – so in a very short space of time we have had experience of all those different ways to operate,' says MSP and former Scottish National Party Cabinet minister Bruce Crawford.

What this has shown is that the consultative steering group that drew up how the Scottish Parliament would operate – a group of politicians, lawyers and others tasked with proposing the new Parliament's procedures, subject to adoption by the Parliament itself – did a pretty good job, according to Crawford.

At the heart of the Scottish Parliament is a committee system that has effectively scrutinized the work of all these governments. While the Westminster Parliament is remote and distant from Edinburgh, these committees of about eight MSPs each are local and highly focused, and can call witnesses from all walks of life in Scotland as they look at proposed new laws and launch inquiries into any topic. Unlike in Westminster, Scottish Parliament committees can even propose new laws themselves, known as 'committee Bills'.

They also often meet in local communities rather than in Edinburgh, and can tailor their methods to their subject matter. In 2012, for example, the Scottish Parliament Finance Committee held workshops on how to improve employment opportunities out in three communities where there is high unemployment; and the Equal Opportunities Committee held special 'round-table evidence sessions' as part of an inquiry into the causes of homelessness where witnesses, including young people who had experienced homelessness, were seated alongside committee members, clerks, researchers, reporters and others around a single table to create a more welcoming environment.

Strong committees and other elements of the Parliament's work such as a robust public-petitions system (see Chapter 13), relate to the body's founding principles of openness, inclusion and accountability, says Patrick Harvie, Green Party regional MSP for Glasgow. However there is always room for improvement, he says.

'Though the committee system works well to scrutinize legislation as it is made, it is not always as good at post-legislative scrutiny – picking up the unforeseen impacts that Scottish laws might be having after passing through our single chamber Parliament sometimes quite quickly.'

Despite a relative openness compared with Westminster, there is more work to be done as well in holding public meetings around Scotland and expanding online debate with citizens to include as many people as possible in the process of government, he says. 'Inclusive processes have slipped back a bit in recent years, and I don't think we yet embody that ideal. The spirit of accountability is something that should be revisited every few years, to see if we can find new ways of recapturing it.'

Moves towards greater devolution of power to Scotland are sometimes characterized as a clash of cultures, highlighted in recent times by very different maps of party-political support. Harvie says clashes between the UK Secretary of State for Scotland and the Scottish government do take place from time to time, but between the Parliaments themselves the relationship works well.

'Tensions between Westminster and the Scottish Government come in peaks and troughs,' he says. 'Policy on less controversial issues like the regulation of charities, or policy on asylum seekers and refugees, or sexual health, is taken forward between the parliaments quietly and methodically, behind the scenes.

'So both parliaments might be working on a similar topic, and there will be telephone or video conferences between committees in Edinburgh and London and links between groups working informally across political parties.'

But when it comes to more controversial, high-profile issues, such as the devolution of further powers to Scotland, or energy companies' obligations on renewables, 'those kind of issues become a bit spikier, and are handled government to government,' Harvie says.

In fact, ministers and officials from the Scottish Government and the UK Scotland Office meet regularly to discuss the whole range of policy issues handled in Edinburgh, not just the high-profile issues such as the independence referendum.

Former Scottish Cabinet minister Bruce Crawford agrees that 'the areas of tension between Westminster and Holyrood are not as great as people might imagine.

'There are policy differences – a prime example is welfare reform. There was significant resistance to its impact in Scotland, and we did not give consent to some of it such as dental charges, or cuts in concessionary travel for people with disabilities. We are also concerned about the fact that no high speed rail network to Scotland is proposed.'

But there are now stronger joint mechanisms for debating these kinds of policy issues, and the advantage is that they can be discussed much more openly, Crawford says.

'There were disagreements before there was a Scottish Parliament, but they were swept under the carpet, and no one knew about them.'

Overall, he says: '90 per cent of the time we rub along OK and come to an agreement on things. There is no benefit to either side to deliberately create tension on any issue.'

This practical approach can be seen in the management of the civil service in Scotland. Although technically a civil servant working for the Scottish government is a UK civil servant, in practice they operate independently and owe their first allegiance to the Scottish government – with the blessing of the UK government and UK civil service.

The Scottish government has increasing power over its own finances, as well – a big point of contention in the past. Until a few years ago, Scotland had very little financial control – as in other devolved areas, its budget total has been largely dictated by the Barnett formula, a system devised in 1978 by a Treasury minister, Joel Barnett.

Intended to be temporary but lasting for more than thirty years because no better acceptable method could be worked out, the formula has automatically increased or decreased funding to Northern Ireland, Scotland and Wales as a proportion of public spending in England. Compared with England, Scotland would receive 10 per cent, Wales 5.8 per cent and Northern Ireland 3.5 per cent (it does not cover all funding, such as social-security payments). The formula reflects population differences and also differences in social need between each area – but only at the time it was devised, in 1978. It has never changed according to changing need over the years, and it also ignores large disparities of need between different regions of England.

This is about to change, however. From 2016, even if the Scots do not vote for their country to gain full independence, the Scottish government would have new powers to set its own income tax rates; to set some other taxes separately, including stamp duty on houses; and to borrow more money independently.

Some of these changes would have little immediate impact, as the Treasury would simply cut its own funding to Scotland by the same amount as that raised by Scottish stamp duty, for example. And there will be no change on national insurance – which is linked to the UK-wide social-security system; VAT, which in any case is being harmonized across Europe; and corporation tax – a big bone of contention, as a separate lower Scottish rate might see businesses migrate over the border from parts of the north of England.

As deeper financial independence takes hold, however, Scotland has been travelling further along the path that meanders somewhere between devolution and independence – what has been termed 'devo max', whereby most tax raised in Scotland will stay in Scotland. This could be the case even if the vote in 2014 is not for full independence.

As more and more powers are devolved, however, what are the implications for England and the other parts of the UK? Can the whole nation remain a strong functioning unit? We will come to this question shortly, but first, a trip to Cardiff.

The Welsh Assembly

As with the Scottish Parliament, openness and transparency are built into the Senedd (pronounced 'seneth'), the Welsh Assembly's home on the Cardiff bay, its light interior merging with the land, sky and sweeping waterfront beyond.

At its heart is the Siambr (pronounced 'shambr'), a circular debating chamber nestling beneath a vast funnel-like construction of glass and red cedarwood stretching up and outwards across the roof. The design represents a tree of democracy, the chamber beneath its roots and its canopy sheltering the building and stretching out beyond the glass walls.

Above the Siambr, a circular public gallery offers a clear view from all sides through glass panels. The whole futuristic space – designed by the Richard Rogers Partnership – has a hint of science fiction about it, like the Jedi High Council or the underbelly of *Avatar*'s Tree of Souls; it is a huge disappointment not to see any of the sixty Assembly members (AMs) shimmering into place by hologram, or flapping off to committee on a winged beast.

Debates in the circular space are polite, informal and understated: it is not unusual for first names to be used, even by the Presiding Officer, and dissent is indicated by a gentle murmuring that in Westminster would barely pass for throat-clearing.

There are laptops at every place and simultaneous translation headsets in both chamber and public gallery (Welsh and English are freely interchanged). As in the Scottish Parliament, voting is electronic and takes about 20 seconds, with the result displayed on plasma screens.

From the floor above the public gallery, in a wide public meeting space where community events – from Shakespeare to beat-boxing – are held free of charge, a peek over the balcony allows people to glimpse through glass the members seated in discussion, deep below. The whole design feels open and interconnected.

The Assembly was created in 1998 following a referendum the previous year, with the first elections a year later. In contrast with Holyrood and Stormont, where powers are general apart from reserved or excepted areas, the body has so far been devolved specific powers by Westminster in around twenty policy areas, including agriculture and rural development, culture and the Welsh language, economic development, education, environment, fire and rescue, health services, highways and transport, housing, local government, social welfare, sport, tourism and planning. Its powers are currently under review, however, with a body known as the Silk Commission (it is chaired by former clerk to the Assembly Paul Silk) recommending in spring of 2014 that it should now expand in size and scope and take on a range of new powers over the next ten years.

At first, the whole Assembly was also the executive or government, and it had powers of secondary legislation only – regulations made under the primary laws from Westminster, allocating money within budgets, or issuing directions to Welsh local authorities or other local agencies. In 2006, the Welsh government, with a Cabinet of up to twelve ministers and deputy ministers, was separated from the wider Assembly, echoing the separation between the Westminster Parliament and the UK government and a similar separation in Scotland and Northern Ireland.

In 2011, following a further referendum, the Assembly gained powers to make full primary legislation – Assembly Acts – amending or replacing UK law for Wales in its subject areas. So ever since it came into being, the Assembly has been steadily growing in power.

Up to now, Assembly elections have been held every four years, though, as in Scotland, the next one has been delayed a year to 2016 to avoid a clash with the first fixed-term UK general election in 2015. And at the time of writing, a further law has been proposed permanently fixing five years as the Assembly term, to avoid future election clashes with Westminster. The voting system used means a large majority for any party is almost impossible: out of sixty seats, forty are elected using first past the post in constituency areas, and a further twenty according to a party list preference system across five regions. The regional system is designed to balance power: adjustments are made to ensure that the more members a particular party wins in the constituencies, the fewer it is likely to see elected in the regions. So, for example, in the South Wales West region in 2011 seven constituency members were elected, all from Welsh Labour; but of the four regional members from exactly the same area, two were from the Welsh Conservatives, one from Plaid Cymru and one from the Welsh Liberal Democrats. It's not surprising, therefore, that of the four governments to be formed so far, two have been coalitions.

As in the other devolved bodies, committees are a vital part of the way the Assembly works, but in Wales they scrutinize proposed new laws and reach out to the public at a particularly early stage.

Welsh laws pass through similar stages to the UK Parliament – consideration of general principles, detailed consideration and a final stage. But most of the time, general or specialist committees of members are asked to look at an Assembly Bill first, and to run open hearings with experts and consult the public, before producing a report for the Assembly and moving to the second stage of detailed consideration.

'Welsh bills receive quite an examination before they even reach the second stage, which is a positive feature of the way our procedures have developed,' says Keith Bush, the Assembly's chief legal adviser. 'For one thing, it enables a committee to consider if a bill could be strengthened before it is considered in detail, and ministers have the chance to respond positively to that – so they aren't having to defend every dot and comma of their bill right from the word go. They can take on board changes before it gets very confrontational.'

Public input into these hearings is taken not just through the usual modern channels of email and social media but using the much lower-tech means of the Assembly's Outreach bus – 'democracy on the move' – which tours the land scooping people in for consultation and video evidence for inquiries.

The Assembly's second Presiding Officer, Rosemary Butler, has made it a priority to connect the body's work more directly with the public through initiatives like the bus and to allow more time for debates on topics of wide cross-party interest brought by individual members, such as control of payday loans companies, or the smacking of children. The smacking debate was the subject of a media frenzy in 2011, driven by popular misunderstanding that the Assembly was about to ban all smacking – in fact, the topic was just the subject of general discussion, though Assembly officials were happy to gain the publicity.

The Welsh Assembly might be the smallest of the UK's devolved bodies with just sixty members, but it is a global pace-setter in at least one respect.

In 2003 the Assembly hit 50 per cent representation by women (30 of 60) – the first lawmaking body in the world to do so (the previous best had been the Swedish Rikstag, where women accounted for about 45 per cent).

It went even further: following the Blaenau Gwent by-election in 2006, the Assembly held 31 women and 29 men: a female majority. However, the proportion of women to men has since slipped back to 42 per cent (25 members) – still the best of the UK's four legislatures, but now overtaken by a few other nations, including Sweden and the Rwandan Parliament (56 per cent women members, thanks partly to a new 2003 post-genocide constitution which sets aside a minimum of 30 per cent of seats for women). In the Scottish Parliament the proportion of women members is currently about 35 per cent – much higher than Westminster's 22 per cent. The ratio is worst in Northern Ireland, however, with only 18.5 per cent (20) female Assembly members following the 2011 election.

As for the future, the devolution of further fundraising powers seems likely after the UK government accepted a recommendation from the first Silk Commission report that the Welsh Assembly – subject to a referendum – be granted powers to vary income tax in Wales and set a few other tax levels, including stamp duty and business rates, up to a total of about 25 per cent of its own budget. Adding further financial independence, if the tax powers are passed the Assembly will also be granted more powers to borrow money to fund major schemes such as road-building. The question of whether to increase the Assembly by another twenty seats to reduce members' workloads is another reform that seems likely to take place as and when more powers – in areas such as youth justice, transport and education – are devolved. As this might change the Assembly's party-political balance, it is sure to generate some lively debate.

England and the West Lothian question

So much for the devolved areas of the UK – but what about England? Does it matter that of all parts of the UK, the largest does not have its own parliament or assembly, while the others do?

This is the riddle that has come to be known as the West Lothian question, after the former MP for West Lothian Tam Dalyell, who high-lighted the issue in the 1970s. Dalyell pointed out that as a Scottish MP, he – along with more than a hundred other MPs from outside England – was entitled to vote on new laws that would affect only England, so it was possible that a law affecting only England could be passed or thrown out on the strength of votes from outside England. However, in many key policy areas MPs from England no longer had the same power over the devolved places.

In reality, the issue does not arise much as a practical problem in Parliament: as 82 per cent of MPs are currently from England and issues are more often disputed on party rather than national lines, it is hard to imagine a situation where MPs from outside England would want to or be able to gang up specifically to block a law affecting only England. Nevertheless, the more power that is devolved, the more power the question seems to have. There is a fear that, with creeping change happening in bits and pieces, we might end up with an 'asymmetric' system that makes no sense overall.

The most complete way of solving the West Lothian question would be to create a new parliament or assembly for England. The UK Parliament in Westminster would remain as the overall seat of power on UK-wide issues such as defence, and the controller of the rules and powers of all the various devolved bodies.

One problem with this idea is that there is very little support in England for the creation of a new English Parliament. Perhaps because Westminster is in England, most English people feel they already have a Parliament and they don't want another one.

There is another problem, too: the fact that England is home to 85 per cent of the total UK population means there might still be an imbalance of power between the various devolved bodies. An England-wide Parliament in London would also remain quite remote from many of its citizens, for example in the north of England and the south-west.

One answer to this might be to create a series of regional assemblies across England, dividing the UK as a whole into more of a regional patchwork. But again, there seems to be very little public appetite for this: a recent previous attempt to create regional assemblies was shelved in 2004 when a referendum on the establishment of the first one in the north-east was rejected by a whopping 78 per cent of voters. In any case, regional assemblies as they were proposed would not actually have solved the West Lothian question, as they would not have been passed anything like the same powers as the Scottish, Welsh and Northern Irish devolved bodies.

Nigel Smith, who chaired the 'Yes' campaign in the 1997 referendum for a Scottish Parliament and has gone on to advise on referendums worldwide, says: 'I was a supporter of regional government in England but as soon as I read the bill I realized it would lose. The reason is that London was not prepared to give it sufficient powers and the public were not going to elect 40 new politicians to do very little.

'In my view, the wrong conclusion has been drawn from the failed referendum for a North East regional assembly: it is not that people reject regional government, but they don't want weak regional government. Regions will only get democratic approval if they are given the powers to make a difference.'

Yet another solution would be to create a system such as an 'English Grand Committee' to allow only English MPs to vote within the Westminster Parliament on issues affecting only England. This solution would bring its own new problems as well, though, as the MPs sitting for England would still also be UK MPs, whereas in the other devolved areas the elected representatives are usually different people who have no seat in Westminster. English MPs might thus sometimes be divided in their loyalties and be working within completely different party-political balances in the same building.

Nevertheless, an English Grand Committee might be the easiest solution, since it would be flexible and easy to change or improve, with no need to set up a completely new parliament or assembly which nobody wants. But is a solution needed at all? Couldn't it all be left as it is, to muddle along?

Susan Dalgety, former chief press officer to Jack McConnell when he was Labour First Minister of Scotland, says that to ignore the West Lothian question altogether would be a grave mistake for England. She believes that the UK as a whole must adapt to take account of the recent shifts in power to devolved parts of the UK, for everyone's benefit – and that stronger regions in England could be a part of this.

'When the Scotland Act was passed, it was the biggest shake-up of the British constitution for 300 years: but it was not that Scotland was changing, it was that the UK was changing.

'It is about trying to create a UK for the twenty-first century that reflects the different regions, economies and cultures but keeping that within the most effective social, economic and cultural union. It should be the people of the UK together deciding what the shape of the UK is, but people are not looking at it as a coherent whole, they are just looking at the elements.'

The UK government has recognized that some change is needed, which is why in 2012 it set up the snappily named 'Commission on the consequences of devolution for the House of Commons', also known as the McKay Commission. The commission has now reported, recommending procedural changes that would mean laws only or mainly affecting England would be debated by committees representing the party balance in England. Separately, the Political and Constitutional Reform Committee of MPs has published its own report recommending England gain its own assembly with similar powers to the other devolved bodies, such as powers to raise taxes. So the problems are not being ignored, but they can be expected to take a long time to sort out, not least because the situation in each of the existing devolved areas is still changing and settling in, and the UK government wrestles with a range of public interests and views.

Whatever happens, the UK in the twenty-first century is set to develop as a colourful patchwork of assemblies and parliaments working alongside various systems of local government, law, party politics and social policy. There is the referendum on full Scottish independence to come, but whatever happens in this, all these myriad differences do not have to be seen as a source of weakness within the UK as a whole or within the UK and neighbouring Scotland. Instead, they could and should be seen as strengths.

After all, the most urgent needs in all parts of the UK are to address our deepest social problems, from unemployment to inequalities in health and education. In a well-functioning devolved UK, more and better use could be made of local knowledge and expertise within each devolved area to tackle these issues, with better sharing of ideas between the devolved areas as well.

The UK's expanding democratic institutions are already learning from each other, with elected representatives from Westminster and the devolved bodies looking to each other for new ways of engaging and helping the people they serve and represent. Whatever happens in the future to all parts of our patchwork democracy – devolution, independence or all points in between – a strong, creative exchange of ideas will help build the way ahead.

Chapter 7

Local government – the front line

People grumble about national politicians, but there are only a few hundred of those. There are about 23,000 councillors in the UK – more than twenty times as many as all other kinds of elected representative combined. Local government is the front line of British democracy.

The fact that local services are managed by locally elected people is meant to ensure they reflect the priorities and identity of each place. Local councillors are people who live in your community and understand the problems residents face, city by city, town by town, street by street, farm by farm, business by business. They understand how a place works.

'There are some services that are best delivered for a local area rather than across the whole country,' says Paul Bettison, leader of Bracknell Forest Council in Berkshire.

'It would be unthinkable that you would try to organize street cleansing – sweeping streets, and picking up litter – across the entire country, for example. You have to do it by breaking it up into smaller areas, and if we're going to have services delivered over these smaller areas, we need someone to plan them and keep an eye on how it is being done on behalf of residents.'

Their role as people's champions in a relatively small area means that our elected councillors are much more accessible than national politicians and there is a lot of contact through surgeries, public meetings and in person, Bettison says.

'We are far more accessible than MPs and we also cover smaller areas, so we know each street, we walk each street before each election and many of us in between as well. Every councillor's contact details are very well publicized, so people will call you at home, sometimes at midnight. They will come and see you, and they will ask for you to come and see them.

'We are very, very available, and that is important. It is amazing how many people you bump into in your local supermarket queue and they while away the time haranguing the councillor they happen to be standing next to'.

Despite their accessibility, there remains a widespread lack of understanding about exactly what services councils provide.

Part of the confusion stems from the fact there are often two or three layers or 'tiers' of local government in the same place. In many rural areas of England, for example, there is a top tier of larger county councils providing wide-area services such as education, library services and social services, sitting above a middle tier of smaller district or borough councils providing more localized services such as rubbish collection and planning. Below that, there is a lowest tier of parish and town councils – the smallest units of local government, closest to the people but with only very localized powers such as running cemeteries or managing footpaths. We will take a closer look at parishes towards the end of this chapter.

Elsewhere in England, and everywhere in Scotland and Wales, instead of the two layers of county and district there are 'unitary' councils that provide almost all local services to their area, from running schools to collecting the bins. There are still parish councils here, at the very local community level.

London has slightly different arrangements: there are thirty-two London boroughs – which are similar to unitary councils rather than county and district – plus the City of London Corporation which run most services. However, strategic planning for transport and development has been taken over by the Greater London Authority (GLA). This is made up of an elected mayor who takes decisions about policy and sets budgets, and an elected assembly whose main job is to oversee the work of the mayor (elections for the mayor and assembly are separate, but they take place on the same day). We will come back to elected mayors later on in this chapter.

In Northern Ireland, because of past direct rule from Westminster and the sensitivities of the peace process, the twenty-six main or principal councils are similar to unitary councils but they provide fewer services than in the rest of the UK. They do not provide education services, for example, partly because the schools system has mirrored the deep social divisions in Northern Ireland society and is judged to need higher-level, less localized control. In fact, five education and library boards cover the whole of Northern Ireland, and there have been moves to centralize further to a single education authority. Now, however, local government in Northern Ireland is strengthening and taking on new powers, as part of the peace dividend, and a reorganization is underway to create fewer but stronger principal councils. From May 2015 a new structure of just eleven of these councils will be created, with powers similar to English district councils.

Of course, the average citizen neither knows nor cares what the structure of local government is in their area, nor wants to tell one tier from another; he or she just wants the bins collected on time, the graffiti cleaned from their walls, or the swimming pool opened early in the morning. Or any other of hundreds of council services, from education to planning, street-cleaning, refuse collection, library services, social services, transport, highways, street lights, parks, economic development, restaurant inspection, trading standards, cemeteries, local records and archives, port and harbour facilities, electoral registration . . . all the way through to pest control, dealing with asbestos and licensing the storage of poisons. Local councils are also responsible for creating plans to respond to emergencies such as floods, large-scale road problems, aircraft crashes or any other unexpected crisis or disaster. While a core team of emergency staff will manage the process, other council staff will often volunteer their time to man hotlines twenty-four hours a day, help residents evacuate or staff shelters when something out of the ordinary happens. They also have increasing involvement in health services, with new public health duties being handed to them as part of recent NHS reforms. All in all, councils play a huge part in improving the quality of everyone's lives, every day, often without us noticing.

Different parts of the UK use different election systems for local government. In England and Wales (apart from the Greater London Authority) they use first past the post, the same system as for MPs; in Scotland and Northern Ireland they use the single transferable vote (STV). At the time of writing, Wales is also considering switching to STV for local government elections.

Whatever system they use, however, local elections are also suffering from the same problem of falling voter turnout as national elections – worse, in many cases.

In most recent years, turnout has dropped below 40 per cent for local elections, and as low as half that amount or less in some poorer areas and inner cities. In local elections held in May 2013, the average turnout was about 31 per cent. Can it be true that fewer than a third of UK citizens care who runs their communities?

Local elections analyst Colin Rallings of the University of Plymouth says people's motives for voting in local elections vary widely.

'In some places, it's almost an exact match with national voting patterns, but in others different choices are made, either to send a signal to the government, or simply because the election is for a different job,' Rallings says.

'The electorate is happy to pick horses for courses. Some parties or independent candidates are seen as doing a good job locally, though people might not vote for them to run the country.'

Councillors in Britain are also slightly more representative of the population in gender terms than national politicians – though only slightly more. Overall about 30 per cent of local councillors in England are women, though this rises to 36 per cent of councillors in London boroughs and 40 per cent of councillors in metropolitan authorities. Outside England, about a quarter of councillors are women: 25 per cent in Wales, just over 24 per cent in Scotland and 23 per cent in Northern Ireland.

It is easy to see why many people would struggle to become councillors, or stay on for more than one term, particularly younger people: as with other kinds of political activity, the demands on a person's time can be great and the pay is minimal. There is a history of councillors being volunteers, running local services in their spare time – and then finding they don't have any spare time.

Some councils do offer a liveable wage – one typical medium-sized authority in the north of England, for example, offers councillors a basic allowance of £11,500, with extra pay for those taking on more responsibilities, adding up to more than £40,000 in total for the council leader. However, there is no consistency between councils, and many still offer much lower allowances and expenses, which can tilt the balance towards older or retired people becoming councillors, or people with other sources of income.

'The government has allowed councils to raise allowances, but they have to do it themselves, and it is difficult for councillors to raise their own wages,' says Paul Bettison of Bracknell Forest. 'We are caught between the devil and the deep blue sea.

'My cabinet members receive around £17,000 – not a king's ransom – but in some councils, some members can still work seventy hours a week, more than most full-time jobs, and get just £2,000 a year.'

So how exactly does a council work?

A local council is divided into its political part – the groups of elected councillors, who take key policy decisions such as creating and approving new local plans for libraries or the environment, and approving spending; and the operational part, which manages and runs services from day to day.

In this, the elected councillors – also often referred to within local government as 'members', or members of the council – are distinct from the council managers, or 'officers' – who are the ones that run the council's day-to-day operations. The members are the politicians, setting policy and strategy, and the officers are the local equivalent of civil servants.

To carry out their work, there are various different ways that councillors can organize themselves.

Before 2000, all local services were overseen by committees of councillors, with a different committee deciding on every issue such as planning or housing, and different councillors on each committee. Many councillors could be involved in decision-making, with most sitting on at least one committee.

The Local Government Act 2000 replaced this committee system in England and Wales with a choice of either a Cabinet headed by a council leader or an elected mayoral system. For now at least, most councils and local voters chose to have a local Cabinet system.

Under a Cabinet system, the council as a whole votes for a 'leader' – a bit like a prime minister, locally – and the leader then appoints a Cabinet of typically eight to ten councillors. Most strategic decisions are then taken by this Cabinet or 'executive' – similar to the Cabinet system used in national government.

In the Cabinet model, the other councillors outside the Cabinet – who are known as non-executive members or backbench members – take on the role of scrutinizing the work of the council on behalf of the residents. These backbench members sit in scrutiny committees that work a bit like select committees in the parliamentary model

In both the old committee model and the newer Cabinet model, there are also regular (usually monthly) meetings of 'full council', attended by every councillor. Full council takes certain key decisions, like approving key local policies such as an area's transport plan, the annual budget, and regulatory and legal functions like overseeing planning, licensing of premises and elections. It is also the full council's role in a Cabinet system to help hold the Cabinet to account.

Then there is the elected mayor system. Elected mayors – the other option offered under the Local Government Act 2000 – have so far not proven very popular in most places outside London, since the arrival in 2000 of the UK's first directly elected mayor – Ken Livingstone, running at the time as an independent candidate.

The London-wide mayor is a special case, however, as most local services in the capital are still controlled in a layer beneath, by the London borough councils. In other parts of England and Wales, however, and even within these London boroughs themselves, councils have been offered the chance to create even stronger directly elected mayors.

These super-mayors, or so the argument runs, have powers to hack through dusty old, bureaucratic, party-political local government, taking decisions far more quickly, for everyone's benefit. The idea is that they will also be much better known (can you name your council leader?), and hence more accountable. They can innovate, experiment, and they take no prisoners. These are not the old-fashioned Lord Mayors and Lady Mayoresses, passive figureheads driven from dinner to dinner in their ceremonial chains. They are a new breed who replace an entire council Cabinet with their own advisers or councillors, whom they appoint personally.

There are limits to the power of elected mayors: many of their decisions, in fact, are 'co-decisions', which need to be approved by the full council as well. The mayors can also appoint their own Cabinet of councillors to take some decisions. The details can get complicated and, this being local government, they also vary from place to place. But the key point about an elected mayor system is that the mayor has a great deal of scope to make decisions personally: it is more like a local version of a president than a local version of a prime minister.

Of the mayors elected so far, several of them are independent candidates, not linked to any political party – most memorably in Hartlepool, where a man in a monkey suit – H'Angus the Monkey, the mascot of football team Hartlepool United – swept to power in 2002 on a ticket including free bananas for schoolchildren. The man beneath the costume – local twenty-nine-year-old Stuart Drummond – initially ran simply to get publicity for the football team, and was amazed to win on a protest vote against the main parties. However, once elected the 'monkey mayor' ditched the fancy dress to concentrate on serious local politics. Hard work and perseverance – initially he knew nothing about local government – paid off, and the plain-speaking Drummond ended up shortlisted for an international award for best city mayor (despite backtracking on the bananas promise – too expensive, though fresh fruit has been made available in all local schools). He was subsequently re-elected twice, the first UK mayor to achieve this. And while the post of elected mayor was removed once more in April 2013 following a referendum the previous year, Drummond had made his mark in the history of UK local government. The best headline on this topic was probably the *Guardian*'s: 'Gorilla tactics'. But behind the jokes lies a serious message about a local person with no political background connecting with the residents of a place and being chosen to represent them, beyond party politics. And making a success of it, for a decade at any rate.

A 2012 report on elected mayors and city leadership by the Warwick Commission, a panel of experts convened by the University of Warwick, found that switching from a council leader to an elected mayor can create a buzz around local politics and democracy that can energize debate about a place.

'There is now a real sense of momentum, direction and purpose,' says the Labour city mayor of Leicester, Sir Peter Soulsby, quoted in the Warwick Report. 'There are now cultural debates – a real buzz in the city – it's not just about buildings but what happens around them.'

This sounds fantastic. The only problem is, for the moment there does not seem to be a big appetite for elected mayors.

So far, only seventeen places have elected super-mayors, a club now reduced to 16 with the loss of Hartlepool: namely Bedford, Bristol, Doncaster, Hackney, Leicester, Lewisham, Liverpool, London (Ken Livingstone, then Boris Johnson), Mansfield, Middlesbrough, Newham,

North Tyneside, Salford, Torbay, Tower Hamlets and Watford. And in referendums held in 2012 on the introduction of elected mayors in nine other cities – Birmingham, Coventry, Manchester, Leeds, Nottingham, Bradford, Sheffield, Newcastle and Wakefield – the residents all said no, thanks.

The reason the widespread reticence seems to be that there is no strong case yet that directly elected mayors bring better local government to an area, and there are risks as well – what if you get the wrong person in charge? Understandably, if people are not well persuaded, they rarely vote for more politicians, or more change.

But the reason for introducing the mayors – to energize local democracy – is still valid, and urgent. As there are now a good few elected mayors, if they are seen to do a good job the concept is likely to continue as a locally decided issue. So the few elected mayors there are have the future of all elected mayors in their hands.

In fact, the way local councils are run in England has now been opened even wider, to more choice, since the passing of the Localism Act 2011. This has now offered councils at least four options on how they want to run themselves: a Cabinet system, an elected mayor, back to the old committee system, and a hybrid between Cabinet and committee (which councils can propose and which must then be approved by the government).

So local choice about the way councils are run is increasing; if you live in England, expect more stories in your local paper about how your council is run, and more referendums.

Another innovation in local democracy was the appearance in 2012 of forty-one elected Police and Crime Commissioners across England and Wales (Scotland and Northern Ireland have not adopted the model, with Scotland shifting to single national police and fire services).

The commissioners are elected on four-year terms to set objectives for policing in their areas, theoretically providing strong local accountability for policing priorities, because to be elected they will have to set priorities that will be popular locally. They do not run the police forces directly – that is left to chief constables, though the latter are appointed and dismissed by the commissioners.

Previously, police forces in England and Wales were overseen by police authorities – organizations separate from local authorities but whose membership was usually made up of just over half councillors, with independent members and magistrates. If they do not sound familiar to you, it is not surprising because hardly anyone knew they existed: according to a 2011 report by a think-tank called 'Yes Minister', only 20 per cent of people had ever heard of them. So one of the big jobs of police commissioners, as with elected mayors, is to be noticed and known about – to connect with local people.

It is a concern, therefore, that the early signs are that the new police commissioners are no better known than the old police authorities, and turnout in the first round of commissioner elections last year was incredibly low, at just 15 per cent.

However, it is a new system, and perhaps people were simply confused by what it might mean. The real test will come next time around with the second police commissioner elections in 2016, after people have had more of a chance to see what they do – will they end up capturing people's imagination?

So much for local politicians. How about the council officials that the politicians oversee? Those dreaded town-hall bureaucrats who – if their popular image is correct – would ban two kids from playing conkers as soon as look at them, and dig up your road four times a year for a laugh?

In all, local government employs more than 2 million people across the UK, from front-line professionals such as teachers and social workers to people who run services behind the scenes – the council managers or 'officers'. The relationship between officers and councillors or members is central to the smooth functioning of a council – and varies greatly from place to place.

'Councils all have their own culture, and size is definitely a factor in this,' says Glyn Evans, a former senior officer at Birmingham City Council. At £4 billion, Birmingham's annual budget is the size of a small country's, but Evans has worked in every type of council in his time, urban and rural, all shapes and sizes. 'You can quite easily work for a district council which has one or two qualified accountants, whereas in Birmingham they have one or two hundred, so they have a very different view of the world.'

Whatever the size of council, politicians and managers need to work together well for services to run smoothly, Evans says. The senior officers of a council – the chief executive officer at the top, and the heads of services or departments such as the head of finance, or the director of education – are appointed by the full council or groups of councillors from all parties sitting as selection panels. But once they are appointed, they need to be allowed to get on with the job, he says.

'The relationship between officers and politicians should be a partnership. The politicians are in charge of policy and strategy, of defining the outcomes they want realized – advised by officers. But the officers should be in charge of actually delivering the services from day to day – advised by politicians.'

Council officers – and particularly senior officers, and a council's most senior officer, the chief executive – also have various legal responsibilities for making sure services are run properly, to a minimum level, and that money is spent wisely. These are big responsibilities, but because of the way the public views politicians as responsible for everything, there is a tendency for councillors to want to get involved in day-to-day running of services, to 'micro-manage' in areas they may not know much about, Evans says.

'My view is we've got the balance wrong between local politicians and managers. We've now got a situation where whatever goes wrong then politicians are blamed for it, so that drives them to try and micro-manage.'

What is needed is a clearer code of practice – drawn up by local councils themselves – setting out who is responsible for what, he says. It would state more clearly what councillors are responsible for – and can be blamed for – and what the separate roles and responsibilities of officials are. Evans accepts this would put officers more in the public firing line, creating a 'hire and fire' culture where chief executives come and go according to results. But the benefits would be an environment where local politicians were less fearful of trying new ways of delivering services, and hiring people with the skills and experience to try out new ideas – and would then take more of the responsibility for them if they fail.

Hiring and firing council managers for trying new ideas? If it happens, one of the new breed of pioneers might well be Stephen Baker, who is chief executive of two councils at once: Suffolk Coastal District Council and Waveney District Council.

The idea of having a single management team for more than one council is one example of a growing phenomenon known as 'shared services'. The concept of local councils sharing managers, or computer systems, or fleets of refuse-collection trucks has been around for some time, but is gaining ground in a time when public money is being hugely squeezed. More and more councils are sharing resources, from a cluster of councils in Dorset which have clubbed together to run a shared website, to a huge 'tri-borough' agreement between Hammersmith & Fulham, Kensington & Chelsea and Westminster councils in London, who are sharing management of some £300 million of services, with estimated savings running to tens of millions.

What is never shared is the democratic element – the local elected councillors. So while the two neighbouring councils of Suffolk Coastal and Waveney have shared services including planning, human resources and environmental health since 2010, and have a single set of managers running these services across both their areas, they still have two sets of councillors, two Cabinets, and two council leaders. In this way, the local councillors can set different strategies for their different areas, which is the whole point of local democracy.

'The councils can still have different policies across the two areas – so if one says we want to focus on a higher standard of restaurant inspection, while the other wants to focus more in rural areas, that's fine,' says Stephen Baker. 'But the same team will deliver the services across both.

'The best thing is we can share ideas, and share examples of what works.'

Even with different councils setting different strategies, there are limits to how far sharing of service delivery can go without starting to compromise the essential flavour of local government, however. This is because the way things are run is to some extent determined by the teams running them, not the people setting the policy. So if a system of sharing became too large, and everyone was using the same IT systems, for example, or the same types of road-sweeping machines, the danger is that it would not be local government any more. So there will be more and more sharing of this and that, here and there, with local solutions for local areas; but if the government ever started to push for more systematic sharing across larger areas, local government would be likely to resist.

This may not stop the battle from happening: the tension between government getting bigger at the centre to save money, or becoming more local to respond to local needs, will always be there. It all boils down to cash: while governments always say they want to hand more power back down to local communities, there is so much money at stake that they never quite want to let go of the purse-strings.

In fact, UK councils account for as much as a quarter of all annual public spending, at around £180 billion a year, and only around a sixth of this – £34 billion – is self-financed, mainly through council tax.

Council tax might seem simple – councils raising a bill for their services – but it is not.

Let's take a look at how it breaks down in one sample area: Rushcliffe Borough Council in the county of Nottinghamshire in England. In 2013, the average property in Rushcliffe in valuation Band D – the band used as a medium measure – paid £1,603.93 in council tax. However, only a very small proportion of this – just £113.22, or about 7 per cent – was actually intended to be spent by the borough council itself, the authority which bills and collects the whole tax. The bulk of the amount – £1,193.18 – was passed up to Nottinghamshire County Council for the most expensive local government services such as education, social services and roads. A further £166.41 (more than the borough council charges) was added as a precept by the Nottinghamshire Police Authority; £69.69 by the Nottinghamshire Fire and Rescue Service; and an average of £61.43 by the local parish councils.

Clearly, council tax is a lot more diverse than many people realize. And clearly too, there can be implications for the tax as a whole if just one of the parts of it – the police, say – is asking for a bigger increase than the others.

In the Rushcliffe example, the bill as a whole represented on average a small increase on the previous year's bill – just 0.4 per cent. This is not too bad at all. On the other hand, the county council, the borough council and the fire authority had all frozen their demands at 0 per cent on the previous year: the 0.4 per cent overall comes from a 3.9 per cent rise in the amount required by the police authority. This might all be completely justified – but how many people will realize that in this case and in many others, the rise in their council tax had nothing to do with the council who was billing them for it?

Under the Localism Act 2011, a local authority is now required to hold a referendum if it proposes an increase in council tax by a level set by the government each year (currently 2 per cent). Most councils are avoiding this by setting slightly lower increases, but as and when referendums take place, the way that council tax is assembled could make the issues hard for people to understand. In some areas it is made even more complicated by the fact that some local bodies, such as National Park authorities or port health authorities, can raise 'special levies' which do not count towards the increases that trigger a referendum.

How can you make head or tail of it in your area? Your local council should issue clear information on its website or in printed material on exactly how your council tax breaks down (if it doesn't, kick up a fuss). Brew yourself a strong cup of coffee and take a look.

The great bulk of local government funding is still handed down by central government, through various grants and types of support.

With so little of councils' revenue under local control, it is hard for them to increase their spending much without council-tax levels rising out of proportion – a phenomenon known as 'leverage'. To understand this, imagine your budget was £100 and you wanted to raise it by say 5 per cent – to £105. The problem is the amount you control – your council tax – covers only half your budget, or £50 – meaning you will have to increase it by not 5 per cent but 10 per cent just to raise that extra £5. In fact, councils raise much less than half their own money, so the leverage is actually much higher than this. So they push and push – and the centre squeezes.

In fact the amount of local government fundraising and spending that is controlled nationally in the UK is unusually high compared with most other developed countries, and this, it could be argued, is damaging to local democracy.

Some moves to increase local taxation and spending power in England are being made this year with the return of a small amount of local business rates to local control. At the moment, business rates in England are collected by councils and handed to the government, which then decides how much to give back down to each area. The intention now is to let councils hold on to a proportion of any increase in local business rates collected in future – so that if the local business sector grows, councils will benefit directly. In addition, twenty-eight English towns, cities and regions, from the Black Country to Wiltshire, are in the process of being given more control over transport and other major project budgets in a wave of so-called 'city deals'.

Increasingly, the funding battle might be fought at an even lower, smaller, more local level as well, because the familiar local authority is not always the most local body running public services in our area: there are also some 11,000 smaller – sometimes tiny – town, parish and community councils across England, Scotland and Wales, and their scope is growing.

These miniature councils cover about 35 per cent of the population of England and all of Wales and Scotland (though around a quarter of Scotland's are suspended because not enough local people can be found to stand for election). In England, they are still more commonly found (as the parish council) in rural areas and market towns, but in recent years changes in the law have seen more neighbourhood councils being established in cities, including even in London, to run tiny, highly localized services in another layer even more local than the main or 'principal' local council.

The process for setting up a new community council – known as a 'community governance review' – can be triggered either by a petition signed by local people, or by the primary local authority. A typical neighbourhood council might have around ten councillors elected every four years, with many candidates standing as individuals rather than party representatives. Though many of their powers are less than earth-shattering – cutting grass, watering hanging baskets, maintaining noticeboards, or being consulted on planning decisions – neighbourhood councils in England and Wales can also take on 'concurrent' duties from larger councils with a big effect on local quality of life, such as managing allotments, burial grounds, sports centres, playing fields or libraries.

Community councils like parishes are the closest form of government to the electorate, and often their members are not linked to political parties but run just as independent representatives of the community. Many parish councillors do go on to become councillors at higher levels of local government, however, when they realize where the real power lies and get a feel for how local democracy works. So community councils are a good starting place for anyone interested in local politics.

'Parish and town councils are the only part of our democracy that is growing,' says Justin Griggs of the National Association of Local Councils (NALC), which represents neighbourhood councils in England.

'At the most local level, they really do make people feel as though they can elect their friends and neighbours to be their voice, to be able to collectively say things to other service providers and to provide their own services in a way that's much more responsive, much more alert to very local priorities.'

Small community events, from 'litter picks' to bringing people together at local festivals, fetes or concerts, 'really do make a difference,' Griggs says. 'It improves the social fabric.'

In Scotland, the 1,200 or so active community councils are funded by the larger 'principal' local authorities (to the tune of only about £400 each a year), but in England and Wales neighbourhood councils can raise their own small tax or precept on local people – which, as we have already seen, is added by the principal council on to council tax in that area. The average precept raised is about £45 per person, totalling up to tens of thousands of pounds per neighbourhood council.

Overall, the community wave is gathering momentum, with the extension to neighbourhood councils of a general 'wellbeing' power. In 2000, principal councils in England and Wales became able to undertake general actions to promote the wellbeing of their local area, even beyond powers they had been specifically given by law. This was expanded by the Localism Act of 2011 into an even stronger 'power of general competence' – meaning that councils could now undertake absolutely any action, for any purpose, providing it was not specifically forbidden by law (previously, it had been the other way around: they were only allowed to take actions that had been specifically allowed). This has given local authorities similar legal rights to an individual person.

At first, the new freedom did not apply to neighbourhood councils, but after campaigning by NALC, the power of wellbeing was extended in 2008 to town, parish and community councils where certain conditions were met, such as councillor training. Then in 2011, when the power of general competence came in, neighbourhood councils were again entitled to it, again subject to qualifying conditions. So far about 150 neighbourhood councils have qualified and have been able to use the general power to take actions such as funding cookery training for young vulnerable adults, running local community shops, petrol stations or post offices, or lending money to local businesses.

'It is still very early days, but as the years go forward we will get a feel for how local councils can use their new power,' says Griggs.

In Scotland, too, there are moves for community councils to be given greater powers, with the Scottish government investigating the possibilities. A 2012 survey by the think-tank Reform Scotland found most Scottish people would like to see more powers over planning and community infrastructure passed to community councils, and felt this would boost community participation – though 66 per cent felt they should not be given the power to raise their own money as in England and Wales.

The key to success of all local-government projects is community engagement – capturing people's interest, imagination, energy and support, and, along the way, their understanding of the meaning of local democracy.

Nothing illustrates this better than the Citizen Inspectors project, developed over the past two years by West Lothian Council in Scotland (it just happens to be from the home of the last chapter's West Lothian question – a happy coincidence). The project allows any local resident over the age of sixteen to apply to become an inspector of council services on behalf of the whole community and to suggest improvements to the way services are run.

Following a recruitment process using local papers, the web and social media, the first ten citizen inspectors were selected. In a short training programme, the inspectors learn a bit about the council and are taught a few relevant skills, such as interview techniques. Then they are set loose in teams of four to inspect real council services – initially, winter maintenance services such as gritting roads, and pupil placement in local schools – by interviewing managers, staff and service users; shadowing workers; testing services anonymously in 'mystery shopping' exercises; running surveys and focus groups; dropping in on site visits; and studying performance data and comments and complaints received from the public.

At the end of the process, they write up a report to be sent to the chief executive and relevant council committee, to become part of the improvement plan for each service. Issues they have picked up on include poor levels of communication with the public when roads were going to be cleared of snow, and schools closed – issues that have now been taken up by the council's communications team as well as the service teams.

Rebecca Kelly, quality development officer at West Lothian Council, says the project has helped people understand how their council works – including some who have had a dim view of it in the past.

'We have had people become inspectors who had previously complained about our services, and seen some of their views completely turned around. Once they had spoken to managers and staff, and heard how local decisions are made and how they work, they would often decide we were actually doing quite a good job under the circumstances.

'The project helps people understand what their council is trying to do, and it helps the council understand people's priorities too – it's enlightening on both sides.'

More citizen inspectors are now being recruited, and other councils are looking on with interest.

It is true that exercises like this can directly involve only a very small number of local people, but they might be a good way of showing everyone else that the council is there to serve local people and listen to local people. It is an imaginative approach to local engagement, which is desperately needed because, as with political parties, the big challenge for local government in the years to come is to connect more closely with the people they serve.

In many ways, times have never been harder for councils. They have been on the front line of recent budget cuts to public services and are suffering from the same low levels of approval, engagement and enthusiasm as all parts of the modern political system.

On the positive side, some of the tools they may need to help them fight back were contained in the Localism Act of 2011: the new options for local choices of ways of working politically, for example, might be one way to let local people have more of a say. Another is the 'power of general competence' that we have already heard about, potentially allowing councils to undertake more and more imaginative and innovative local projects without being restricted to offering a certain set of services, defined by law.

What else might be needed?

Early in 2013, the House of Commons Political and Constitutional Reform Committee released a report called 'The prospects for codifying the relationship between central and local government'. As a name for a report, it is hard to think of anything less inspiring to ordinary people, if it had been written in Klingon; nevertheless, the report did contain some interesting ideas.

Among the most intriguing, was one about money: if local government is to become more powerful, and closer to local people, there needs to be a better connection between money raised locally and money spent locally.

'Any attempt to make the relationship between central and local government more balanced would be meaningless without giving local government its own source of revenue,' the committee said.

So the government should consider spelling out more clearly what percentage of everyone's income tax goes to local government, not to raise income tax but just to 'allow local people to see more clearly what their taxes pay for locally and encourage them to hold local councils to account for their expenditure.' But the report also said the government should consider whether and how it could free councils in England to raise their own additional revenue through new local taxes, with the consent of local people.

The committee also suggested that the government should examine whether it would be a good idea to draw up a statutory code for local government, cementing their place in the UK's political system – and dovetailing perhaps with Glyn Evans' idea of a code of practice for councillors and officers within local government itself.

A code could set out the details and limits of relations between central and local government, helping to protect the powers of local government and helping voters understand who does what. The committee even suggested that local government could play the same role in England as the devolved bodies do in the rest of the UK: taking on more powers, and helping to solve the West Lothian question.

This idea emphasizes how closely intertwined are the elements of democracy in the UK that we have met so far: the UK Parliament, the devolved bodies, and local government. Each part needs the other parts, and each part affects the other parts. In trying to improve our democracy, we must always remember this: no one part stands alone.

Soon we will return for a closer look at central government and how it works from day to day. But before we do, let us move even higher up the UK's ladder of power. Because power – legal power – rests above central government in the UK, in an institution that is so rarefied it is centred in just one single individual – the monarch.

It is time to ask some questions about the Queen.

Chapter 8

The monarchy – a free power station?

Any major royal event, such as a coronation, wedding or jubilee, high-lights the British monarchy's position in our lives as a shared national experience. The exact kind of experience varies from person to person, but we all share it. The monarchy forms a big part of what it means to be British: a symbol of our nationality that endures beyond those polit-icians we love, then hate.

Nevertheless, the Queen herself does not appear to have much say in anything. How does this work?

The British monarchy is not an absolute monarchy, where a sovereign is in charge, but a constitutional monarchy. This means that, while the monarch is the legal source of all national power, in practice the monarch's power is only exercised according to our constitution – the laws set down by Parliament and conventions established over time.

The monarch is our head of state, however, so when a visiting leader arrives on a state visit they often stay in a palace and dine with the Queen, which adds a touch of magic. But to achieve anything political, they must meet the Prime Minister and other ministers, who make all the decisions that matter.

The legal powers retained by the monarch are known collectively as the Royal Prerogative. Some of these powers are very impressive, like making war or dissolving Parliament; others are smaller and relate to fish.

In our constitutional monarchy, however, most of these powers have either been passed over to politicians or government agencies acting 'on behalf of the Crown', or they are only ever exercised by the monarch 'on the advice of' the Prime Minister or government ministers – advice which is always taken.

So you might say the monarch has these powers, but always hands them over to the elected government. To have a constitutional monarch is a bit like having a free power station: power for the nation to use, under their control.

How do you become the monarch? Not by being elected – to become the monarch, you must be born in the right place at the right time. Until very recently, it helped to be male as well.

As with most features of a constitutional monarchy, succession to the Crown is governed by law (some of which dates back to 1700) and until 2013 this stated the Crown was passed on to the oldest male child, unless there were none. It was clear, however, that should the first-born child of Prince William and Kate Middleton or any future heir to the throne be a girl, there was no chance in the modern world that the public would accept her being passed over for a male heir.

In fact, the public has supported a change for some time, but the British government had always blocked such a move. This was partly because all the other countries which have the British monarch as their head of state need to agree to any changes and the process was seen as too complicated. The British monarch is separately the constitutional monarch of fifteen other nations, from Australia, Canada and New Zealand to Belize, Papua New Guinea, and various Caribbean and Pacific islands, right down to tiny Tuvalu (population: about 10,700). (The Queen is also the appointed ceremonial 'head' for her lifetime of the wider Commonwealth of nations, although there is no rule to say the British monarch has to be head of the Commonwealth. The Commonwealth nations will decide together whom to appoint as their next head, after the Queen.)

Agreement to change the law to allow female heirs to have an equal claim to the throne was finally reached among all sixteen Commonwealth realms in 2011, with legislation rushed into Parliament at the end of 2012, just as a royal pregnancy was announced. At the same time, changes were made to allow future monarchs to marry someone who is Catholic – though they cannot themselves, as head of the Church of England, be a Catholic.

The episode highlights some interesting features of the monarchy. It shows that it is slow to change, but that it does eventually adapt once public opinion reaches a certain tipping point. It also shows that changing it is not entirely in British hands.

There still remains, too, the hereditary principle – only members of a certain family can become the monarch. Supporters of this principle say it lifts our head of state above the divisive squabbles of party politics and allows everyone to unite behind the Crown. On the other hand, it does mean that the personal qualities of the monarch are generated by nature, at random.

This may not matter too much, since in a constitutional monarchy, most of the time, it is the government that ends up using the Royal Prerogative powers, not the monarch. But the government can also pass – or try to pass – ordinary laws in Parliament to give itself the powers it needs. What's the difference?

In fact, there is not always much difference; but on the whole the reason for the Royal Prerogative – its usefulness, and also sometimes its risk – is that it can enable decisions to be taken without consulting Parliament. So prerogative powers often deal with urgent situations like war, or the machinery of running the country.

Some of the Royal Prerogative powers which have been handed over to the government for day-to-day use include using the army overseas; declaring war or peace; making treaties; organizing the civil service, including the creation of new government departments; taking or destroying private property in a national emergency; and issuing or withdrawing passports.

Other powers exercised by the monarch acting on advice from the government include giving out honours; creating members of the House of Lords; dissolving Parliament and calling elections; appointing or dismissing the Prime Minister and other ministers; and granting assent to new laws ('Royal Assent').

Over the years, a range of laws and conventions has been developed to ensure the powers are exercised in the public interest. 'Royal Assent', for example, has long been a formality: although as recently as the early twentieth century George V considered refusing assent to the Irish Home Rule Bill, no monarch has actually refused assent for more than 300 years (in 1708, Queen Anne refused to pass a Bill creating a militia in Scotland, in case it should become disloyal).

Even longer ago, in the fifteenth century, monarchs had even been known quietly to slip in a few bits and pieces of their own to laws before signing them: the former House of Commons clerk Thomas Erskine May wrote that 'Henry VI, and Edward IV, occasionally added new provisions to statutes, without consulting Parliament' (equal rights for corgis, anyone?).

These days, it is impossible to imagine a situation where a monarch would refuse to assent to a law passed by Parliament. For one or two of the other royal powers, however, there are greyer areas about how they might be used, even in the modern world.

These include the dissolution of Parliament and the appointment of new governments, which might conceivably, in certain situations, still involve genuine choice and judgement on the part of a monarch: for example in a hung parliament, or an unforeseen emergency situation.

Hung parliaments are usually straightforward to sort out, but are potentially extremely complex. The current convention is that after any election with no clear outcome, the previous Prime Minister has the first attempt to form a coalition, even if they are now heading the smaller party. This is what happened in 2010, when Labour was allowed to try first to form a coalition, even though they had won fewer seats than the Conservatives; only when these negotiations were unsuccessful could the Conservatives step in. It can become even more complicated if the party that was last in power wants to try to form a minority government and there is no clear coalition in sight.

Can the monarch, as the only person allowed to appoint a new Prime Minister and invite them to form a government, play an active part in helping sort all this out? Monarchs (advised by their private secretary and others) have played such a role in the past, but it would always have to be within the limits of public acceptance, or the monarchy as a whole could be in danger.

Even without any involvement by a monarch, however – for example, if procedures for forming a new government were handed over to a constitutional court – the process would not necessarily always be straightforward. As with much about our constitutional monarchy, at least the current set-up seems to work.

Some of the exercising of Royal Prerogative powers is undertaken by a group of politicians called the Privy Council, so-called because it used to be a small group of the monarch's closest advisers.

Senior politicians, including all Cabinet ministers, are appointed to the Privy Council for life, and in all there are about 600 current members. However, only a few of those Privy Council members who belong to the government of the day (typically about four at a time) are invited by the Prime Minister to transact its current business on average about once a month, so again this ancient mechanism has become part of the workings of a modern elected government. The council meets wherever the Queen happens to be, so sometimes its members do have to travel out to Windsor or even, occasionally, Balmoral.

Decisions taken by 'the Queen in Council' might include sanctions against countries such as Libya; or matters closer to home such as the approval of royal marriages.

They also include changes to Royal Charters. The granting of charters – essentially, documents that set up a body as a special independent kind of legal entity – is a historic way of managing an organization that is seen as pre-eminent in its field and acting strongly for the public good, such as the BBC and the British Red Cross.

The granting of a charter gives a body stability and an air of permanence. These days, however, most of the elements contained in a charter can also be covered by ordinary modern company law, so new ones are rarely bestowed. The main difference is that, while they operate independently of government, there is a degree of government control over the operations of a chartered body, as the Privy Council has to approve any changes to or renewal of a charter.

Certain Prerogative powers are a bit weirder than others, as the reason for their existence is lost in history. Some have fallen into disuse, such as the Crown's right to 'impress' or press-gang men into the Royal Navy without warning – dormant since the early 1800s, but theoretically revivable tomorrow. Others are lesser powers that have managed to hang around, like the monarch's right to all sturgeon, dolphins, porpoises and whales caught in British waters. Any loyal angler who has offered their sturgeon to the monarch in recent years has been politely turned down, however. With whales, the question arises only when one is beached, with ownership (or disposal) rights now handed over to official agencies such as the Scottish Executive Environment and Rural Affairs Department (SEERAD). But ancient elements of the law still apply, so we find that: 'The right to claim Royal Fish in Scotland allows SEERAD (on behalf of the Crown) to claim stranded whales which are too large to be drawn to land by a "wain pulled by six oxen". SEERAD understand that no stranded whale measuring more than 25 feet from the snout to the middle of the tail could be so drawn to land, and so only intend to review the right to claim stranded whales which measure more than 25 feet.'

Exactly how SEERAD has calculated that a whale measuring twenty-six feet from snout to tail could not be drawn to land in a wain pulled by six oxen is unclear.

The Crown also retains the right to ownership of all wild and unmarked mute swans in open water as 'casual revenue', but the Queen only exercises her ownership for the purposes of an annual conservation census on the Thames known as 'Swan Upping'. The practice dates from the twelfth century, when the Crown took a keen interest in swans, or at least in roasting them at banquets. But every July the Royal Swan Uppers can still be seen pottering upriver, wearing scarlet uniforms, some with feathers in their hats. When a brood of cygnets is sighted, a cry of 'All up!' is given and the boats close in to capture the birds, which are examined for any sign of injury from fishing lines, then weighed, measured, tagged and released. As a US news report once summarized, 'it's a wildlife census in fancy clothes'.

When it comes to all the more archaic Prerogative powers, from time to time someone suggests doing away with them. But the government says 'legislating in these cases would be a questionable use of Parliamentary time' – and unless there are cases when these ancient rules can be shown to be causing a serious problem, it is hard to argue with this.

Another ancient slice of activity under the Royal Prerogative is the awarding of honours for outstanding bravery, long service or achievement. In theory, anyone can receive an honour, and nowadays anyone can nominate someone for one too, including themselves. Following a review in 2005, committees chaired by 'independent eminent people' in relevant fields decide who gets what, and three-yearly reports are published on how they operate.

However, there are a few honours for which the sovereign still personally selects recipients, including the Order of the Garter, for which the monarch by tradition selects twenty-four people, plus herself, some other members of the Royal Family and foreign royals. At the time of writing, holders include one former Prime Minister John Major, and had also included Margaret Thatcher until her death in 2013. Two other former Prime Ministers, Tony Blair and Gordon Brown, are not Knights of the Garter, however – presumably by their choice – a fact which, according to royal protocol, led to them not being invited to the wedding of Prince William and Kate Middleton, unlike the Ambassador to Zimbabwe, a country subjected to sanctions by the UK government.

Most honours are given out at the request of the government, though all are given by the monarch, and the recipients of all honours are generally happy to receive them.

Isn't all this question of who has what power a bit confusing? In fact, it is clear that, overall, Parliament is in charge – and not just by convention, but by law as well.

On taking the throne, monarchs pledge to obey the will of Parliament in an oath set out in an Act of Parliament, the Coronation Oath Act 1688. Each new monarch is asked if they will swear to govern 'according to the Statutes in Parlyament Agreed on', to which they must reply: 'I solemnly Promise soe to doe.'

If a monarch did ever act against the wishes of the people, the power to act in that way would soon be removed, since Parliament is capable of removing any Prerogative power at any time, or replacing it with an ordinary law. In a court judgement dating back to 1610, the Case of Proclamations, the principle was set down that 'the King hath no prerogative, but that which the law of the land allows him.'

Furthermore, where a new law is passed which overlaps with a Royal Prerogative power, the courts will look to the law first and the Prerogative second. In this way, many former Prerogative powers have been superseded over the years.

The Civil Contingencies Act 2004, for example, covers most of the situations where the government might previously have used the Royal Prerogative to enter, take and destroy private property where this is seen as necessary to deal with national emergencies such as terrorism. Where the new Act can be applied, it will be – but as the Prerogative power has not actually been abolished, the government advice is that it could still theoretically be used 'in particularly extreme and urgent circumstances and on a strictly time-limited basis' where there is not time for a government official to contact a minister to fulfil the requirements of the Civil Contingencies Act.

In this case, the government says that the retention of a 'residual' Prerogative power in this area is necessary to guarantee our security.

In a recent review of the Royal Prerogative powers, it said: 'Enacting a statutory power to do this could result in either an undesirably broad statutory power or one that is insufficiently flexible'. However, it is not wholly clear why this should be the case, if a broad statutory power to seize or destroy property was simply being used instead of a broad Prerogative power.

Whatever the legal debates, recent governments have slowly been reforming and reducing the Prerogative powers. The Constitutional Reform and Governance Act 2010, for example, set out new rules whereby most international treaties to be signed by the UK, which in the past would have been signed by the government using the Royal Prerogative, will now first have to be scrutinized by Parliament for at least twenty-one days before ratification, and voted on. Again, however, the government does retain a residual power to sign treaties without pre-discussion in exceptional circumstances.

So reforms of the Prerogative powers are ongoing, but they are not so much about the monarchy as about how far any UK government is free to act without consulting Parliament.

Although we have seen that the monarch has few real powers any more to exercise of her own free will, what about other privileges? Is the monarch and her or his family in any special position when it comes to the law?

It is true that the monarch acting in a personal capacity is above the law, and cannot be prosecuted for anything: were she to bludgeon an orphan to death with an out-of-date library book, she would not even be liable for a fine on the book. This scenario, however, can probably be discounted.

The monarch is also technically exempt from paying tax, although she does so voluntarily.

No discussion of the monarchy lasts for long, however, before money is mentioned. Funding of the monarch's activities is fairly complicated, but the basic chunks are easy enough to understand and they have now been simplified further.

Up to 2013, the Queen and the Duke of Edinburgh received a fixed annual payment from Parliament of about £8 million to help the monarch fulfil her duties as head of state; this is known as the Civil List. No other royals have received a Civil List payment in recent years, although they used to. Around £24 million more in grants had been paid each year from various government department budgets for expenses such as travel, communications and the upkeep of palaces – help with the monarch's costs of acting on behalf of UK citizens, as their head of state. In 2011, however, the Sovereign Grant Act was passed and has now (from 2013) replaced this system with an all-in-one payment to the monarch – valued initially at about £36 million and based on a level the same as (though not directly funded by) a set portion of the profits of the Crown Estate (15 per cent, to start with, reviewable every five years).

The Crown Estate is a vast collection of land and property that, many centuries ago, used to belong entirely to the sovereign but nowadays gives all of its revenue to the state. It includes huge chunks of Regent Street, the entire UK seabed out to twelve nautical miles, and all sorts of other holdings totalling more than £6.6 billion, with net profits standing at more than £200 million a year.

The precise status of the Crown Estate, like many features of our constitutional monarchy, is like something out of *Alice in Wonderland*: technically, it belongs to the Queen, but she cannot sell it; it is 'independent', but every year it gives all its money to the Treasury, which can then decide what to do with it.

The Duke of Edinburgh will continue to receive a separate annuity directly from Parliament, which at the time of writing was set at £359,000 a year.

The Queen is reported to have welcomed the changes, because the all-in-one payment of the Sovereign Grant will allow her to share her money how she wants between palaces, travel, staff wages and other costs, rather than having separate pots of money for each item.

The new Act also places oversight of royal spending for the first time under the same body that audits government spending – the National

Audit Office – and opens it to scrutiny by the Public Accounts Committee of the House of Commons.

Even tougher financial rules could be drawn up for the monarch, but
the more any government were to become involved in the day-to-day
running of the Royal Household, the harder it might become for the
monarch to be impartial when dealing with politicians – an essential
part of a monarchy, as long as we have one.

In fact, Parliamentarians tend to shy away from discussing royal
funding at all, not because they can't, but because the more the monarchy
is discussed, the more it is politicized and so the less point there is to it
in the first place.

This leads to comic dashes for the exit whenever the subject crops
up in Parliament. At a House of Lords debate in November 2010 on the
new arrangements for royal funding, for example, the chamber emptied
in a flash as the Labour peer Lord Berkeley got to his feet – and peers
do not usually do much in a flash. Lord Berkeley noted that the Crown
Estate 'can go up and down in revenue and it does seem a bit odd to
link a long-term arrangement for funding [to] a percentage of such a
volatile revenue, and if the percentage is not fixed, then there's going
to be many fraught and embarrassing negotiations probably going on
every year.'

Defending the changes, the Liberal Democrat Peer Lord Addington
said: 'If we go to an elected president . . . would they be any cheaper to
run? I suspect not. The French President still has a lot of cavalry wearing
heavy armour parading around in front of him.'

Both excellent points, though few were there to hear them.

The new grant arrangements will not affect two other pieces of the
royal funding jigsaw: the Royal Duchies of Lancaster and Cornwall,
separate large holdings which do not form part of the Crown Estate.

The Queen receives income from the ancient 'Duchy of Lancaster',
a huge estate of rural and urban land and property plus financial
investments worth almost £400 million held in perpetual trust for the
sovereign. Although the monarch cannot sell any of its assets, the profit

from the duchy currently amounts to about £13 million a year and is used by the Queen to support her family, apart from the Prince of Wales and his own family.

This is because the Prince of Wales, as heir to the throne, has his own estate in trust: the Duchy of Cornwall, a more rural estate mainly in the south-west of England. This is worth around £760 million, and in 2012–13 earned the Prince £19.1 million from rents and other sources. This income – supplemented with about £2 million in government department funding and other public sources – is used to fund his 'public, charitable and private activities', including his family. The recent Sovereign Grant Act carried a clause which also ensures the proceeds of the estate can now be passed to a female heir to the throne – not the case previously.

Much is also made in the media of the private wealth of the monarch, the extent of which is not known. Some royal artefacts, including the Crown Jewels and some of the Royal Collection of art, is simply held in trust for the nation and so does not belong to the monarch person-ally; but the private estates at Sandringham in Norfolk and Balmoral in Scotland, and much art, antiques, jewels (though not the Crown Jewels), racehorses and even the privately owned royal stamp collection are likely to be worth a great deal. In all, the monarch's private wealth is often reported to amount to hundreds of millions of pounds, though if and how it could all ever be sold off is another matter.

In law, there is no requirement for the monarch to pay tax on most of her income, although tax on the monarch's private income, and income from the Duchy of Lancaster, capital gains tax, even VAT and customs taxes are all mostly paid 'voluntarily'. However, the Queen does not pay death duty.

Prince Charles has also paid income tax voluntarily since 1994. Tech-nically, he does not have to either, though now, as with the Queen, it would be hard for him to stop paying without damaging public support for the monarchy.

Other members of the Royal Family have no special tax exemptions.

Supporters of the monarchy say the royals bring in millions to the UK economy through the value of their palaces, parades and ceremonies as tourist attractions. Whether such attractions would retain their value beyond the existence of a monarchy is debatable. But many tourists and people across the world do seem to see far more romance in queens, kings and princes than in presidents and prime ministers.

Overall, money is a secondary issue when it comes to considering the monarchy. If it is a part of our constitution that we consider valuable for the continuity and stability it brings, then the amounts of money spent on it do not seem large compared with most other areas of public spending. And for opponents of the monarchy, the problem is more what it represents than what it costs: republicans feel that no position of influence should be inherited rather than earned.

Ultimately, however, living in a democracy, the main reason we still have a monarchy at all is that most people want one – or at least prefer the idea of one to any conceivable alternative. Over the centuries, there have been fluctuations in public support for the institution, and as late as the mid-nineteenth century there were still fairly large groupings of 'radicals' in Parliament who wanted to establish a republic. Nowadays, however, most politicians from all parties support the monarchy, not least because it is something that the voters want; and it works well enough not to worry about.

In fact, support for the monarchy is spread widely across all age and income groups in UK society, according to an ICM poll for the *Guardian* carried out in 2012. In common with all opinion polls carried out over many decades, overall this research showed clear public support for keeping our constitutional monarchy for the foreseeable future.

Its findings included that 69 per cent of people think Britain would be worse off without the monarchy (22 per cent said better off, and 9 per cent don't know). In the longer term, people are not so sure: a similar survey the previous year found 89 per cent of people think Britain will still have a monarchy in ten years' time, though only 57 per cent think there will still be a monarchy in fifty years, and just 40 per cent think there will still be one in a hundred years.

Whenever the sands of public opinion do appear to shift from under the monarchy, however, moves are generally made to shore it up. Reforms to the laws of succession, concessions on tax, changes to funding and relaxations of protocol have all been introduced just in time to retain public support. For the time being at least, and for the foreseeable future, this flexible process of royal evolution seems likely to preserve the monarchy as the UK's slow-burning, long-lasting, tourist-attracting power station.

But where most of that power is used – where the power cables run – is in Parliament, and above all, in Downing Street, the focus of our next examination.

Chapter 9

Decisions, decisions – the business of government

A short walk from Buckingham Palace and an even shorter one from Parliament, just beyond the fortress-like Treasury, nestled between the grand Foreign Office and the discreet Cabinet Office and sheltered behind high iron railings, is Downing Street.

In 1732 King George II presented the house at 10 Downing Street to Sir Robert Walpole, considered to be the first British Prime Minister, though the job was not called that in those days. Walpole accepted the house as the official residence of the 'First Lord of the Treasury' (the title still inscribed on the brass letterbox at 10 Downing Street) – an extra role which is still always taken by the Prime Minister, showing that the person in charge controls the cash. These days, suites of offices have been built inside and along the back of Downing Street for people working with the Prime Minister and other units at the heart of government, though the Prime Minister still has a home there as well.

The Chancellor of the Exchequer – the Second Lord of the Treasury – lives at 11 Downing Street. At number 9 is the office of the government's Chief Whip, and number 12 houses the Prime Minister's press office and research unit.

The last-known private resident of 10 Downing Street (or part of it) was a Mr Chicken, about whom nothing is known beyond his name: and some might wish the same of some of its more recent occupants. As a job, however, being Prime Minister is not easy. What exactly does it involve?

The job of Prime Minister, like the role of the Cabinet and many other aspects of the UK government, is not set out in law, but is just convention – the accepted way of doing things. As such it can be changed radically at any time without passing laws.

Potentially, pretty much anything and everything can be examined by the person in overall charge. With so much possible, the difficulty is to step back and take the wide or long view. In an age of twenty-four-hour news and the internet this is getting harder and harder, as David Cameron told the Leveson Inquiry into the behaviour of the press in 2012.

The danger as Prime Minister, said Cameron, is that 'you are fighting a permanent battle of issues being thrown at you hour by hour, where responses are demanded incredibly quickly'. Political leaders 'have got to get out of the 24-hour news cycle . . . focus on long-term issues, and be prepared sometimes to take a hit on a story they don't respond to so quickly.'

So that is the aim: the leader of the government will try to focus on strategy, looking at detail only where it is unavoidable. As head of the nation, the Prime Minister will also spend a lot of time on world affairs and on the economy.

Like any leader, the Prime Minister also needs to appoint the best people possible to take on chunks of the national workload. As well as appointing Cabinet and (with advice from whips and officials) other government ministers, he or she takes a hand in or approves the appointment of the heads of the Security Service MI5 and the Secret Intelligence Service MI6, military leaders, ambassadors and other top civil servants.

UK government is to a large extent Cabinet government. While the Cabinet has no legal powers of its own, and is really just a way of facilitating meetings and making decisions, it controls the leading group – the government – in the real seat of power: Parliament. All the government's most important policies are agreed in Cabinet, a group of about twenty-five of the most senior government ministers picked by the Prime Minister.

As well as picking the most competent people to serve in a Cabinet, the trick is not to just appoint those who represent one type of view: it is essential for Prime Ministers (and First Ministers) to carry as many factions of their party with them as possible, for fear of creating enemies. John Major was overheard in 1993 referring to 'Lyndon Johnson's maxim' in relation to rebels in his Cabinet: US President Johnson had said of FBI director J. Edgar Hoover, 'it's probably better to have him inside the tent pissing out, than outside pissing in'.

There is a limit in law to the number of paid Cabinet posts, at twenty-two, though other unpaid posts are possible. Non-Cabinet ministers (including ministers in the House of Lords), along with relevant advisers and officials, can be invited to attend all or part of meetings, which typically last for an hour and a half on Thursday mornings, though they can be held more often and last longer. The same basic Cabinet system on a smaller scale has been put in place in the devolved governments of Scotland and Wales, while in Northern Ireland there is a slightly different 'executive' system, which includes more parties in government to reflect the pattern of their seats in the Assembly and also the presence of compulsory coalition (see Chapter 6).

Shaping the Cabinet agenda and chairing the meetings is another key part of the Prime Minister's role. Ministers can say in advance which issues they would like to be discussed, and the PM, working with advisers and Cabinet Office officials, selects which ones will be covered and which other issues should be raised.

Most items are quick and, with time to discuss only two or three issues in any detail, the main focus of Cabinet meetings is always on current parliamentary business; the economy; and defence and foreign relations, though sensitive areas of national security are not discussed in full Cabinet, but reserved for a special Cabinet committee – a smaller group of relevant ministers and officials – called the National Security Council and its sub-committees (more on these shortly).

The meeting style depends a lot on each Prime Minister – some allow any minister in the room to express an opinion on any subject, others are less tolerant.

Formal votes are hardly ever taken in Cabinet – to close each item the PM summarizes the point reached and the Cabinet Secretary – a top (arguably, the top) civil servant – records the conclusion, or what seems to be the conclusion. It is not always clear.

So Cabinet is brief. In fact, many key central government policy decisions take place in Cabinet committees and sub-committees – smaller groups of ministers and officials whose decisions usually carry the same weight as full Cabinet decisions.

Until recently, like all matters relating to the Cabinet, very little was formally revealed about these committees, but the government now publishes a list of Cabinet committees and their membership.

Early in the twentieth century there were several hundred Cabinet committees: it seemed that every issue, however small, was an excuse to form a new one, but policymaking is now more devolved to the different government departments, with less happening at the centre.

Most of the time, when questions are raised about policies or disagreements arise within government, ministers and civil servants are encouraged to sort it out between themselves by letters or emails sent between departments, or by meetings of senior civil servants or other less formal meetings. Where an issue cannot be sorted out in this way, however, or where a very important policy is at its early stages and all ministers involved feel it needs to be discussed more formally, then a Cabinet committee or sub-committee meeting will be called by the chair of that committee.

There are currently about thirty Cabinet committees, including permanent or standing committees such as the National Security Council; the Home Affairs Committee; European Affairs; Economic Affairs; Public Expenditure; and the Parliamentary Business and Legislation Committee. A few sub-committees, acting beneath or reporting to these committees, look at specific issues of prime importance, such as the Social Justice (Child Poverty) sub-Committee; and 'ad hoc' committees are formed to cover temporary issues such as the 2012 Olympic and Paralympic Games. Sub-committees beneath the National Security Council, for instance, currently include one to handle strategy on national threats and emergencies, including an even more restricted sub-group to consider intelligence matters, one to consider nuclear deterrence and security, and one examining the UK's relationship with emerging international powers such as China.

In the most urgent situations of national crisis, another type of committee is set up, known in government as a Cabinet Office Briefing Room (COBR) or in the media by the racier, James Bond-like name of 'COBRA'. These are similar to Cabinet sub-committees but draw in other relevant agencies such as the police, the UK devolved administrations and local government.

Some Cabinet committees on key topics like the economy and defence are chaired by the Prime Minister, but most are chaired by other ministers. Publication of membership of UK Cabinet committees is quite a recent innovation: until 1992 they were kept secret, a situation which pleased ministers because no one knew whom to hassle about which issue, but did not please anyone else, for the same reason.

Most Cabinet papers, such as background papers, meeting conclusions and the Cabinet Secretary's notebooks, are still kept secret, subject until recently to a thirty-year rule before they were published in the National Archives; this is being gradually reduced between now and 2020 to a twenty-year rule.

Is it right in a democracy for such important documents of state to be kept secret for so long?

The reason for most of the secrecy surrounding the Cabinet is to enable free debate – an essential condition to allow ministers and officials to debate options, argue and disagree without worrying about media headlines, before uniting on a single national policy.

The outgoing Cabinet Secretary Gus O'Donnell, for example, told *The Times* in 2011 the Cabinet should be a 'safe space' for free discussion, and that more transparency would lead to less debate and hence poorer government. Others fear that if the main meetings were more open, meaningful debate would be driven into smaller, less formal meetings involving even fewer people, on the margins.

The secrecy or privacy of the Cabinet is seen by its supporters as an essential part of one of the core principles of Cabinet government – 'collective responsibility'. Under this principle, whatever and however strong are any disagreements between ministers behind closed doors, they must always end up agreeing a single policy to which they must all stick in public – or leave the government.

To disagree with their government on any key issue, therefore, ministers must resign. And if many people within a political party disagree with the leadership on an issue, they must form their own party. The reason is clear: if a government could present different policies to the public at the same time, how would anyone know whom to support, or how to vote? A government is a single, collective entity – in the face it presents to the outside world. Disunited, it is not a government – and it will usually fall.

This convention of collective responsibility is also observed by the Scottish and Welsh governments and the Northern Ireland Executive – though the devolved leaderships sometimes do things a little differently as well.

The Welsh Government Cabinet – with nine members – is unusual in openly publishing the minutes, papers and agendas of its meetings unless there are overriding reasons to withhold material, for example if it is commercially sensitive. For instance, detailed discussion of the awarding of a council contract to a business may not be released where some information is handed by a company to the council in confidence – such as detail of a company's pricing policy that it does not want its competitors to know about, or other trade secrets.

The Scottish Cabinet also currently has nine members, who meet weekly in Edinburgh while Parliament is sitting, and in the summer break it holds fortnightly meetings at other locations, from cities to the far-flung Highlands and Islands (not to be outdone, the UK government has taken up the same practice, with occasional meetings in locations such as Birmingham, Exeter and Aberdeen).

There is more openness in some aspects of how the Scottish government works: for example, a list of 'Scottish ministerial preferences' is published online. This is an internal briefing document for Scottish government officials, with guidelines for officials on how each minister likes to receive their briefings, notes and speeches, including how they like letters to be written by officials on their behalf, and what times the ministerial boxes close each day to be taken home.

They offer an insight into the demands on a minister's time: guidance for officials submitting papers to the office of Scottish Finance Secretary John Swinney, for example, are advised: 'A short, focused, concise submission can often do the trick and move an issue along. Think about it – how would you feel if someone handed you fifty 20-page submissions to wade through overnight? How far would you get before deferring the material to another day?'

Other notes detail preferred formats for letters to be signed by ministers, or speeches to be delivered. Notes on speeches written for Scottish Culture Secretary Fiona Hyslop, for example, state: 'Ms Hyslop speaks at approximately 150 words per minute and requests that approx 10 per cent of her speaking time is left free to allow her to take interventions/add anecdotes.'

Cabinet ministers are at the top of the tree, but there are many other jobs in government. In Northern Ireland there are two junior ministerial posts, in Wales three, in Scotland thirteen; and in Westminster there are some seventy-four MPs and twenty-eight peers who are ministers outside the Cabinet.

With the Cabinet and the Prime Minister, this makes about a hundred MPs in government. Furthermore, nearly half of all these ministers are each assigned another MP to be their unpaid general assistant or Parliamentary Private Secretary (PPS). The PPS is a minister's 'eyes and ears' in Parliament, watching out for how policies are being received by backbenchers; this can sometimes be a first step towards government, allowing a backbencher to see how a minister works – and a minister to see how the backbencher works. So at the time of writing, the total number of MPs involved in government in some way – in Cabinet, outside Cabinet, or working as a PPS – is 146. At 23 per cent of MPs, some say this is too many, and it is many more than in the past: up from ninety-five in 1950 and just forty-two back in 1900. But still, four-fifths of MPs are in Opposition or on the backbenches: a comfortable majority.

For MPs who do become ministers – whether in Cabinet as a secretary of state or as a more junior minister – life becomes very busy, very fast. Even junior ministers cover many different policy areas, and for most there is a lot to learn in next to no time.

Lynne Featherstone, former junior minister in the Home Office (she has since moved to the Department for International Development), arrived in government for the first time after the 2010 election to be handed a portfolio covering everything from domestic violence to missing people, prostitution and wheel-clamping on private land. She remembers a flurry of briefings in her first few weeks in post from teams of officials in all the various policy areas. 'Each one seemed clear at the time, but there was such a volume that five days later it was hard to remember details of all of the new subjects.'

Though it is a huge privilege to be part of a national government, with the power to put political ideas on improving people's lives into practice, the workload is unrelenting, Featherstone says. A typical ministerial working day runs from 6 a.m. to 11.30 p.m., answering questions in Parliament, attending meetings, sitting on policy committees or inter-ministerial groups.

'Every half an hour there is something different that you need to be briefed on. As a minister, you sit on top of a large machine that spends its time organizing things to come to you, because often only the minister can take a decision.'

For Cabinet ministers, the workload and pressure are even higher. Zoe Gruhn, director of leadership and learning at the Institute for

Government, says many politicians are unprepared for government and could be better supported.

'For many ministers, their apprenticeship is through working as lawyers, barristers, maybe running a small business. They do not tend to be people who run big corporates. The expectation is that you learn on the job, but to go from a university background through having an office of two people as an MP to having an office of 30,000 as a minister in charge of a government department is daunting, and not many people know how to do that effectively.'

The situation is not helped by a reluctance for politicians to admit they need support, says Gruhn. 'It is difficult because they have been elected to be competent, so they don't want to show any weakness. But while that's fine for constituency work, it does not prepare them for government, where they must cover a wide range of issues.

'Ministers need not just induction but ongoing training and development as normal custom and practice, in the way you get businesspeople going off for training to make them more effective leaders. Even famous sportspeople have coaches, because they always need to be better than the competition.

'It is not something that should be seen as weakness, and to say politicians are unique and different is nonsense.'

As well as overseeing the running of public services, ministers also form a key part of the process of developing new ideas, policies and strategies for the government. They do this through central structures like the Cabinet sub-committees, and also within their departments, with their officials and by bringing together their own groups of experts and advisers to consult.

'In my policy areas of science, technology, broadcasting, multimedia, and space exploration I identified groups and individuals within each field who I felt could come up with innovative ideas,' says Ian Taylor, former Minister for Science and Technology from 1994 to 1997. 'So in the space industry, for example, I asked my advisers to develop a national space strategy which looked at all aspects of the sector. This doesn't mean to say you accept everything that comes back to you, but [it] provides a much stronger policy platform and a much greater understanding of the priorities you should take.'

There will always be limits for manoeuvre when it comes to developing new policies, such as the government's overall strategies on spending (or not spending) and the impossibility of doing everything that everyone would like you to do, Taylor says. There is also the problem that major changes such as the establishment of a new public agency would usually require new laws to pass through Parliament, which is time-consuming. But within these restrictions there is a great amount a canny minister can achieve, he says.

'Any wise minister tries to do as many things that don't require parliamentary approval as possible, such as improving existing policies or enhancing their reach, because primary legislation will take at least a parliamentary session, and may take several sessions.

'But there are a lot of initiatives you can take which – while they might require collaboration with other departments – do not require primary legislation. Such things for example, in the fields I covered, as setting overall priorities for scientific research, or encouraging changes in the way science and technology is taught in schools.'

Ministers can also look to restructure their department to support their priorities, and must always fight for their budgets within the government as a whole, Taylor says.

'Departments have an overall budget which is agreed with the Treasury, so to an extent ministers compete within that total for their own budgets. It's a process of negotiation between ministers and officials, persuading each other of the priorities. Fighting for your budget is an important skill.'

When policy priorities are higher profile or do require new laws to be passed, or were pledges in a government's manifesto, the centralized power structures of the Cabinet Office and the Prime Minister's office play a bigger role in driving plans forward.

At the heart of government sits the Prime Minister's policy unit, a small group of civil servants, political advisers or some combination of the two that acts as the Prime Minister's key advisory group on policy and strategy. It is up to each Prime Minister to create his or her own unit – that builds relationships with all the departments of government.

This powerful unit in Downing Street sits very close to the Prime Minister as an individual. It often reviews ideas from departments and ministers before passing them to the Prime Minister, and helps to set overall priorities and policy themes for the government. To be acted on, however, any new ideas will usually have to be passed by the Cabinet, and ultimately by Parliament, before being carried out by ministers in their departments. So all parts of the system need each other and must work together – along with research teams in political party headquarters, policy think-tanks and ministers' own policy advisers – the special advisers or 'Spads' we will meet in the next chapter.

Cabinet government – and policy formation – is close to party politics, but it is not always the same thing, most clearly when – as currently in the UK, and formerly in Scotland – there is a coalition government with two or more parties combining to rule. This might seem a recipe for chaos, but in fact, according to one UK Cabinet minister, agreements can be strong.

Sir George Young, the Government Chief Whip and a Conservative member of the current Conservative–Liberal Democrat Cabinet, says the Coalition Cabinet works differently from a one-party Cabinet, but it does work. In effect, there is an extra layer of 'coalition machinery' that sits above the traditional Cabinet machinery, with the aim of resolving any cross-party disputes ahead of Cabinet meetings, he says. 'It's very collegiate. If you sat at the Cabinet table, most of the time you wouldn't know what party people belong to. You could argue it was more cohesive than a normal Cabinet.'

The system is replicated within government departments, with ministers from both parties in the Coalition building consensus and taking any disagreements outside to a Cabinet committee for Coalition dispute resolution co-chaired by the Prime Minister and Deputy Prime Minister.

Outside government, however, the parties separate back out into their traditional separate roles, Sir George says. 'As you get further down towards the constituencies, you get a different atmosphere, because we are contesting elections, and we all want outright victory next time around.'

Whether working in a coalition or for a single-party government, the most important aspect of any minister's work in a democracy is accountability.

Ministers are held responsible for whatever happens in their department, and across their whole policy field, such as education or healthcare. In a sense, that is their point. They are in charge, and they are elected politicians, so they stand or fall on their record, and they are part of a government that the people can either vote back in next time around or not, depending on how well they do.

The accountability of ministers takes many forms, from being grilled by TV journalists to responding to written and oral questions from backbench MPs. Sometimes, as we will see in Chapter 11, they face court cases against their decisions. In Parliament they must steer Bills through debates to become law and appear before select committees.

One key committee that scrutinizes the work of different departments at different times is the Public Accounts Committee. This independent-minded body picks its own topics, focusing laser-like on whether the relevant departments are spending public money well and achieving what they should efficiently and effectively. At one time or another, most ministers will be called to appear: topics of PAC reports last year, for example, ranged from looking at whether money was spent well around the Olympics and Paralympics; matters to do with the sale of the former bank Northern Rock; and issues as detailed as the contracting out of language translation and interpreting services by the Ministry of Justice.

A similarly daunting experience for ministers is appearing before the

Public Administration Select Committee (PASC), another watchdog that examines the 'quality and standards of administration within the civil service' – basically, how well the government as a whole is doing its job. Recent PASC inquiries include public procurement – how well the government purchases goods and services – and public engagement in policymaking.

Ministers' activities are also measured against the Ministerial Code, which sets out standards of conduct expected from them, such as declaring financial interests. Versions also exist for Scottish and Welsh government ministers and Northern Ireland executive ministers.

One widely perceived problem with the code, however, is that it is up to the Prime Minister to decide if it has been violated. The current and the previous Prime Ministers have appointed independent advisers to rule on whether or not this has happened, but it is up to the PM to decide whom to appoint as the adviser, whether or not to refer a minister to the adviser, and whether to take the advice – all areas of ongoing debate.

Another perennially controversial area, which has been hitting the headlines again in 2013, concerning ministers and public trust is that of 'lobbying'.

Lobbying – a word derived from the historic practice of people standing around in the lobbies at Parliament waiting to talk to politicians – will always be part of politics, and in a free society the ability for individuals and organizations to put their case directly to politicians is essential.

Usually, lobbyists will simply be trying to present information to ministers on how policies that are proposed will affect businesses or citizens; but where they are lobbying solely on behalf of an organization or interest group that is paying their salary, they will be putting across only one side of each case.

What does it matter? After all, charities and citizen campaign groups often hire their own lobbyists.

There is a perception, however, that bigger, richer organizations are able to hire greater numbers of lobbyists, generating a wave of influence over politicians whose power is disproportionately large. After all, many consultation processes are quite esoteric and, let's admit it, not too high on the excitement scale: it is no surprise then that when a meeting is called in Westminster (or Brussels) to debate a policy issue, for example, the room is often mostly full of people who have been paid to go along, and paid to take a certain line.

This would all be fine if it were clear to see who was doing what on behalf of whom. The main problem, say those calling for tighter regulation, is that there is simply not enough information available about lobbying activity, with the result that even very big campaigns to influence politicians might be taking place without anyone even knowing they exist.

Until recently, the lobbying industry had been wholly self-regulated by three separate organizations: the Association of Professional Political Consultants, the Public Relations Consultants Association and the Chartered Institute of Public Relations. Each of these bodies has drawn up codes to which it says responsible lobbyists should stick, and each has (different) routes that people can take if they want to complain about a member possibly violating one of the codes. The problem was that all the codes were (and still are) voluntary, and because there are three, the suspicion is that organizations and lobbyists can pick and choose which one they want to follow, or which bits of which one.

Following a scandal in the summer of 2013 involving allegations of an MP taking money to support a cause, however, the government proposed a law to create a single compulsory register of lobbyists by 2015, and says it will also enforce more transparency about who is meeting ministers and what they are talking about.

The law – the Transparency of Lobbying, Non-Party Campaigning and Trade Union Administration Act – was duly passed early in 2014. The new law, however, will only require third party or external professional lobbying agencies to sign up, which some say will only capture a small fraction of the general activity of political lobbying. Tamasin Cave, for example, of the Alliance for Lobbying Transparency – a group of campaign organizations including Greenpeace and Friends of the Earth – says that third party only represent about a fifth of the activity going on. Most lobbying is carried out by in-house lobbyists and other staff working inside organizations, she says.

Registration should be wider, to cover all lobbyists, and organizations should also have to register 'good faith' estimates of how much they are spending overall to lobby on certain issues, Cave says.

'They have been doing this in the US for years, so they know for example how much the healthcare industry has been spending to fight Obama's healthcare plans. So then you can have a proper debate about it, and see whether money has the power to change the nature of the debate.'

As for ministers releasing details of the meetings they hold, they simply need to comply properly with existing rules, Cave says. 'They are supposed to record all meetings on a quarterly basis, but a lot of the big departments take nine months to get those published, and then they give very little info about the subject of the meeting.'

Her group accepts the importance of ministers consulting with organizations of all kinds including big business, she says, but more openness is needed to make sure they are fairly balancing competing concerns.

'We are all lobbyists, and proud to be so. Lobbying is an essential part of democracy – it is a lack of transparency that is the problem.'

The House of Commons Political and Constitutional Reform Committee has backed the call for regulation to be expanded to cover everyone who lobbies professionally, including in-house employees lobbying on behalf of businesses, charities, trade unions and think-tanks.

This move is also supported by many lobbyists. For example Michael Burrell, Chairman of the Association of Professional Political Consultants, has written in the *Huffington Post*: 'The public needs to see who we are and better understand what we do. A statutory register of all lobbyists would give the public the chance to find out for themselves and let us and our activities be judged and scrutinized.'

In Scotland, plans are also in hand to introduce a statutory register of lobbyists to the Scottish Parliament, so this could be another area where Westminster can look to the newer devolved bodies for inspiration. However the new reforms are implemented, this subject will not be closed. Clearly, as well, whatever lobbying rules are put in place for companies, must also be observed by MPs. As this book went to press, a new lobbying controversy was breaking in which an MP was accused by undercover journalists from the BBC of failing to disclose money received for lobbying work promised. So for the benefit of all sides – citizens, corporations, charities and lobbyists – more transparency about who is spending what money in putting their case to politicians would surely be a good thing.

In the meantime, campaigners for reform will wait to see what happens, and will continue to press for change . . . by lobbying ministers.

Chapter 10

Yes, minister – the civil service

Government minister Jim Hacker (apoplectic at being sent into a meeting without a proper briefing, to civil servant Sir Humphrey Appleby): 'Humphrey, do you see it as part of your job to help ministers make fools of themselves?'

Sir Humphrey (suavely): 'Well, I never met one that needed any help.'

Yes Minister, Series 1, Episode 6 – 'The right to know'

The classic BBC series *Yes Minister* from the 1980s was much loved by the then Prime Minister Margaret Thatcher for its uncannily accurate lampooning of the civil service. But if not quite to help ministers make fools of themselves, what is the job of a civil servant supposed to be?

In part, the job is in the name – a civil servant is employed to serve our society. Specifically, they serve the government which has been elected to represent everybody – and as soon as new politicians are elected, they must serve them with equal energy.

In the widest definition of public servant, it is a big group of people. Counting everyone who works for some kind of public service body, there are some 6 million workers, including those in local government, education, police, NHS, public corporations like the BBC and other special cases – such as, in recent years, the odd bank or two.

The term 'civil servant', however, is usually used to refer to the group of public sector workers that works directly in or for central government departments and agencies, ranging in size from a few hundred staff to 80,000 or more within the big UK government departments such as the Department of Health or the Ministry of Defence. It is also now used to refer to people working in the devolved UK governments.

There are currently around 420,000 people (full-time job equivalents) who are counted as working for the UK civil service, though this is set to reduce to around 380,000 by 2015 as part of a reform plan. The vast majority of these officials work in 'front-line' services, working directly with the public in roles such as advising people on their benefits, or issuing passports. Many more work inside the departments and agencies as managers for these services, or carry out specialist jobs such as being a government lawyer.

At the higher levels, however, civil servants are more involved with policy work, at the interface between front-line service delivery and politics. The role of the civil service at these higher levels is to help government ministers improve those front-line services, gathering information about how they are working, developing new ideas for how they might work better, briefing ministers (see *Yes Minister*, at the start of this chapter), and offering choices and decisions for ministers to take.

This is an important role, but as civil servants are not in overall control, it requires patience – and stoicism.

'Senior civil servants have the freedom to analyse, and think, and make recommendations,' says Anthony Zacharzewski, founder of the Democratic Society – a non-partisan body which aims to boost engagement with democracy – and himself a former civil servant. 'But you are not in charge. You can make recommendations all you like, but if they are ignored, then you have to take it.

'On many occasions I created what I thought was a good policy idea, but it was knocked down because it didn't fit with what senior management wanted, or it conflicted with some new policy announcement, or the politicians simply did not agree. The first time it happened, my boss's boss just changed his mind about the direction he wanted to take the project. I was young and a bit naive, and it was teeth-grindingly frustrating.

'A few years and plenty of knockbacks later, I just thought "Oh well".'

The core values of the civil service are set out in a code which is drummed into all new recruits: integrity, honesty, objectivity and impartiality. In particular, civil servants must not allow their personal political views to guide any of their actions at work.

A similar code has been drawn up for civil servants working for the Scottish and Welsh governments and for the Northern Ireland civil service. These officials are still UK civil servants, and their core values are the same, but the devolved code for Scotland, for example, adds in a clause on 'recognition of the importance of co-operation and mutual respect between civil servants working for the Scottish Executive and the UK Government . . . and vice-versa.'

Ultimately, it is fair that it is the ministers who take final decisions. After all, they are the ones who will have to defend themselves publicly and run for re-election. They are the ones who are held to account. So when it comes to giving advice to ministers, and to most of the rest of their work unless things are going wrong, civil servants are anonymous and their advice is usually kept private. Again, this is largely so that it can be left to the politicians to decide how and when to act.

As the civil service code says: 'You must not disclose official information without authority. This duty continues to apply after you leave the Civil Service.'

Where matters are more sensitive, such as those relating to national security, defence, international relations and crime, the Official Secrets Act applies, making it a criminal offence for civil servants to disclose information. It is often said that civil servants have 'signed the Official Secrets Act', but it does not need to be signed: people may sign something saying they understand that it applies to a certain job, but whether or not they sign, it applies anyway. It also applies to everyone who might come across restricted information by accident.

None of this means that civil servants of the more senior, advisory kind do not have any influence. As they usually last longer in a specific field, such as health or education, than their politicians, they add stability and continuity to the management of public services.

So who are the top civil servants? The most senior job in the civil service is Head of the Home Civil Service, a post currently held by Sir Bob Kerslake. His role is to make sure civil servants are properly recruited and trained, with the right skills to do their jobs, and that their working conditions are good and fair.

Other top jobs include the Cabinet Secretary (the civil servant in charge of running the Cabinet – see previous chapter); and Permanent Secretary for the Cabinet Office (the civil servant in charge of the Cabinet Office, the government department which helps drive policy and services across the whole of government).

Moving down through the civil service, there are currently thirteen pay grades, which also act as ranks of seniority (the number of grades may soon be cut to ten, as part of reforms). The highest rank includes the heads of the big government departments, known as permanent secretaries (the word 'permanent' has a telling ring to it, compared with their more transient masters – the politicians). Permanent secretaries are very senior positions: they work very closely alongside ministers, and in a sense they really are the people who 'run the country'. In *Yes Minister*, the wily Sir Humphrey Appleby is the permanent secretary of Jim Hacker's department and the mad manoeuvrings of their relationship are the source of all the entertainment.

Below that the grades cover such job titles as director general (of which there can be several in a department, often mirroring the portfolios of ministers), directors and deputy directors. The 'senior civil service' is usually considered to cover Grade 5 and above, which includes around 4,000 people – about 1 per cent of the civil service.

As a general rule, people working in the higher grades move around a lot more between jobs and departments, or in and out of the civil service, while at the lower grades, down to Grade 13 (administrative assistant, or AA), it is less unusual for people to stay in the same job for longer periods. As well as reducing the number of grades, however, it is part of reform plans to break down the barriers between grades, allowing even more people at all levels of the civil service to move around and advance.

People used to talk – sometimes scathingly, sometimes longingly – about 'jobs for life' in the civil service. Is it still such a stable career move?

'At junior levels, civil service jobs are desirable as they're generally better paid than jobs in the wider economy and with better conditions,' says the Civil Service Commissioner Jonathan Baume. 'And generally – despite recent contractions – if you want to stay there, you can.

'At a higher level, jobs are more precarious – about a fifth of all senior civil service jobs have gone in the past couple of years – but it's an exciting challenge.'

The Civil Service Commissioners (and separate commissioners for Northern Ireland) are independent experts appointed to make sure recruitment of civil servants is fair and open. They also approve the most senior appointments.

Since 2008, hearings have also been held by Commons select committees for appointments to the top posts – with applicants being grilled by MPs. The results are only advisory, though they have sometimes led to people withdrawing voluntarily.

For many, the way in to the higher grades of the civil service is through the 'fast stream', a way for graduates with good degrees to gain quick experience right across government.

Fast-streamers are offered a personally tailored four-year training programme including as many as six different placements: they might spend time working in a minister's private office, helping take a Bill through Parliament, or liaising with the private sector, all in different departments. After that, they will usually jump into a longer-term job at around Grade 7, the first management level.

You don't have to come in through the fast stream: managers can also work their way up through the ranks, running teams of clerical staff.

Overall, there is no shortage of people wanting to come into the civil service, says Baume.

'If you want to go into a management role, there are some very big jobs. And if you have an interest in politics with a small "p", you can have a front row seat in big national issues, or international negotiations.'

The government is a diverse employer, running everything from driving-test centres to coastguard stations; it is the biggest single employer of barristers, not to mention tax inspectors, statisticians, economists and school inspectors.

Around 80 per cent of civil servants overall work outside London (though not so many of the more senior grades), and then, of course, there are the devolved governments.

The civil service is still unified across all parts of the UK, but this does not mean that the civil service in each devolved area does not have its own flavour and its own loyalties.

'Civil servants in Scotland were always working to a separate secretary of state, and their own ministers, so there has always been a bit of a difference,' says Bruce Crawford MSP, former Scottish Cabinet Secretary for Parliamentary Business and Government Strategy. 'But now we have a Scottish government and parliament which they are required to serve, so inevitably the Scottish civil service – and rightly so because it has been accepted by UK government – takes a slightly different perspective.

'In fact, sometimes it might be carrying out a completely different policy direction to the UK government. But there is little tension – Sir Bob Kerslake has made it clear that civil servants in Scotland are there to serve the manifesto of the government in Scotland.'

The pros and cons of keeping the devolved arms of the civil service inside a single unified family were examined by the House of Lords Constitution Select Committee in its 2003 report 'Devolution: Inter-Institutional Relations in the UK'.

The advantages of a single Home Civil Service described in this report include that 'it serves as a guarantor of impartiality against politicians who might seek to co-opt or undermine it, because members of the devolved institutions do not have the power to interfere with it.' Other advantages include that staff can move between all parts of the UK civil service, spreading knowledge and expertise.

The committee did acknowledge that the effects of devolution may in the long term create significant pressures for the ending of a single civil service. However, it said: 'Given the pressures that may result from administrations of different political persuasions existing in the UK, the case for a single civil service has so far, in our view, strengthened rather than weakened.'

There has been a trend over the past few decades to bring people into senior civil service jobs from the 'real world' outside to inject a bit of fresh air into dusty bureaucracies, such as businesspeople and dot.com entrepreneurs. At one point, two out of every five senior civil service posts was filled in this way, but more recently enthusiasm has waned. These days, 'direct entry' is less frequent and there is more of a focus again on developing people's talents and skills up through the civil service. Businesspeople are still brought into government, but often now as ministers or advisers in the House of Lords.

Another intersection between the civil service and the world of politics happens in the private offices of government ministers.

Ministers preside over their departments, or chunks of their departments, with thousands of people working beneath them. They need to communicate with all these people and also across government, with other ministers and other departments. They manage all this through their private offices, staffed by up to five civil servants led by a principal private secretary. The office will also handle relations with other parts of the public sector and relevant outside groups with an interest in each policy area.

'It is really just a communications network – these days, a big email machine – communicating your minister's views throughout Whitehall, down into the department, and receiving views from other ministers and from the Treasury,' says author and former senior civil servant Martin Stanley. 'You are trying to make sure your minister has the right advice from the right people and that he or she knows what colleagues around Whitehall and in your department think about an issue as he or she makes a decision. Everything changes very rapidly and you have to keep on top of it.'

Private offices play a big part in developing the two main ways ministers promote their ideas: writing correspondence and writing speeches.

Ministers do not write their own speeches from scratch: they might rewrite them, or finish them off, but early drafts are usually written by officials. Being neutral civil servants, however, the officials can only say that a new policy is fantastic – not that the old one was a disaster. To add the party-political bit of the speech, a different type of semi-official will jump in: the ministerial special adviser, or 'Spad'.

Spads are not quite civil servants and not quite party officials. They are 'temporary civil servants', appointed by ministers to work alongside the private office, who 'are exempt from the general requirement that civil servants should be appointed on merit and behave with impartiality and objectivity'. So they can happily politicize and attack the record of a previous government.

Special advisers are chosen by ministers and approved by the Prime Minister, or the First Ministers in devolved areas. There are one or two per minister, with the last reported total at ninety-five; since 2010, special adviser numbers have had to be reported annually by law.

The situation is slightly different in Scotland and Wales, where special advisers work for the centre of government rather than for individual ministers, and are limited in number to twelve, with responsibility for policy development and speech writing in specific subject areas. In Wales, the five or six special advisers to ministers are appointed by open recruitment, working alongside civil servants in a Strategic Policy Unit (though they cannot give instructions to the civil servants). In Northern Ireland there are sixteen special advisers in total, one per departmental minister and three each for the First Minister and Deputy First Minister.

Civil Service Commissioner Jonathan Baume says special advisers have a relationship with their ministers a bit like the 'daemons' of Philip Pullman's fantasy trilogy *His Dark Materials* – spirit manifestations of a human, in animal form, that are separate from but never stray far away from their owner and mirror his or her personality.

'You never find two the same, and they are used by secretaries of state in very different ways,' Baume says. 'Some are used as a sounding board, to check ideas, others are highly politicized.

'Where the system works, they are an asset: if you are in a busy department, it can take a week to get a meeting with a minister – so one of the things you can do is talk to a special adviser. But it can be a risky position, too, as part of their job is to be the fall guy – to protect the minister in times of crisis.'

Spads do have to comply with some parts of the civil service code – like the bit on honesty – but also have their own Code of Conduct for Special Advisers, which allows them to add party-political knockabout to speeches. Beyond that, each Spad is granted different powers by their ministers, such as reviewing policy papers for political implications; contributing to policy planning within the department 'with a political viewpoint in mind'; and acting as spokespeople for their minister to the media.

There are limits to their powers, however, when it comes to dealings with civil servants: they can convey a minister's views and work priorities to officials, for example, but they cannot directly issue instructions, authorize spending or handle budgets. They may also hold meetings with officials to discuss the advice they are giving to ministers, and comment on such advice – but not suppress or supplant it before the minister has received it.

Above all, civil servants, Spads and ministers must all play clear and separate roles and stick carefully to their own codes.

For all their neutrality, civil servants have a clear role to play in the process of democratic accountability, and a fair amount of power in their own domain of running and managing public services.

Democratic accountability requires officials to keep notes and minutes of ministers' meetings, for example, in case a politician is called in front of a parliamentary committee. Civil servants are also responsible – with approval from ministers – for drawing up many kinds of regulations: under most laws passed, legal powers are handed to government departments rather than to the government itself. And although ministers will do most of the explaining when it comes to policy, civil servants do have to explain themselves sometimes to Parliament. In particular, like their ministers (see previous chapter), senior civil servants often dread appearances before the Public Accounts Committee, the committee of MPs charged with making sure public money is spent well.

Responsibility for services is not always straightforward, however, when the basic structure of government is changing all the time. Although many of the core tasks of government – such as running the education system – remain steady and stable, the way they are organized into departments often changes as political priorities change.

There are around twenty-four UK central government departments, but their size, shape and responsibilities tend to change from government to government, with some coming and going and others splitting and merging.

The current Department for Communities and Local Government, for example, was established in 2006, and at the time this was its fifth name change in just nine years, along with changes in its coverage and responsibilities.

With local government having once been managed within the Department of the Environment, in 1997 it had become the Department for Environment, Transport and the Regions; then the Department for Transport, Local Government and the Regions (2001); then a year later the Office of the Deputy Prime Minister (2002); and finally (for now), in 2006, the Department for Communities and Local Government.

This final change prompted one insider to comment (anonymously) on the *Guardian* newspaper website: 'At the last name change in 2001, the then Permanent Secretary Sir Richard Mottram was reputed to have proposed that the lettering outside ODPM's Eland House HQ should be replaced by fridge magnets. Sadly this proposal didn't find favour.'

While extreme, such changes are by no means unusual: the department covering business and trade has undergone almost as many transformations in recent years, to name just one other. While such frequent change might be good for logo designers and stationery printers, or the makers of fridge magnets, it can be bewildering for everyone else. Why does it happen?

Often, departments are changed around when a new government comes into office, to reflect its political priorities – departments are linked, after all, to ministers in the Cabinet. New laws do not need to be passed to change departments around: it takes place under government exercise of a Royal Prerogative to organize the civil service (see Chapter 8). For the Opposition, there are bigger battles to fight, so changes do not tend to be opposed.

For new Prime Ministers, therefore, it is a chance to express their views on what the most important issues are. Do issues like energy or the environment merit their own department? How should policies be grouped? Where does higher education belong – with schools, or with business? And as each new department is created, others may need to be merged or split to keep the numbers right in Cabinet.

Of course, there is a limit to the number of big changes that can be made to the main structure of government. Some policy issues that touch on several different topic areas have to be handled by committees that cut right across government. And the departments themselves are broken down into more than a hundred Executive Agencies (sometimes known as Next Step Agencies), ranging from Her Majesty's Prison Service to Jobcentre Plus, with their own management structure and (often huge) budgets.

The complexities do not end there. Executive Agencies are still inside government departments, but there also exists a huge ecosystem of other government agencies, commissions, boards, regulators and advisory bodies, usually lumped together under the name of 'quangos' – quasi-autonomous non-governmental organizations.

Quangos are independent, arm's-length bodies ultimately controlled by government but set up by law to allow technical experts to be in control of an important issue unaffected by the hurly-burly of day-to-day politics. There are hundreds of such bodies, from the Arts Council to the UK Statistics Authority. Some have a professional or regulatory role, such as the General Medical Council or the Architects Registration Board; and this is not to mention more than a thousand other less formal advisory bodies, set up by ministers or departments ad hoc to advise the government on issues ranging from nuclear safety to the design of coins, medals, seals and decorations.

The removal of control of an area from politics to a quango can be good for the field concerned, and good for the politicians as well, as they do not have to take such direct responsibility if things go wrong. However, that same strength can become a weakness if the quango comes to be seen as unaccountable and cannot be changed other than by passing a new law.

Martin Stanley, the former head of a quango – the Competition Commission – says life outside departmental government is very different.

'The absence of a minister makes a big difference. You lose the fun of politics, but what you gain is the traditional civil service job without the politics added, where you can analyse issues in depth, consult widely and defend your own decisions.'

What you do also lose in a quango, however, is the flexibility to change what you are doing without changing the law.

'If you work in a department, there is more flexibility to change,' Stanley says. 'But quangos are governed by what is referred to as black letter law – clear and undisputed, black letters on white paper. So when you go and work in a quango you read the relevant Act that set it up, and do what it says. If you are consistent with the law and reasonable, you cannot be challenged. If ministers don't like it, they have to change the law.'

An example might be Ofcom, the UK's regulator for the communications industries, including TV broadcasting. One of the duties Ofcom has, set down in law, is to ensure TV news is politically balanced: so that is what it does, sticking as closely as it can to the letter of the law. To change this duty, ministers would have to try to change the law in Parliament.

These days, 'quango' is often used as a derogatory term for something inefficient and undemocratic: the current government, for example, lost no time in axing nearly 200 quangos and merging more than 100 more, in the biggest act of quangocide ever seen.

On the other hand, the creation or removal of a quango does not necessarily make much difference to whether or not the government actually does something, or pays for something. When quangos are scrapped, for example, the government often simply creates a unit within a government department to do the same job – with the same people in it. It does change the way the job is done, making it more accountable to ministers – but it does not necessarily save a lot of money, and the independence is gone.

The complex world of quangos is a good example of why reform of the civil service is so hard.

Apart from the fact that it is not a high public priority – people want to know what a government will do, and don't care so much how they do it – the size and complexity of the government machine make it hard to get a proper grip of the controls.

Some might say that the fact that it is the civil service itself that is in charge of making any reforms work means that it is too easy to resist changes it doesn't like. So reform tends to happen drip by drip, piece by piece.

One recent reform – introduced in 2010 – was the strengthening of departmental boards. Government departments each now have a board, a little like a company board of directors, except the board is not in direct charge – control still rests where it should, with ministers – but acts as a guiding, strategic, advisory body. Their remit is to advise and challenge ministers on strategy, planning and performance management for their departments.

Departmental boards are chaired by the secretary of state and are comprised of other ministers, senior officials and non-executive board members, largely drawn from the commercial private sector. Examples of non-executives – a key new role – are Lord Browne, former chief executive of BP at the Cabinet Office – who has also advised the government on the appointment of other non-executives; Sir Andrew Witty, chief executive of GlaxoSmithKline, at the Department for Business Innovation & Skills; Sara Weller, chief executive of Argos, at the Department for Communities and Local Government; and Barbara Stocking, chief executive of Oxfam, at the Cabinet Office.

The innovation of boards has the potential to be hugely powerful, revolutionizing the professionalism of government.

Is it working? The truth is, it is still too early to tell. Some ministers who have brought in non-executive directors have found them very supportive, but as they are just advisers, or reference points, it is still a role that is in development – a work in progress.

The latest reform ideas include introducing more performance management into the civil service, so top performers may be rewarded with better pay or promotions and low performers might be warned and, eventually, sacked.

There are also moves under way to open up the culture of the civil service, bringing in more ideas and people from business or other areas of public service. The government has described this aim as 'A new presumption in favour of open policy making, with policy developed on the basis of the widest possible engagement with external experts [such as] businesses, charities and think-tanks, and those who will have the task of delivering the policy once announced.'

The government has also expressed an interest in letting ministers pick their own departmental permanent secretaries from a shortlist, and to appoint civil servants on fixed-term contracts, in what would be a huge change to the culture of a neutral, independent, permanent civil service.

Such a move would be highly controversial. The House of Lords Constitution Committee, for example, said recently that such a move 'could risk undermining the impartiality of the civil service, threaten the principle that appointments are based on merit and make it harder for officials to give honest advice to ministers.'

But many analysts see changes in that direction as inevitable – with top civil servants becoming associated much more closely with the policies they implement.

'There is a change in the air to make civil servants more public figures, with more of a US-style civil service and a more political appointment system,' says the Democratic Society's Anthony Zacharzewski.

'I think it is inevitable because if you have openness and transparency to the extent the government wants to have – with open policymaking – you will have to have a higher profile for civil servants. And as soon as senior civil servants become more public figures, you are going to get more pressure towards them being political or publicly visible appointments.

'It is better to have a conversation and do it in a transparent and thought-through way rather than just let it evolve unplanned.'

All sides agree, however, that there is a need to preserve the independence of the civil service overall and to support its strong public-service culture, built up over centuries. This culture is designed to deliver services fairly, impartially and continuously, smoothing the path of the UK government between one temporary lot of politicians and the next.

And so to another field where independence from politics, and continuity through different governments, is essential to democracy. This is a field tied inextricably to the work of civil servants and politicians, yet also standing completely separate, with the ability to exert power over them and even punish them, if they deserve it.

We turn now to the rule of law.

Chapter 11

The rule of law – freedom's foundation

It was 11 November 1762. The drunkard lying by the side of the road barely looked up as the four men in their dark uniforms moved determinedly along the filthy street and turned the corner by the gambling house. Rich customers, no doubt, looking for a good time. But they stopped by one of the tumbledown houses and the first man shoulder-charged the door, which exploded off its hinges, the frame splintering as they charged past up the stairs. 'John Entick – you are suspected of acts of libel against His Majesty's Government. We are here on command of Lord Halifax, Secretary of State, to search for evidence of these deeds.'

A small crowd gathered outside as they set about their work: levering open the locked drawers of Entick's writing desk, prying open the front of his precious old bureau, opening boxes and rummaging in the linen chests. The more they searched, the angrier grew Entick himself, confined in a back room shocked and trembling with rage. In the end, it took the men four hours to search every corner. Before they left, they gathered up as many books, pamphlets, letters and other papers as they could carry and passed back out into the street through the broken door, shedding paper into the gutter as they went.

The state had acted: and what could anyone have done to stop it?

The second part of this story comes three years later, in 1765. Here are the same people: John Entick and the same four state officials – a man called Nathan Carrington and three others.

This time, however, all five are dressed smartly, even Entick, and they take their places alongside a throng of black-robed lawyers, clerks, reporters, spectators and *others beneath the high benches of Westminster Hall. The King's Messengers – now known by their official title – seem different from the toughs who smashed down John Entick's door and charged the stairs; they appear cowed and apprehensive sitting down below the Lord Chief Justice, Lord Camden, perched high above the proceedings.*

The case has been brought by Entick himself, accusing these officers of the state of trespassing on his property without legal authority.

The lawyers for the government agents put their case: the 'gross and scandalous' contents of Entick's Grub Street newspapers attacking the government and both Houses of Parliament were so serious, they say – amounting almost to treason – that it was proportionate and necessary to break into his home to investigate.

Entick's lawyer is equally eloquent: 'If [the warrants] are held to be legal the liberty of this country is at an end,' he says. 'No power can lawfully break into a man's house and study to search for evidence against him; this would be worse than the Spanish Inquisition; for ransacking a man's secret drawers and boxes to come at evidence against him, is like racking his body to come at his secret thoughts.'

Some hours later, when all the arguments have been heard, the judge, Lord Camden, draws his robes around him and surveys the room. Sunlight streams through the high windows on to the heavy green velvet curtains beside the witness benches. No one yet knows the outcome: this could go either way. The packed court-room is silent as he begins to speak.

What does Lord Camden say? We will return to this case at the end of the chapter, when we come to consider how the law must apply to the government in the same way as to everyone else.

Because the ability of courts to decide independently whether or not people have broken the law, free from political interference – including the government itself, or people acting for the government – is essential to democracy. Partly, what it boils down to is the value of our elected Parliament. If the laws passed by Parliament cannot be applied to absolutely everyone, then what is the point of Parliament?

In the UK, as a general principle Parliament – or legally speaking 'the Queen in Parliament' – has the right to make, change or abolish any law about anything. This principle is called the sovereignty of Parliament.

Almost all other democracies have a higher national law than their parliament or lawmaking body – a constitution. The UK does have many laws relating to what are known (even without a constitution) as constitutional issues – issues relating to how the country is run, such as elections, for example, or the powers of the House of Lords – but these are all passed by Parliament itself, and there is no separate, pre-existing single constitution which is different from ordinary parliamentary laws. So a new law made in the UK can never – as it can in other countries – be described as or even blocked for being 'unconstitutional'.

Nevertheless, there are a few grey areas for legal power in Britain. Outside England, the supremacy of Parliament has rightly been qualified by devolution of lawmaking power to the Scottish, Welsh and Northern Irish elected bodies. Scotland also has its own legal system, and Northern Ireland is a separate legal jurisdiction as well, all operating under similar principles but as self-contained systems.

Technically, unless and until any parts of the UK were to become fully independent countries, the UK Parliament does still have the power to pass laws overriding these bodies, and also to change or abolish them. In practice, however, it is hard to conceive of a situation where it would do that other than as it might be seen as necessary to maintain peace in Northern Ireland. So the UK operates within a patchwork of legal systems.

Then there is the ferocious ongoing debate about whether European law of one kind or another is now overriding the sovereignty of Parliament. We will come back to this subject in Chapter 15, but one of the key points here is that the UK Parliament has passed its own law – the European Communities Act 1972 – which allows European Union law to override UK law. So European law is supreme, as long as the UK is an EU member state: but a UK Parliament law makes it so.

The other Euro-legal furore rarely out of the news relates to the European Convention on Human Rights, which the UK has signed.

Not everyone realizes that this convention has nothing to do with the European Union. Instead it is a treaty of a larger and looser human rights and democracy organization called the Council of Europe. The council has forty-seven members, including all twenty-seven EU countries plus twenty others such as Norway, Switzerland and Turkey. The UK is an active member and played a key part in fostering, drafting and promoting the convention, much of which is based on British law.

Having signed the convention, UK ministers and Parliament must now take its provisions – from freedom of expression to the right to a fair trial – into account when drawing up new laws. Interestingly, UK judges also now have the power to declare that a new law created by Parliament is incompatible with the convention, and therefore violates (or could violate) human rights – making the convention almost like a UK constitution, or part of one. However, the court cannot then throw out the law, which would interfere directly with parliamentary sovereignty. When one of these 'declarations of incompatibility' is made, it is up to ministers to make any changes of their own accord.

According to a 2011 report from the Ministry of Justice, in the first ten years since the Human Rights Act came into force some nineteen declarations of incompatibility were upheld by the courts. They related not to entire laws but to aspects of how laws work in sensitive areas, such as detention of terrorist suspects, the involvement of politicians in sentencing of prisoners and the rights of mental health patients. In all cases so far the government has taken steps to alter the law as appropriate to tackle the issue – though it is not forced to do so.

If any individual does feel their human rights have been violated however, and they have not been supported by the UK courts, they can take their case to a European Court of Human Rights, and if they win, the UK must comply with the court's decisions.

For some, this represents another controversy about loss of sovereignty to Europe. Again, however, it is a voluntary loss, because the UK has signed up willingly to the Human Rights Convention; and again, the

UK Parliament has also passed its own law, the Human Rights Act 1998, embedding the European convention into UK law.

Perhaps the most controversial ruling from the European Court of Human Rights affecting the UK was made in 2005 after a challenge from a prisoner, John Hirst, that the UK's ban on voting for all prisoners violated his right to vote, which is protected under the convention. The court did not say that all prisoners had to be allowed to vote: it said a blanket ban was illegal, and the UK needed a new policy allowing at least some categories of prisoner, for example people serving short sentences for less serious crimes, to vote.

At the time of writing, the issue has not been resolved, but the likely outcome seems to be that Parliament will pass a new law complying with the European ruling – though in principle it does have the power to carry on with the voting ban. If a full ban is continued, the outcome is likely to be fines on the UK from Europe, further legal challenges and general confusion. It is an interesting case because the law itself seems clear; but the matter has run beyond the law to issues of sovereignty. Few people, too, would say that prisoners have no human rights – or else there would be no laws on torture, for example.

We can already see that legal issues can be complex and subtle, and that different people can have different views on them. How are these complexities resolved in practice?

One practical way the law proceeds is by the rule of precedent. The UK has what is known as a common law system, which means that each court ruling creates a precedent for future similar cases (this does not apply to magistrates' courts, which try less serious offences, but to all higher courts, which are 'courts of record' – more on the hierarchy of courts shortly).

So whenever courts deliberate, it is assumed that if the same or very similar facts have arisen in the past, particularly in a higher court, then the same decision should be taken this time. And whenever a new decision is taken, it becomes part of the new common law, or case law. It is also referred to as 'judge–made' law, since it is made by judges, as compared with statute law – laws passed by Parliament or the devolved bodies, which are made by politicians. So the law upheld in British courts is a mixture of judge–made law with statute law.

Law is divided into various fields. Criminal law relates to how individuals and organizations are ordered to behave, by Parliament or a devolved lawmaking body. The restrictions of criminal law exist to protect people and property and to ensure society works well and peacefully. Usually, if someone commits a criminal offence they will be prosecuted by a public agency – technically, by the Crown, which represents the nation as a whole. Private criminal prosecutions are sometimes possible too, but they are rare. In England and Wales criminal prosecutions are brought by the Crown Prosecution Service, in Scotland by the Crown Office and Procurator Fiscal Service, and in Northern Ireland by the Public Prosecution Service.

Another field of law is civil law, which includes cases in which citizens or organizations take action against each other for alleged wrongs, such as divorce, libel, or breaches of contract, and if the accused is found guilty then a remedy is ordered, such as payment of compensation.

Other categories of law include what is sometimes called con-stitutional law, which, as we have heard, determines how the state is run. There are other terms too – family law, for example. These different categories are generally straightforward to understand, although they often overlap. But the most important fact about all of them when it comes to democracy is that the legal system and the judges who administer it must be independent from Parliament, the government and other official bodies. It is vital that all of their rulings must be respected, obeyed and enforced by the government, the police, local councils and all other official bodies, even – or particularly – when these rulings are made against them.

Although politicians and the courts do therefore live in different worlds for most of the time, these worlds do intersect whenever a new law is made.

Clearly, politicians are involved with making a new law. They have plenty of legal advice: teams of lawyers are employed inside government departments, working with a central specialist team of about sixty lawyers in the Cabinet Office – Parliamentary Counsel. Together they write the Bills that will become laws if passed by Parliament.

Once a law is passed, it is the courts that will have to rule according to the exact wording of that law, whatever it says. But what if the wording is not clear? What if it clashes with other laws? And what if so many new laws are made each year that the legal system struggles to keep up, and the law becomes less effective?

All these dangers are real.

Paul Bowen QC, a barrister specializing in cases involving public services, says that, from a lawyer's perspective, all governments tend to make too many new laws.

'Politicians see law as a manifestation of power, and they want to exercise power, so they make more laws. Everything has to be done in a hurry too, to fit it into the life of a government. But laws written in a hurry do not tend to be well-written.'

There is still more temptation to over-legislate because politicians do not always trust the courts to behave in the way they want, Bowen says. 'The perception in government is sometimes that the courts will interpret the law in a way that runs against their will. So yet more bits are needed, to tie the details down.'

The problem can be that, as complex new laws pile up, some replacing little bits of earlier laws with unpredictable results, it becomes harder and harder for anyone to make head or tail of them. This makes them harder to enforce – which makes them pointless – and it can also make it harder for people to hold the government to account if it ignores or misuses its own law.

The House of Commons Political and Constitutional Reform Committee has been looking into ways of ensuring new laws are made to the highest standards. In the course of this inquiry, committee member Paul Flynn MP accused politicians of often being too quick to respond to media scares.

'Dogs bark, children cry and politicians legislate,' said Flynn. 'It is our answer to every problem on earth and in heaven.'

Lord Butler of Brockwell, a former head of the civil service, told the committee that government departments also tend to try to cram too many extra provisions into a Bill because they are not sure when they might get the chance again to pass a new law: 'When a department has a slot, they add things to it like Christmas trees.' All this leaves very little time to prepare and consult on draft Bills, he said.

One proposal studied by the committee was to set up a new Legislative Standards Committee in Parliament to report on each stage of making a new law, from concept to implementation. Some analysts suggest Westminster could learn more from the devolved legislatures of Scotland, Wales and Northern Ireland, which have taken extra steps to explain why new laws are needed and consult more widely on them before they are passed. Not all of these working methods could necessarily be transferred to the larger and busier UK Parliament, but valuable lessons could still be learned.

Once laws are passed, they enter the domain of the courts.

HM Courts and Tribunals Service, the Scottish Court Service and the Northern Ireland Courts and Tribunals Service together run the UK's courts and tribunals – special courts that rule in areas such as tax, employment and gambling.

The service in England and Wales alone handles about 2 million criminal cases as well as 1.8 million civil claims, more than 150,000 family law disputes and almost 800,000 tribunal cases a year. Some of these are settled without a court trial, but even so that represents nearly 5 million cases of all kinds every year: quite a few, in a total population of about 50 million adults.

On the front line of this huge operation sits a fascinating and democratic part of the UK legal system which has been around since the eleventh century: magistrates' courts. Most cases are decided by magistrates; and magistrates are ordinary people, and volunteers.

Almost anyone between the ages of eighteen and seventy can apply to be a magistrate. They work part-time, are not paid (though may claim expenses) and have no formal legal qualification whatsoever – though they are trained, mentored and supported in court by a legal adviser.

Magistrates – or Justices of the Peace (JPs), as they are also known – deal with more than 95 per cent of all criminal cases in England and Wales. Scotland and Northern Ireland also have some lay or non-professional Justices of the Peace, though in Northern Ireland they sit alongside qualified judges. While many other justice systems do also feature 'laypeople' or ordinary citizens as part of the process, the UK (outside Northern Ireland) is unusual in having lay magistrates administering criminal justice on their own: deciding on guilt and innocence, and then sentencing.

Each year 5,000 people in England and Wales apply to become magistrates, though only 25 per cent are successful. Some magistrates do have an interest in the law, and can even be lawyers, though not criminal lawyers practising locally, to avoid people appearing in a court as a lawyer where one of their magistrate colleagues might be presiding. Serving police officers may not be magistrates either, for similar reasons. But they do come from all walks of life. One typical current county 'bench' – the term given to a local pool of magistrates – includes a law student, an ambulance driver, a plasterer, a train driver, two teachers, a vet, two people who are unemployed, a local authority officer and a professor of education.

The interview panels for people applying to become magistrates do not expect candidates to know the law. Instead, they are trying to rate a candidate's ability to listen, learn and consider the facts – for example, in deciding whether it makes it more or less excusable if a person was drunk when they punched someone. The panel will also try to detect prejudice.

Michael Hocken, an Oxfordshire JP who is also on the council of the Magistrates' Association, says the fact that magistrates are ordinary people makes the judicial system fairer.

'It is intimidating enough for most people to come into court, but with lay magistrates, they can at least see their case is being heard by people like them, who are dressed like them, not in gowns and wigs, and who talk like them, asking questions in non-legalese'.

More serious or more complex cases are not heard by magistrates – partly because it is unfair for volunteer magistrates to have to sit on cases which will last more than a few days. These will either be sent to higher courts, or heard in magistrates' courts by district judges, who are similar to magistrates but full-time and legally qualified (they used to be known as stipendiary magistrates). Some more serious cases, such as murder or rape, are automatically sent to the higher or senior courts, but with some others in the middle (known as hybrid or 'triable-either-way' cases) it can be left up to the magistrates or the defendants to decide what kind of trial they would like.

The higher courts in England and Wales are the Crown Court for criminal trials and the County Court and High Court for civil trials. These courts are presided over by judges, and they are where jury trials take place. Beyond these courts, verdicts or sentences can be appealed even higher to the Appeal Court – which usually sits with three judges – and finally to the Supreme Court – created in 2009 as the final court of appeal for most UK cases (other than those that can be appealed to the European Court of Justice and the European Court of Human Rights).

Where someone is not satisfied with the verdict of any court, they can try to gain permission to launch an appeal to a higher court. Rights of appeal can be granted by the courts on either a point of law – where the original court may have made a mistake in applying the law – or (much less usually) on a point of fact – some compelling new evidence that has appeared. People do not have an automatic right of appeal, but need first to explain convincingly to the court why they feel a mistake has been made.

The UK's final court of appeal used to be the House of Lords, sitting as a court with senior judges known as the Law Lords, until the Supreme Court was created in 2009 to separate the justice system more completely from the political system.

Another relatively recent move to ensure the separation of the judiciary from government was the changing role over the past ten years or so of the Lord Chancellor, the government minister who is responsible for running the legal system.

Before 2003 the Lord Chancellor was also the most senior judge and the Speaker of the House of Lords, straddling government and the law in a way seen by many as a threat to the independence of the legal system. Following reforms in 2003 and 2005, however, the Lord Chancellor is still the Cabinet minister in charge of law – in a role now known as Justice Secretary – but is no longer a judge or the House of Lords speaker. In Scotland, the similar Lord Advocate role combines advising the government and acting as a public prosecutor, prompting calls for separation of these roles as well.

Since 2006 the Lord Chancellor has also been given less of a say in the appointment of judges, with the establishment of an independent Judicial Appointments Commission to appoint most of them. Usually, a new judge will have been a barrister for twenty years or so beforehand, and then be promoted up through the courts.

The commission – whose members include judges, lawyers, magistrates and members of the public, but not politicians – is busy: there are some 42,000 people holding judicial office in England and Wales, and in 2011–12 some 750 new appointments were made. The Lord Chancellor can reject a nomination, but not help select one.

Judges serve until they are seventy years old and cannot easily be dismissed beforehand. Their rulings can be overturned on appeal, they can be ridiculed in the media or by politicians (though they have no right to respond) and they can be reprimanded by more senior judges, but they are very hard to dismiss. This is to shield them from pressure from the media or politicians, to protect the independence of the legal system.

In the past, this meant that the occasional outbreaks of even the most regrettable behaviour from ageing judges was ignored to protect the system as a whole. Since 2006, however, an Office for Judicial

Complaints was set up to investigate complaints against judges' personal behaviour. The office can recommend judges' discipline or dismissal – but only if both the Lord Chief Justice (the most senior judge) and the Lord Chancellor jointly agree.

Sanctions are rare but they do happen: in 2011, for example, the deputy high court judge Judge James Allen was dismissed after being convicted for assaulting his wife. Only a few other higher court judges have been removed in six years, though around thirty less senior judicial officials, including magistrates and tribunals judiciary, are removed or resign each year following investigation into allegations that they have failed in their duties, broken the law (including driving offences), misused their office or otherwise brought the judiciary into disrepute.

Judges can seem remote, but at least one key aspect of the UK's judicial system is quite well known and understood by large numbers of ordinary people, because many of them have been a part of it: the jury system.

Jury trials are intended for more serious criminal cases, where people run the risk of being put in prison for a long time, as well as for some civil cases, including defamation.

Until as recently as 1974 only people who owned or rented property were allowed to sit on a jury, so many women and people on lower incomes were excluded. Now, juries in the UK are made up of twelve people in England, Wales and Northern Ireland and fifteen people in Scotland, aged between eighteen and seventy, selected at random from the electoral register.

According to government figures, in 2011 about 340,000 juror summonses were issued in England and Wales, resulting in about 170,000 jurors being 'supplied to the court' – the rest either not being needed, or being excused duty for reasons such as childcare.

Rough calculations show, therefore, that most people will not serve on a jury. (You are eligible for fifty-two years of your life. If a different 200,000 people served every year for fifty-two years it would total about 10 million, out of about 50 million adults in the country – and some people serve more than once. So very roughly, one in five would serve.) It is also clear, however, that many millions of people do serve.

In England, Wales and Northern Ireland, a unanimous verdict is preferred and juries will be encouraged to continue debating in secret until they can all agree. If they are still deadlocked after a certain time, however, the judge may allow a majority verdict of, say, 10–2. In Scotland, where there are fifteen jurors, a simple majority is all that is required: so 8–7 is fine, and there can be no such thing as a hung jury.

There are other differences, too, in the Scottish jury system – which is not surprising, as Scotland has a separate legal system from the rest of the UK. For example, there are three verdicts available to a Scottish jury: guilty, not guilty and not proven – the last of which acts exactly as a 'not guilty' verdict in the sense that it acquits the accused, but – controversially – can carry the implication that if guilt has not been proven, neither has innocence, quite, either. Following a review by senior Scottish judge Lord Carloway, however, the Scottish government is currently considering scrapping the 'not proven' verdict and increasing the size of jury majority needed for a verdict.

The experience of being called to sit on a jury is usually memorable. For many people, entering a court for the first time, it can feel like stepping into a Hollywood movie or TV drama. By the end of a case, a juror has often heard about situations of violence or desperation which shock and disturb. Although the judge will always offer detailed guidance on points of law, when a jury retires to debate a case in secret no one else is present and the responsibility is real.

While there can also be long periods of boredom and waiting around, when a person finds themselves part of a jury which convicts someone and sends them to prison, the experience of holding such power over a fellow citizen can be humbling. As the foreman of the jury stands to announce the verdict there can be gasps, cries, tears and fury. Nothing can prepare you for that experience, which drives home that you, a set of randomly selected ordinary people, are at that moment powerfully affecting people's lives. And then it is all over – and more often than not, you will never see your fellow jurors, the judge, lawyers or defendants again.

Stephen Jakobi, founder of Fair Trials International, says the participation of ordinary citizens in serious trials is of immeasurable value to defend those few innocent people who do sometimes find themselves in court.

'Justice is about innocent people, not guilty people,' he says. 'Anyone who's had anything to do with the criminal justice system knows it's boring, because 95 per cent of defendants are guilty – and that's being generous. But you need a trial for the 5 per cent of the cases where there could be reasonable doubt, and the jury system is absolutely key to this.

'If you are a judge and have sat through a hundred burglary cases, you are case-hardened. You've heard it all before, and you are likely to think: "Same old story, same old solution. Three years. Next!" The jury's job is to come to things fresh. They haven't seen twenty-five burglary cases played out, they've only seen one: this one. So with fresh eyes, they apply their common sense based on the evidence.

'The jury is the democratic principle applied to law.'

There can be problems, though, with a jury system, Jakobi says – it is expensive and hard to manage, and can also fail in highly complex cases, as in some fraud trials or trials featuring medical evidence, 'where frankly you would do better to have accountants and professors sitting with a judge'.

But for most cases, he says, to have a cross-section of ordinary people who have heard everything that went on does usually work. 'I have never had a client convicted who I was privately convinced was innocent. At times I've been desperately worried, and couldn't see how a jury could understand – but they did.'

Juries are one key aspect of the legal system that keeps it accessible to ordinary people, at least for some cases, but even more important is the issue of funding. Court cases are expensive, for all concerned, and while people do not usually have a choice about attending their own criminal trials, in other areas of the law – civil law – they do have a choice when it comes to bringing a court action themselves, and their choice can be hugely limited by money.

There are various possible ways to fund a court case.

One way is out of your own pocket: but given the costs of legal action, realistically this is open only to rich people, big organizations, or campaigns with a large amount of donations behind them. Property development companies, for example, might choose to fight a planning decision in the courts and fund it themselves. Smaller organizations, however, and individuals who are not so wealthy, face the risk of being ruined by taking legal action, since if they lose they might have to pay the legal costs of the other party.

These days, one way to cut the costs of an action is to find a law firm that will take on your case on a 'no win, no fee' basis. However, you will need a very strong case, and you may also need to take out what is called 'after the event insurance', an expensive kind of legal insurance to cover any costs incurred if the case is lost.

But the main way people without access to private funds can support a court case is through legal aid. Legal aid is aimed at people of limited means facing serious problems such as housing eviction and cases relating to debt (information on who is eligible can be found online at www.gov.uk/legal-aid).

Funding for legal aid amounts to more than £2 billion a year, with separate systems in England and Wales, Scotland, and Northern Ireland. This sum, however, is set to be cut by around a sixth under new reforms. On 1 April 2013 the main agency previously responsible for legal aid, the Legal Services Commission, was replaced by the Legal Aid Agency under the Legal Aid, Sentencing and Punishment of Offenders Act 2012. This removed several kinds of civil (non-criminal) cases out of the scope of legal aid, including divorce and child residence cases, other than ones involving aggravating issues such as domestic violence; some employment law cases; some cases involving challenges to benefits decisions; and some repeat challenges of immigration status. Subject to further consultation, legal aid may also be removed from households with more than a certain amount of disposable income.

Of course, the main reason for the cuts is to save costs – and funds are always limited. The UK has a relatively generous legal aid scheme: according to Council of Europe figures, the percentage of public spending per person allocated to legal aid in the UK in 2010 was 0.21 per cent, more than three times that of the next highest in the Netherlands (0.06 per cent).

On the other hand, once fewer people receive help each year under the new system, there will be a social cost to those people. And this may lead to wider social costs, if problems such as housing eviction challenges can no longer be sorted out in the courts and are left to fester.

Sometimes, if a case raises a general point that is considered to be in the public interest – for example something relating to human rights – another special type of support is available called a Protective Costs Order. This will cover you against having to pay costs if you lose a case, because the courts consider it is in the public interest to have the arguments heard. But these orders are available only for certain cases where strong general issues are involved, not for cases that may matter the world to an individual but do not raise any big new points of law. And they will not pay the costs of your own lawyers.

As with many aspects of a functioning democracy, the whole subject of cost is clearly an area for ongoing consideration, debate, reform – and balance, says Paul Bowen QC.

'As eligibility requirements for legal aid have become tighter and tighter, essentially the only people who are entitled to help are those on benefits', he says. 'So it is there for some vulnerable or marginalized groups, although this is under threat as the budget has recently been cut by 25 per cent. But for most people the idea of getting involved in legal proceedings is about as realistic as a trip to the moon.

'There is a danger here,' he says. 'Our justice system is predicated on the fact that we are all equal before the law, not as equal as we can afford to be.'

One area where access to funding is of particular importance for a healthy democracy is judicial review.

Judicial review is where an individual or organization is able to challenge the actions (or inactions) of a minister, the government or any official body. This is essential to any democracy, and to the rule of law: it is the way a citizen can make sure that the government can do only what it is allowed to do, and that it always does it in the right way. Remember Entick versus Carrington, from 1765, at the opening of this chapter? We will come back to that case in a moment, because this is where it is relevant.

Possible grounds for judicial review include that a state agency lacks the legal power to make such a decision; that the procedure it followed was incorrect; or that the decision itself was unreasonable or unfair.

The standards set to allow a review are quite high – which is reasonable, since a system where anyone could challenge any tiny decision by the government in the courts would quickly descend into chaos. First, the person who is challenging has to be directly affected by the decision, and they must have exhausted any other appeal processes that might be available in law, such as a relevant tribunal or ombudsman. A complaint that a government department has mishandled your personal data, for example, would be taken first to the Information Commissioner's Office, which is the proper place to lodge a complaint like that for the first time; only once a complaint has run through all the official channels and a person is still dissatisfied might it come to the courts.

Second, it is not enough simply to disagree with a decision, or to argue that another decision might have been possible. A review will be allowed only if it seems like it might be possible to show that a minister or official body acted unreasonably or illogically based on the case and on the powers they have, or that they may have acted against European Union or human rights law.

Although justifiably hard to carry off, however, the power of judicial review is essential to democracy, as it means the government can do only what the law allows it to do, and follows the correct processes.

An example of a successful challenge happened in 2010 when campaigners won a High Court battle reviewing government plans to build a third runway at Heathrow Airport. Lord Justice Carnwath found the Transport Secretary had passed over several issues that ought to have been taken into account in making the decision, such as public-transport access to Heathrow – and so the process used to take the decision had been unreasonable.

While their decisions can be reviewed, however, ministers and some public bodies are generally protected against civil or criminal liability while carrying out their public duties.

Historically, government ministers and civil servants enjoyed widespread immunity against criminal prosecution, known as 'Crown immunity'. This arose partly because criminal prosecutions take place 'on behalf of the Crown' in the first place and, since civil servants and ministers also act on behalf of the Crown, it was considered impossible for the Crown to prosecute itself.

In modern times, however, Crown immunity has been removed or reduced in many areas. In 1947, for example, the Crown Proceedings Act made the government generally liable in civil law, such as contract law, employment law and property law. From the mid-1980s, the immunity of prosecution has been removed in stages from NHS bodies, so the health service can be sued for negligence in the treatment of patients. Ministers and civil servants can also sometimes run the risk of being sued as individuals, if they might have committed criminal offences. Further modifications of immunity are likely to be made in years to come, to make sure public bodies can be held to account, while always trying to preserve their freedom of action where they are genuinely acting reasonably within their powers.

From time to time, legal rows do become politicized and politicians are forced to square off directly against the courts. Recent battles between judges and politicians have happened in cases such as the deportation of terrorist suspects, or the hasty sacking of public officials which is later found to have been illegal.

In cases like these, ministers will thunder that the courts are out of touch with public opinion, or that they will look into changing the law to make sure that next time whatever it is can't happen again. But generally what happens then is that the matter will be quietly dropped, the courts will have their way and the law will be upheld. Politicians and governments understand that they cannot be seen to break the law, which, after all, was created by governments in the first place. They can rant and rave, and the debate is healthy – just as we need an Opposition in Parliament, open debate about whether and how a law needs to be changed is necessary in a democracy. Politicians, too, can always try to change the law after they lose a case – and they often do. But they cannot defy the law.

All of which brings us back to the case of Entick versus Carrington, the story which opened this chapter.

To the astonishment of many people present, Lord Camden supported the individual citizen – Entick – over the state, ordering the government to pay him compensation.

The state said it was allowed to force its way into someone's home to find evidence against them, said Lord Camden: ' . . . but no such law ever existed in this country.' So in the end, the judge made his decision based only on one consideration: on whether something was allowed by the law, or whether it was not. In doing so, he noted that Entick might well have been libelling the state in his low-life newspapers, and if he had been, this was not good. But this was irrelevant to the requirement for the government, like everybody else, to act only within the law.

The case of Entick versus Carrington is often cited to this day. It even influenced the passing in 1789 of the Fourth Amendment to the United States Constitution, supporting 'The right of the people to be secure in their persons, houses, papers, and effects, against unreasonable searches and seizures'.

The ability of one, single, centuries-old lawsuit to have such a huge impact demonstrates the supreme power of the courts in a properly functioning democracy.

It also shows vividly why in a democracy, where the state exists to serve the people, it is so important for the courts to be independent of government. Judges such as Lord Camden must be free to be able to make a ruling for anyone – even a seedy character like Entick, who invented fictitious academic credentials to sell more books – against the government, or against anyone else. Of course, they might rule for the government in a case; but they might not. It is this independence which creates the rule of law.

The case of Entick versus Carrington happens to raise another interesting topic that is still the subject of ferocious debate, today as much as ever: the freedom of the press. John Entick printed newspapers that were on the edge of what was acceptable for the time, and the boundaries are still being debated today. Why does this matter so much in a democracy? That is the subject of our next chapter.

Chapter 12

The media – our right to know, and to be heard

It is an image that horrified, shocked and inspired the world. In a wide, deserted street in the centre of Beijing a column of squat, menacing tanks daubed with orange and khaki camouflage came to a halt in front of a lone, frail-looking man in a white shirt. The tanks tried to move around him, but the man moved too, and would not let them pass. To do so, they would have to run over him.

The year of this image was 1989, the tanks part of an overwhelming and ruthless force on its way to Tiananmen Square to suppress growing student pro-democracy protests. The man knew he could not win, but was willing to sacrifice his life in a simple act of political protest. A short while later, he 'disappeared', quietly removed by security forces, and nothing more is known.

Perhaps most shocking of all is that most young people in China today would not even recognize this image. The Chinese writer Yu Hua writes in his riveting book *China in Ten Words* that soon after the event, 'Tiananmen vanished from the Chinese media. I never saw the slightest mention of it afterward, as though it had never happened . . . Twenty years later, it is a disturbing fact that among the younger generation in China today few know anything about the Tiananmen Incident, and those who do say vaguely, "A lot of people in the streets then, that's what I heard".'

Disturbing, but not surprising. China's state-controlled news agency, Xinhua, will cover a story only if the government agrees it can be covered. The reason is clear: if everyone in China had known what was happening in 1989, the pro-democracy movement could have become irresistible. To control the country, information and people are continually wiped out together, like the 'tank man': no name, no trial, no past, no information.

For that reason alone, an independent media sector – press, TV, radio and online – is essential to democracy.

For elections to work, citizens must be able freely to discuss both their system of government and what each government does. While there are some legal restrictions in every country on what people can say or write, to prevent one person's freedom from unnecessarily harming another's, in developed democracies such as the UK the press is free to comment on most issues, including the activities of the government. Stories about possible wrong-doing by politicians, in particular – such as the MPs' expenses saga – are headline news instantly, and for weeks.

When any major event is happening that affects our lives, we rely on media reports to find out the details of it, and in the UK people rely on one media organization more than most for news. Most countries have a state-funded broadcaster, but the UK has the largest and (many would say) the best in the world, particularly when it comes to reporting clear, independent news – the BBC.

The British Broadcasting Corporation is not a government body, but it is publicly funded and publicly owned under a Royal Charter. Charters are a historic way for the state to set up or preserve an independent organization acting over a long period of time for the public good, like the Royal National Institute of Blind People and the British Red Cross (see also Chapter 8).

Most charter rules are the same as for any ordinary company or charity, but there is more government control over a chartered body, as the charter comes up for review at regular intervals. The BBC's charter currently has to be reviewed every ten years. It was last renewed in 2006, so will be reviewed again in 2016. Each review is a chance for the government to make changes to how the organization works: at the last BBC review, for example, the charter set up the BBC Trust, a body replacing the old board of governors to run the BBC more independently in the interests of licence-fee payers.

The BBC does not sell advertising or sponsorship, both so it can stay impartial and so it will not take money away from commercial broadcasters. It receives most of its funding from the TV licence fee – at the time of writing, £145.50 for a colour licence. Licences are needed to watch TV on any device, including laptops, tablets and mobiles, whatever channels you watch (if you never watch BBC channels, you still need a licence). Free licences are issued to people aged seventy-five and over, with a 50 per cent reduction for people who are blind or have severe sight problems.

Total BBC turnover is around £5 billion a year, with around £3.6 billion from the licence fee and the rest from government grants and limited commercial activities such as selling programmes overseas. Not all of this goes on Jeremy Clarkson's salary: £1.3 billion is spent on BBC 1; around £1 billion on all other BBC TV channels including BBC 2, BBC News Channel and BBC Parliament; around £0.6 billion on national and local radio and less than £0.2 billion (around £190 million) on BBC Online – the BBC news and other websites.

Overall, the BBC reaches more than 90 per cent of the population, and its news coverage is more trusted than other sources. Richard Sambrook, director of Cardiff University's Centre for Journalism and former director of news at the BBC, says this trust is a direct result of the BBC being publicly owned: not government-owned, but as a stand-alone part of UK democracy.

'Without a media organization acting in the public interest, debate can become skewed, with the richest voices being the loudest voices,' Sambrook says.

'The size of the BBC is a real advantage to the UK because public debate is essential for people to be informed citizens, able to make free choices not only about who they support and vote for, but all sorts of other choices about how they run their daily lives.'

This view is backed up by research. A 2008 study led by James Curran of the University of London found public service TV devotes more attention to news and public affairs than commercial channels. This helps to narrow a gap in knowledge of the news between advantaged and disadvantaged sections of society: essential for a fair democracy. Commercial channels, in contrast, have less incentive to provide wide-ranging, high-quality news to a general audience, for its own sake, tending to lean towards more populist entertainment to ensure they can deliver big audiences for advertisers.

Public service broadcasting in the UK reaches wider than the BBC, however.

Channel 4 and its Welsh-language offshoot S4C are also publicly owned broadcasters. Though they are partly funded by advertising, they are owned by the nation and their boards are government-approved. Because of this, Channel 4 has been required to dedicate part of its output to minority-interest programming that might not be covered by the more mainstream BBC or by commercial channels – such as gay-interest or ethnic minority-interest programming.

When it comes to news and current affairs programmes on TV, all broadcasting on the UK's main news stations – including ITV, Channel 4, Channel 5 and Sky News – is regulated to be impartial by the communications regulator Ofcom. Although individual programmes can take one side of an argument, over time no particular viewpoint or political interest can be favoured.

For commercial stations such as ITV and related stations STV in Scotland and UTV in Northern Ireland, and Channel 5, there is a deal: they accept public service duties in return for being guaranteed prime positions in broadcast bandwidth and TV listings – Channel 5 will always be listed as the fifth main channel, for example – and in the case of ITV, it has also been granted regional franchises to compete with local or regional BBC services.

Commercial radio stations, including local community stations, also have some public service obligations, but these are not as strong as for TV channels.

Overall, though, how aware are members of the public that there are these public service deals, made and funded in their name, with commercial broadcasters? Should UK citizens be more demanding of the public service elements of commercial stations like ITV? Who knows what these elements even are? The public service broadcasting licence for ITV is coming up for renewal – or not – at the end of 2014, so a good time to expand this debate would be now.

Of course, it is not as simple as saying that publicly funded programming or reporting is good and commercially funded programming or reporting is bad. Far from it: private companies are often much better placed to invest more money in innovative ideas.

And while it might seem odd that competitive, private, profit-making media companies play as important a part in a functioning democracy as elections and the legal system, ultimately our freedom to choose whichever newspaper or news source we want should guarantee a diverse selection of offerings, from all sides of the political spectrum and with some competing hard for accuracy and quality of news.

For this to work, however, we do need a real choice of different news and media sources – and this means newspapers, TV channels and other providers of news, information and debate must be owned by a wide range of different companies – and different people.

This is the issue that is known as media 'plurality'. The government accepts – and it is written into law – that, in order to maintain quality, it needs to restrict the number of media channels that can be owned or controlled by any one company or person; avoid any one person or company being able to put too much pressure on politicians; and ensure that a range of audiences – including poorer, less educated and more socially vulnerable people – are served and their voices heard.

Most potential problems with plurality arise when one media company wants to take over another. Where these deals are very big and might cut competition, bodies outside the government can have a say – the European Commission, the Office of Fair Trading and the Competition Commission. But once those organizations have approved a deal from the point of view of competition, the government must still be happy that it would not threaten plurality.

Some of the UK's media plurality rules are very precise: for example, newspaper groups with more than 20 per cent of the national market cannot buy more than 20 per cent of a major broadcaster such as ITV. But even where deals are smaller, the Secretary of State for Culture, Media and Sport has powers under the Enterprise Act 2002 to step in if the public interest might be threatened by media mergers.

The Secretary of State can consider plurality of media ownership, accurate presentation of news and free expression of opinion in newspapers. This 'quasi-judicial' role – the politician must try to act completely impartially, as if he or she were a judge – has proved hugely controversial in recent years. Between 2010 and 2012 two different secretaries of state – Vince Cable and Jeremy Hunt – were the subject of huge rows over whether or not they could be impartial in deciding whether to allow a takeover of UK satellite broadcaster BSkyB by global media giant News Corp. The takeover attempt was later withdrawn after News Corp became embroiled in phone-hacking scandals, but not before several grey areas had been exposed in the rules on media plurality, such as whether politicians can ever be as impartial as a judge; how political lobbying could affect an outcome; when a government should refer deals to the Competition Commission; and whether or not a company can always be trusted to keep promises about news coverage.

Clearly, this area could benefit from a lot more work, but it is not often in the spotlight until big deals come around. In 2013, however, the government launched a new consultation into media ownership and plurality, and at the time of writing it was sifting through the responses with a view to looking at new ways to measure plurality.

What changes are needed? The House of Lords Select Committee on Communications suggested in 2008 that Ofcom, not just the minister, should be able to refer a bid to government officials for public-interest scrutiny, and that would be one change to look at. Another already being considered by the government is whether the law should be reformed so plurality issues could be looked at independently of mergers and takeovers – for example, when companies just happen naturally to grow so large that dominance might become an issue. In the age of huge digital companies that come out of nowhere to become global giants, this is a live issue.

A good starting point for looking at these kinds of issues might also be to ask the question – who exactly owns the UK media? Surprisingly, no one has been compiling this information in a clear way, and publishing it regularly to the public, on the web – a gap the government has now acknowledged needs to be filled. Following its recent consultation, it will be looking to draw up a new measurement framework or 'benchmark' for media plurality which might for the first time include the BBC and digital news on the internet. Clearly, such a benchmark or map will look very different now than it would have done just ten or fifteen years ago. In this high-tech age, the media picture is much wider than the 'old media' of print, TV and radio.

Since the birth of the web, and more recently of widespread mobile access to the internet, it is not always so clear what constitutes a publication, for example, or what makes something a piece of news, or who is a journalist. Sometimes this confusion causes officials to panic. In 2012, nine-year-old Martha Payne from Argyll began posting photographs of her school lunches on her wonderful school food blog, 'NeverSeconds'. One cheeseburger lunch was awarded a damning 2 points out of 10 – though the reviews were not always bad. Most people would be overjoyed if their child showed such independence and creativity, not to mention awareness of what is good or bad to eat. The council, however, said the school's catering staff had expressed concern about their jobs after one local headline read 'Time to fire the dinner ladies', and asked the school's headteacher to ask Martha to stop reporting.

After the story was picked up again in the press, however, the story went global and millions of people saw Martha's website – more people than read many newspapers, these days – and criticized the council for being heavy-handed. The council and school soon backtracked and Martha was allowed to carry on, using her new-found fame to help raise money for schoolchildren in Africa.

This case might seem straightforward, but how simple is it? Would it be acceptable for any child to post any picture from inside their school on to a public website? Or for any employee, such as a person working in a care home or a mental-health facility, to report on their day at work? These are not simple issues, and Martha's story is simply one of the first of what is sure to become a growing wave of similar controversies.

Existing news organizations face their own challenges from new media, but they are seeing benefits as well.

The rise of the 'citizen journalist', sending in reports and pictures of fast-breaking stories such as riots or floods, can combine powerfully with traditional methods.

In a speech to an 'electronic democracy' conference in London in 2008, the then director of BBC News Helen Boaden described how the *10 O'Clock News* had asked people to send in photographs after the head of the army had voiced concern about military housing conditions.

'Journalists were unable to film on MoD premises,' said Boaden. 'So the programme used the BBC website and sites that soldiers use to offer families affected an open platform to tell their own story.

'The material sent in exposed the squalid state of much of the soldiers' accommodation. We were then able to show the pictures we received to the Army – and they had to respond.'

However, not all 'user-generated content' is particularly thoughtful or adds much to a debate, and editorial control or systems whereby readers rate each others' comments are still sometimes needed, warned Boaden. 'We must guard against mindless interactivity replacing genuinely useful debate and insights.'

To understand this point, consider how journalism was changed by an older 'new technology' – the telephone. All of a sudden, phone-in shows on the radio meant large numbers of people from anywhere in the country could take part in a discussion. But such programmes do not just throw open the lines to everyone at once, or to anyone at random, as some internet discussion seems to do: calls are vetted by a producer and moderated by the host. The technology enhances public debate, but it is not chaos.

When it comes to the internet, media organizations are still feeling their way. The new possibilities are powerful, but just because something is written by a blogger rather than a big corporation does not make it fearless, true or even honest. Cases have emerged which show bloggers can be just as subject to hidden influences as any profit-led media organization.

In August 2012 a judge in the US uncovered cases where both newspaper reporters and technology bloggers had written positive stories about giant companies such as Oracle and Google while – unbeknown to their readers – they were also receiving money from these companies to act as 'consultants'. While the bloggers denied they ever directly wrote stories for cash, the dangers are clear: if you read something online, who knows who may be paying the person who wrote it, or even who that person really is?

A different kind of hidden influence may be of more concern not to people reading blogs but to those writing them: the UK's libel laws.

'Libel' is the legal term for something that is written (and read by a third party), published, broadcast or put online about a person that is damaging to their reputation and is not true (the wider legal term is 'defamation', covering both libel and slander, which relates to speech). There are various defences for publishers, one of which – not surprisingly – is truth, although this may be hard to prove in court.

While details of individual cases are often kept confidential – most cases settle before a final court judgement – the cost of settlements and judgements to UK media organizations is known to run to many millions of pounds every year.

'The big concern is over what is known as the "chilling effect" of libel law,' says Judith Townend, a researcher at the Centre for Law, Justice and

Journalism at City University London. 'If people are overly worried that saying something bad about a company or person will mean they end up in court, they might be scared of writing about certain topics and certain people or corporations.'

The problem is worse for smaller publishers, including many online publishers, who do not have legal insurance or in-house lawyers, Townend explains. 'In the end a court may find in your favour, but just to get to that point can be very expensive.'

And social media have raised new concerns, she says. 'Anyone having a conversation on Facebook could, in the eyes of the law, be a publisher, and some celebrities have bigger audiences on their personal Twitter feeds than newspapers. Maybe you don't have lots of followers – but what if you are retweeted by someone who does?'

On the other hand, few think a free society could do away with defamation law entirely. If we did, what would prevent any media outlet from setting out to destroy someone's life simply because they wanted to, or a company from attacking its competitors with made-up stories?

Faced with a struggle that is impossible to resolve completely – freedom of speech versus protection from malice and lies – the debate over possible reforms will never end. As specific new challenges like the internet arise, however, new reforms will be developed to try to keep the balance between competing interests as fair as possible.

The new Defamation Act 2013, for example, requires a claimant to sue over a libellous statement on the internet within a one-year limitation period. Previously there had been no limit while a statement was still accessible online, so in effect every time it was viewed or downloaded it could be considered as a new libel, on and on. This is a sensible change that takes account of the nature of new technology. The Act also includes protection for scientists and academics publishing articles in respected journals, and protection for people publishing information they reasonably believe to be in the public interest.

More controversial are rules to protect websites that carry other people's comments, such as social media sites, from being sued for libel, as long as they take reasonable steps to address a problem, such as helping to put the person mentioned in touch with the author or removing the content. This means website owners will no longer be responsible for all content as soon as it is published, but it could make them the judges of what is allowable and what should be taken down.

All these issues are complex, and above all website users, website owners, individuals and organizations must be clear at all times what the law is and how it applies to them. The government would do well to create a simple, one-stop site for advice in this field.

Battles over freedom of speech do not begin and end with the libel laws, however. Most notably in recent times, outrage at phone hacking by tabloid newspapers led in 2011–12 to the first stage of an inquiry by the senior judge Lord Justice Leveson into the culture, practices and ethics of the press (the second part, into how specific hacking cases came about and were investigated, is on hold pending the outcome of separate legal action).

The Leveson Inquiry (part one) uncovered a shocking stream of stories about hacking, burglary, blackmail, bribery of police officers and other public officials, payment of criminals for stories, entrapment, compromising of protected witnesses, spying, destroying evidence, lying under oath, and invasions of privacy – part of an ingrained hidden culture of malpractice in at least some sections of the British press.

Such practices often do already break existing criminal laws (no one is allowed to pay a public official for information, for example), but their extent sparked calls for new laws specifically to regulate the press.

Throughout history, most democratic governments have shied away from creating such laws, for fear of restricting the freedom of speech and the independence of the media that is so essential to a functioning democracy. Instead, they have relied on trusting newspapers to set up systems to regulate themselves – with mixed results. The most recent such move before the Leveson Inquiry was the creation in 1991 of the Press Complaints Commission, a body led by editors and other senior figures in the press whose job – as its name suggests – was mainly to respond to complaints from the public.

As it was controlled by the same people it was trying to regulate, however, the PCC was not really that 'independent'. And while the commission did draw up a code of practice for editors, it had no powers to enforce it. Finally, no one even had to join the system at all – newspapers could just walk away from it and nothing would happen to them.

Following part one of the Leveson Inquiry, both the government and the press accepted the need for a new system of regulation. Although they disagreed and continue to disagree strongly on the details. At the time of writing the government had successfully set up a Royal Charter to create an official regulator of regulators – a 'watchdog' body that will examine new independent regulators to be set up by the press, and make sure they follow certain guidelines. Many newspapers and media organizations tried to fight this move in the courts, arguing there should be no legal body at all interfering directly in press regulation: but their bid was rejected by judges. Defiantly, the media bodies have gone it alone anyway, setting up a new Independent Press Standards Organisation (IPSO) separate from the rules of the Royal Charter, which theoretically could expose them to huge fines if they fail to regulate themselves properly. Everyone is now waiting to see what happens next.

Whatever happens, no one wants a return to the scandals of phone hacking and bribery. You can be sure, however, that the new Royal Charter system will be tested: whatever the boundaries set by government, the press will push against them, in the name of free speech, entertainment and profits – and not necessarily in that order. And because free speech must be protected, the controversy will never disappear.

The whole picture is complicated still further in the digital age by confusion over what a newspaper actually is these days, and who should be regulated. However, Martin Moore, director of the Media Standards Trust, says this problem is best avoided by focusing on the larger media companies.

'We should focus on the real danger – the potential for big media corporations to abuse their power, whether this is to influence public policy improperly, to corrupt public life, or to "monster" ordinary people and squelch those who try to challenge them,' he says.

'By focusing on the bigger, multi-million-pound media organizations, you sidestep the whole issue of how to regulate TV, as opposed to print or the internet. You leave individuals and small publishers free from any regulation beyond the law, and concentrate on ensuring big organizations – who can cause serious harm – are accountable for what they publish.'

The government is trying to go down this route, restricting regulation to companies that edit and publish news for profit, not people writing blogs on their own.

Time will tell if all this is enough to ensure we never see a return to the corrupt cultures that led to phone hacking and other criminal practices in the darker corners of the British press.

Controversy is certain to return at some stage, however, since most people accept that as a democratic nation it is better that we allow some bad things to be published by keeping regulation as light as possible, rather than that important investigations should ever be blocked for the wrong reasons. As barrister Sadakat Kadri wrote in 2012, in the *London Review of Books*: 'Although it's easy to look on News International's predicament with some satisfaction, we shouldn't forget that intrusiveness is a requirement of good journalism. It was muckrakers at the *Guardian* and *New York Times* who uncovered the phone-hacking story in the first place; [and] the *News of the World*, less than a year before it closed, won plaudits for a sting that exposed corruption in the Pakistan cricket team.'

So the problem will never disappear completely. Freedom of the press, unfortunately, will always come with an unpleasant aspect. How much unpleasantness, intrusiveness and crudeness should we put up with, as a price worth paying for that freedom? The debate continues, and like all good debates about the meaning of freedom and democracy, will continue for ever.

Another key issue for a healthy democracy is the need for a thriving local media sector. Just as local government is the front line of democratic politics, local and regional media – and devolved media in the UK's devolved nations – are vital for informing people about, and allowing them to question, democracy at a local level.

The UK's local and regional newspapers, however – until recently, a cornerstone of local media – are not in a good way.

Local papers, from the *Edinburgh Evening News* to the *Tavistock Times Gazette*, used to make a lot of money from classified advertising. These days, however, online listings websites and free newspapers with online editions have removed much of this cash, and their problems do not end there.

John Thompson, founder of UK media news website Journalism. co.uk, says the key problem for local press centres is concentration of ownership, with local news businesses becoming part of bigger groups over the past few decades.

There are now just four main players in UK local newspapers: Northcliffe Media, part of the international group that publishes the *Daily Mail*; Trinity Mirror plc; Newsquest, the UK arm of the unfortunately named acquisitive US publishing group Gannett; and Scotland-based Johnston Press, publisher of the *Scotsman*. Between them, these four publish more than 600 local and regional papers across the UK and hundreds more local websites.

Together, however, the four have taken many businesses that were previously local and independent and 'systematically asset stripped, cut jobs and centralized operations,' Thompson says. Centralization to cut costs is not always a bad thing, he points out, but when editorial processes such as sub-editing – which includes checking facts in stories and writing headlines – is taken away from a local area, big problems can be created.

He cites the example of one local paper – the *Argus*, in Brighton and Hove – which was bought by Newsquest and had production moved to a team based sixty-five miles away in Southampton. In the first issue after the move in 2012, the fairly important local word 'Brighton' was misspelled not once but twice in a picture caption about a young singer (and 'Brighten' Institute of Modern Music graduate) set to perform in a London concert.

'So it all makes financial sense, but it alienates local readers. Our local press has become estranged from communities.'

However, it is not all doom and gloom in local journalism, Thompson says. A new buzzword – 'hyperlocal' – refers to websites written by a new breed of community reporter. These 'citizen journalists' – often without any formal training, and in their spare time – are carrying out the sort of local research, interviews and investigation that used to be the domain of the old school of better-funded local newspapers, and are gaining audiences fast.

'The problem now is making it pay,' he says. 'Will these hyperlocal sites become businesses, or will local newspapers manage to embrace them, bring them into the fold and pay their writers?'

At the level of the UK's devolved nations, there are additional problems for the news media. When it comes to political coverage – and in particular coverage of what goes on in the new devolved legislatures – many feel the UK national press is simply not that interested.

Ella Taylor-Smith of Napier University in Edinburgh says that while Scotland's own newspaper industry is strong, the UK national TV and newspaper coverage, including BBC coverage – the BBC has dedicated services for Scotland, Wales and Northern Ireland – tends to be London-focused and to view Scottish politics as a minority interest. 'For them it's like local news – somebody's cow stuck in the barn.'

Officers at the Welsh Assembly feel similarly ignored by UK national media. Despite pioneering work with audio and video releases, National Assembly for Wales media relations officer Alex Feeney says his team focuses most often on Welsh media, including devolved channels like BBC Wales, the *Western Mail* newspaper, the Welsh-language magazine *Golwyg* and even a freelance blogger in the Assembly lobby – Gareth Hughes, a former political correspondent for ITV Wales.

'The UK national media tend to only cover us during times of elections – trying to make any sort of headway at other times is very tough indeed,' says Feeney.

'It is very frustrating. When a story was breaking recently about how the UK Parliament in Westminster works, I contacted one political editor of a broadsheet with information on how the Welsh Assembly works in a different way, as the differences were relevant. All I got back was an email saying: "please take me off your mailing list". That is not atypical.'

In Northern Ireland, years of community–engagement work and its position with access to both UK and Irish media have combined to help create a vibrant media sector. However, as mentioned in Chapter 6, wider national coverage has fallen here too, following the end of the Troubles.

When and how might the UK media ever properly come to terms with devolution?

One expanding way the media can adapt to different local audiences – whether devolved, regional, or much more local, in cities, towns and smaller local communities – is through local broadcasting.

The BBC and other national broadcasters have developed a few local services for some time, but with the modern explosion of digital TV and radio channels combined with broadband internet and other new technologies, a more diverse local broadcasting scene is now emerging.

Community radio stations, for example, are experiencing a boom since Ofcom began licensing them in 2005. Since the first licence was granted in that year to Forest of Dean Community Radio, more than 200 have been granted (about 230 at the beginning of 2013 – so there is likely to be one near you).

Community radio stations are non-profit organizations, typically covering a radius of just five kilometres and catering for tiny communities or sub-groups, such as a particular age group or interest group. They offer training opportunities to local people, and many staff are volunteers.

Now, local TV is catching up. In 2011 the government and the BBC worked out a deal to slice off up to £40 million of BBC licence money to kick-start a new generation of more diverse local stations – £25 million for technology set-up costs and up to £5 million per year (in total, across all channels) over three years to fund local content. The government's vision for the stations is specifically to boost local democracy by telling people more about what is happening in their area.

In August 2012 Ofcom revealed it had received fifty-seven bids for the first wave of nineteen twelve-year licences to run local TV services on digital terrestrial television in cities and towns across the UK. These licences have now been awarded in Belfast, Birmingham, Brighton, Bristol, Cardiff, Edinburgh, Glasgow, Grimsby, Leeds, Liverpool, London, Manchester, Newcastle, Nottingham, Norwich, Oxford, Preston, Sheffield and Southampton. The first channels (led by 'Estuary TV' in Grimsby) are now coming on the air and are set to exploit a modern mix of broadcast TV and internet video.

'Local TV could and should bring about a major boost to local democracy in the UK,' says Fred Perkins, chief executive of Information TV, a national digital channel that is divided into 'micro-channels' including some local services. 'Changes in technology now mean there are lots of different ways you can broadcast, and there is the ability for local people to make their own "citizen producer" content. You can create something that is of great value to the local community, at minimum cost.

'However, there is a risk that the combination of regulatory require-ments from Ofcom and the low level of the BBC's financial contribution could nip in the bud the energy and excitement around local partici-pation.'

In Perkins's view, local TV will be sustainable only on a low-cost model that builds viewer loyalty around weekly or daily programmes, rather than trying to run 24/7. 'The financial numbers are smaller than traditional TV broadcasters are used to, but by starting small they can make a profit, and grow from there.'

One fact which can safely be predicted about the future of local television stations is that local politicians – councillors, and local MPs – will be keen to appear on them. Because just as we need a free, diverse and independent news media for citizens to stay informed, it is also necessary in a democracy for politicians to have a strong relationship with the media. As far as possible, there needs to be fair coverage of politics on the one side, and open communication from the other. This relationship, however, has not been straightforward in recent times. Problems such as phone hacking, accusations of political 'spin' and the perception that big business in the media is looking to influence politicians are leading to a three-way breakdown in trust between public, media and politicians.

'The government has a responsibility to communicate its policies and its work to the population, because we are a democracy,' says Martin Moore of the Media Standards Trust.

'In decades gone by, this was not such a problem, as the press used to cover politics and government statements more widely as a matter of course – it was a sort of unspoken bargain.

'Nowadays the bargain is not working any more, as the press becomes more and more competitive. In many newspapers, parliamentary news is now virtually non-existent – a lot of Bills go through the house and you would have no idea.'

Recent governments have responded by trying to professionalize their relations with the media, with ever-growing armies of press officers, but this has now backfired, Moore explains. 'The papers understandably said this is "spin", and we're not reporting what you want. So we are in a messy period – the trust between the government and the media has broken down.'

At the same time, however, Moore says, there are an amazing number of new methods for people to communicate with each other online about what the government is doing, and to find out information about politics and public services.

So are we entering an exciting new world of political news, where people have more access to information about politics – national, devolved, regional and local – than ever, or is there now so much information that more and more people will simply become confused and switch off?

The media sector is certainly undergoing huge change, and coverage of politics is changing too. More and more people are accessing information instantly, anywhere, any time, on tablet computers, smart-phones, e-books and laptops.

Like all other areas of our democracy, in the end it will be up to us what use we make of these new opportunities. But the scope of all these technologies to revolutionize our access to political news is powerful and exciting. Even more exciting is the potential of these new technologies to access politics and social action directly. And that is the focus of our next two chapters.

Chapter 13

Rights to protest, rights to demand

Less than twenty years ago, the right to hold protest rallies – also known as the right of assembly – and the right to join campaigning organizations like trade unions and political parties – known as the right of association – did not exist in the UK.

That is not to say these activities were banned: protest and campaigning have a long and proud history in the UK. But these rights were not fully protected either; they were simply allowed to happen by default, in that people can generally do whatever they like, provided no laws are broken.

Since 1998, however, assembly and association have been made legal rights. Article 11 of the European Convention on Human Rights, as passed into UK law by the Human Rights Act (see Chapter 11), says: 'Everyone has the right to freedom of peaceful assembly and to freedom of association with others, including the right to form and to join trade unions for the protection of his interests.'

What difference does this make? One difference might be that people have stronger rights now for these activities to be protected, for example against potentially violent counter-demonstrations trying to stop a peaceful protest from taking place.

However, the rights of assembly and association are not unqualified rights. As with many aspects of free democracy, one person's freedom is not allowed to endanger or impede other people unfairly, so restrictions on these rights are allowed 'in the interests of national security or public safety, for the prevention of disorder or crime . . . or for the protection of the rights and freedoms of others.' The law also allows the government to prevent some types of public worker, such as soldiers or police officers, from joining trade unions, where strikes might threaten national security – and it does do so.

To help balance everybody's rights – the rights of people to protest, the rights of people's property to be protected from damage and our right to use public roads and pavements, for example – the standard advice for people planning a protest is to let the police and local authorities know where it will be and how many people are expected to turn up.

For a standing protest, you do not have to let anyone know – though it is preferred – but if you are organizing a march from one place to another you are required by law to notify the police six days in advance (twenty-eight days in Northern Ireland), or as soon as you reasonably can, as roads may need to be closed.

The right of assembly and protest does not hold on private land: it might be tolerated, but gatherings of twenty or more people can be prevented from taking place in private areas as 'trespassory assemblies', a criminal offence under the Criminal Justice and Public Order Act 1994 (if there are fewer people, trespassing is only a civil offence). There are also designated sites such as royal properties and military bases where it is a criminal offence to trespass; and special rules apply to the area immediately around the Houses of Parliament, where camping overnight by protestors and the use of amplified noise (such as speakers and loudhailers) is banned.

Despite this, the cases where clashes happen between protestors and the police most often are where violence or property–damage erupts, or seems likely. In this case, police have powers to stop or move a march or protest, even if it is held on public land.

Feelings can run high. People can feel hurt, angry and betrayed by politicians. And acts of protest, like acts of opposition in politics, are vital for democracy: they are part of the process of challenge, debate, and a display of people's strength of feeling about an issue which is much better expressed out in the open than bottled up or hidden.

But in a democracy, protest is not allowed to become physical. Democracy is rule by persuasion, not fear or force. In a democracy, the most effective protest of all can be registered by removing a government or council at the ballot box, so if enough people protest loudly enough between elections, it ought to be enough to win changes.

So rallies and marches are important. But they are not the only means that ordinary citizens have to try to create political pressure. Another less spectacular but sometimes just as effective way to focus people's calls for change is by launching a petition – a much older right for UK citizens.

The right for a group of citizens to petition the people in charge directly (at first the monarch, and then Parliament), to ask them to put right something that they feel is wrong, dates back to the Middle Ages. Its use grew until in the early nineteenth century tens of thousands of petitions were presented to Parliament every year (and one Chartist petition, as we heard in Chapter 1, received more than three million signatures).

Through the twentieth century, however, their use in Westminster dropped off, which is not surprising since they were rarely seen to have much effect – and many still don't. Paper petitions are presented to Parliament by MPs on behalf of their constituents: the MP can make a short statement (not a speech) and drop the petition into a green bag that hangs behind the Speaker's chair. As we saw in Chapter 4, petitions are listed in Hansard, and a government department responds to each one with an 'observation' – which does not have to include any promise for action. 'By and large, paper petitions disappear into the petitions bag . . . without attracting much comment or notice,' according to one report from democracy charity the Hansard Society.

In recent years, a bit of the old magic has returned to the system, however, with the appearance of electronic petitions, first introduced on the website of the Prime Minister in 2006. Anyone could sign one at any time of the day or night, from their own home, mobile phone, or anywhere else they could access the internet. When Downing Street switched on its first 'e-petitions' system, 26,000 were created in the first year: a return to nineteenth-century levels of excitement.

When MPs protested that people should be petitioning Parliament as a whole, not just the Prime Minister, e-petitions were switched over in 2011 to the main website for the government (www.gov.uk/petition-government) and linked to the business of Parliament.

A rule was introduced that if any petition receives more than 100,000 signatures in the time it is open (they can be left open for up to a year), it is considered for debate in Parliament; and so far, a debate has taken place on the dozen or so cases that have reached the threshold. The numbers of people putting petitions forward have zoomed even higher: in the first year of the new system some 36,000 petitions were submitted, attracting 6.4 million signatures. They make fascinating browsing: from huge mainstream issues such as returning VAT on air-ambulance fuel payments, to petitions with one lonely signature, such as a plea to paint all cars in bright colours to reduce accidents.

Sir George Young, Leader of the House of Commons at the time the e-petitions system was introduced, says it is an 'enormous improvement' to paper.

'A paper petition is put in a bag behind the Speaker's chair and nobody knows what happens to it. An electronic petition creates a trail. It's relatively easy to set your name to one, so it has helped build a stronger link between people and Parliament.'

Sir George cites the 2012 release of government papers relating to the 1989 Hillsborough football crowd disaster – a demand made at least partially through an electronic petition – as a milestone in proving their effectiveness.

In autumn 2012, the system was enhanced by a government undertaking that any e-petition signed by more than 10,000 people would have a response published, including a statement of the government's policy on the issue, and details of any other relevant parliamentary processes on the go that people might be able to engage with.

However, the Westminster system, with its high signature threshold for full debate and lack of any other mechanism for investigating issues raised, remains at the weaker end of what is possible.

Elsewhere in the UK, more powerful petition systems have been set up. While the system in Northern Ireland is similar to (or weaker than) that operating in Westminster, the Welsh Assembly and Scottish Parliaments both have special petitions committees of elected members who can refer any petition to other committees or carry out their own inquiries.

In Wales, members of the public can present their petitions directly to the Assembly, which has led to various media-friendly events involving horses and fancy dress; the petitions committee is then free to launch inquiries into either the petition or the general topics it raises, take evidence, hold debate, visit sites and recommend action to the Welsh government.

The Scottish Parliament petitions committee has similar powers, inviting petitioners to come and put their points directly, and summoning ministers to respond.

With greater powers come greater effects. Petitions in Westminster might have helped push the government to release the Hillsborough documents and delay an increase in fuel tax, but in Scotland petitions have more regularly led to deeper inquiries being set up in areas as diverse as superbug infections in hospitals, knife crime and child abuse in care institutions, after the voices of people who had suffered or lost relatives were heard repeatedly and directly in the media following petitions committee investigations.

Even more significantly, a Welsh petition needs only ten signatures to be considered, while in Scotland there is no minimum number at all.

'Here, petitions are treated no differently if they have five hundred signatures, or just one,' says Anne Peat, clerk to the Scottish Parliament's

Public Petitions Committee. 'Petitions driven by media campaigns are not always the best ones to look at.'

There is no fixed end to the process of consideration by the petitions committee, either, says Peat: it continues, sometimes for years, until the committee is satisfied that all important issues raised have been properly addressed. 'We have two petitions about school bus safety and signage that were lodged in 2007 and 2009. The petitions raise a number of issues some of which relate to powers still currently reserved to Westminster. Discussions have taken place about a transfer of functions but these matters take time. The committee continues to press the Scottish Government. In the meantime, the petitions remain open.'

The Hansard Society, in a 2012 report 'What next for e-petitions?', suggested the House of Commons could learn from the Scottish and Welsh systems, setting up its own petitions committee with powers to question ministers, invite petitioners and others to public hearings, raise issues with select committees and commission their own inquiries.

At the moment in Westminster there is 'no common agreement about the purpose of e-petitions and as a consequence, public and media expectations of the system are confused', the report found. The promising of a debate – or a possible debate – only if 100,000 signatures are received 'is a very thin form of public engagement . . . and is almost entirely one-directional', it said.

The problem with a single threshold is that petitions can still attract considerable support, but if they are one signature short of the threshold – and are 'only' signed by 99,999 people – there is no guarantee of anything happening at all, a fact which must put many people off starting a petition in the first place.

The report accepted that Westminster would need a different model to Scotland and Wales, since the number of petitions received is so much higher: in one recent year, the Scottish Parliament received 120 petitions and the Welsh Assembly fifty, compared with tens of thousands filed at Westminster.

However, a single high threshold is not the only answer. If a

Westminster petitions committee were set up, it could consider petitions at a lower threshold of around 10,000 signatures, and some with even lower levels of support could be passed to MPs or offered some quicker feedback, the report suggested.

Ultimately, the key to any successful petition system is to set up a clear process and publicize it properly, says University of Lincoln academic Catherine Bochel.

'It needs to say you can achieve this, this and this – so people are realistic about it.

'Clearly a petition is not a way for people to get anything they want. But if people feel they have been listened to and treated fairly, and if their issue has been discussed, they are much more likely to accept the outcome.'

Petitions can be local, too, though progress here has been mixed. A legal requirement for local authorities in England to set up formal processes to respond to petitions was introduced in 2009, then scrapped in 2012 as part of 'localism' plans to allow councils more freedom to pick and choose between local activities. Accordingly, some councils (such as Mid Sussex District Council and Melton Borough Council in Leicestershire) subsequently voted to stop running e-petition services, deciding not enough people were using them to be worth the money. But more and more other councils are continuing to introduce e-petition systems, and as technologies become cheaper they are likely to have a growing part to play in the strengthening of UK democracy in the future.

One aim of starting a petition or other form of campaign can simply be to try to find out more about what is going on, and this overlaps with another right which has been strengthened in recent years – the right to access information held by public bodies, under a law called Freedom of Information.

In years gone by – and some might say it is often still the case – public officials in the UK have been used to operating in an atmosphere of confidentiality. Our bureaucracies were built in a Victorian age of public deference to the people in charge, with many official papers locked away in secret. For many papers, there was a thirty-year rule: thirty years before any chance of release – now in the process of being reduced to twenty years (see also Chapter 9).

But with growing pressure for things to change, the Freedom of Information Act 2000 and the Freedom of Information (Scotland) Act 2002 were passed, giving citizens across the UK a clear right to access information produced by public bodies unless there are strong and specific reasons not to release it, as with medical records or intelligence information. Environmental information is covered by Environmental Information Regulations (EIRs), which provide similar rights of access.

These are not woolly rules: once you have requested a piece of information, anyone who destroys that information to stop it being released is committing a criminal offence.

In fact, any request for a piece of information from a public body is now counted as a Freedom of Information or FOI request, whether or not you call it that – though it doesn't do any harm to use the magic letters 'FOI' in your request, to speed things along.

For the law to apply, a request for information (outside Scotland) must be in writing, though an email is fine; and in Scotland, video and audio requests are allowed, including voicemail messages.

The authority must supply information you request within twenty working days, or give a valid reason why it cannot. Most responses will be by email and free of charge, though reasonable printing, copying and postage charges can sometimes be made.

The 'unusual and distinctive' democratic role of FOI law, says Maurice Frankel, director of the UK Campaign for Freedom of Information, is that 'it does not depend on elected representatives or anyone else acting as intermediaries on your behalf. If you as an ordinary citizen want to know what justification there was for an action taken by a public body, you can ask in your own name.'

There are several benefits to this direct approach, according to Frankel. 'At one level, it is something individuals can use to check whether they are being treated fairly by an authority which has refused to provide a service or benefit for which they have applied. They could ask to see the authority's internal guidance to see whether it has been properly applied – and check that the guidance itself is in line with the law.

'Second, at community level, it allows people to challenge a decision to build a factory, or change a road layout, or close a hospital – people can see if what they are getting is a version of the truth that has been doctored to help an authority get its way with the minimum of objections.

'And third, it helps to hold public authorities to account, to keep them honest: if they know that what they tell us can be checked against internal papers, they know it is better to tell us the truth.'

Frankel offers one 'very telling example' of how the simple act of asking for information can have a major positive effect on how services are run.

'A few years ago, the charity Action against Medical Accidents used the FOI act to obtain health care safety information from what was then the National Patient Safety Agency,' he says. 'The agency had a system of sending out medical alerts to NHS trusts in England when safety problems arose, and then asking trusts to confirm they had taken action. The charity used FOI to ask for details of these responses, and made a shocking discovery – in 2010, 75 per cent of trusts failed to comply with at least one of those alerts, and 15 per cent of trusts failed to comply with ten or more of them.

'When they asked for the same information the next year, however, levels of compliance had improved. The likely explanation is that publicity for their findings – the release of the information – had ensured a change.'

Authorities do not always have to release information. They can refuse to supply it if the cost of staff time in finding it out would exceed certain limits (£600 for government departments), and there are various types of information that are exempt from the law – or can be exempt.

'Absolute' exemptions include information held by courts and tribunals; security and intelligence records; materials gathered by journalists working for the BBC and Channel 4; and – a recent addition – communications with the three most senior members of the Royal Family (currently the Queen, Prince Charles and Prince William – so letters from Prince Charles to government departments are not obtainable, for example).

In some other cases, information will be exempt only if it is decided that it is in the greater public interest to withhold it than to release it. This includes where release of information is likely to 'prejudice' key interests such as international relations, law enforcement or trade secrets. The test is tougher in Scotland, where information can be withheld only if it would 'substantially prejudice' these kinds of interests.

Information can also be held back if it relates to the formulation of government policy – private discussions between ministers and advisers while they are making up their minds what to do about something. And another exemption – again subject to a public-interest test – applies if the release of information would be likely to 'inhibit the free and frank provision of advice.'

Several ministers and top civil servants have argued that the whole process of government could be wrecked if politicians and officials can't discuss sensitive issues frankly, in private – and so all discussion of policy should be held back. Others have said that if this kind of private discussion starts to be released, officials and politicians will end up never writing down their true thoughts and views, meaning the policy process would actually end up being even more hidden than it was before.

However, there is still a public interest test, and sometimes the decision could go the other way and policy discussion could be released.

In the first instance, it is the public body that holds the information that makes this judgement itself; after that it can be referred to the Information Commissioner or Scottish Information Commissioner, then to the tribunal and then to the law courts. Finally, at the end of this long and complex process, if ministers have been ordered to release information and they still simply do not want to do so, there remains a right of ministerial veto – so in other words, in the end, the government can still just say no to the release of any information.

This veto is used only rarely, and in exceptional circumstances – though it has been used several times. It was used in 2012, for example, when an Opposition MP asked the Department of Health to publish a 'risk register' it had created analysing the possible consequences if proposed NHS reforms were to fail. The government refused, saying that this was information used to develop policy. After an appeal, the Information Commissioner backed the release of the register, saying that it would be in the public interest to publish it; and a tribunal supported him. But in the end, a veto was used by the government and the register remained unpublished. Another veto was used last year to block the publication of letters from Prince Charles to seven government departments, in a case that was brought before absolute exemption was introduced for communications with senior members of the Royal Family.

Clearly, these are very sensitive issues. Not everyone likes the veto on FOI; but without it, the very existence of FOI law might be jeopardized, since governments of all parties might turn against it.

A review of how FOI law is working, carried out by the Commons Justice Select Committee in 2012, concluded that it is generally working well, and has made public bodies more open, accountable and transparent, while preserving a 'safe space' for private policy discussions. The ministerial veto was an acceptable part of this, the committee found, though the whole system needs to be more widely known about. More people need to be aware of their FOI rights, and more people need to use them.

There are many other complexities to FOI law (does an authority have to say if it has information, even if it doesn't release it, for example? And what about private firms contracted to provide public services? Is it fair that the law doesn't apply to them?), so anyone thinking of making an information request should take a look at the guidance available from the information commissioners or the Campaign for Freedom of Information.

The rights and powers UK citizens have to protest, petition and uncover information are all possible aspects of another activity central to a free democracy: the campaign.

Politicians might have most of the power in a democratic society, but they can be urged to use it in a different way. People and organizations campaign all the time to get things done, or to get things changed.

So what makes a good campaign? A campaign that works?

One powerful example from the recent past shows that, with the right tactics, a small group of people can sometimes make a big difference.

You may not have heard of the Campaign for Unmetered Telecommunications – or even its easier-to-use acronym, CUT – but you will be familiar with how most UK citizens now access the internet: we pay a monthly fee to a broadband company and we can use the internet as much as we like.

But it has not always been like this.

In the early 1990s, UK telephone companies charged by the minute for dial-up internet access. This involved using a maddening little box called a dial-up modem that plugged into your phone socket in the wall. Every time you wanted to use the internet, you used this to dial up a special number, and wait, and wait . . . and wait for it to connect. What is more, unlike in the US – where local calls were already unlimited within a flat fee (hence 'unmetered') – the longer we stayed online, the more it cost.

One Canadian cable company which was operating in the UK at that time, Videotron, *was* offering free local calls in some parts of UK, and some internet providers used it for flat-rate internet. But when Videotron was taken over by Cable and Wireless, this service was ended.

CUT began in 1998 as a group of enraged Videotron customers campaigning to keep their unmetered access, but they ended up fighting for the same rights for everyone, nationwide. In the space of just three years, and with the growing support of other campaigners and politicians, this dedicated band of about a dozen people used a range of campaigning tactics to take on some of the UK's biggest companies, and win.

One of CUT's founders, internet entrepreneur Nick Mailer, says the key to the campaign's early momentum was hard work on the detail: hour after hour put in to research, planning, and responding to all the technical points that the telecommunications companies were making to support their claim that unmetered access would lead to overuse.

'We had lawyers helping us with research, and people from the US who knew how the regulatory system worked over there. When the companies made a claim, we would refute it with evidence.'

The group's members were a diverse collection of people – 'from students to an American oil magnate' – who held meetings every Monday evening to discuss strategy, after which they went out for a meal. 'We would go to an eat-all-you-like Chinese buffet, which we referred to as the unmetered Chinese. After all, as we pointed out, if a buffet could run a flat-price policy, surely a telecoms company could do the same? Sure, there will be one or two people that eat too much crispy duck, but it all balances up in the end.'

In fact, humour can give a huge boost to a campaign, Mailer says. 'We would stand outside the headquarters of Cable and Wireless and sing a parody of their advertising slogan, 'getting to know you'. We held a festival of free calls there, handing out free sherbet lemons and candyfloss. Parody is hugely important – it helped us get thousands of supporters.

'An effective campaign is peaceful: it can't be threatening, because then you lose people's sympathy.'

As the campaign gathered pace with an 'internet boycott day', it gained some famous supporters – including the inventor of the web, Tim Berners-Lee – bringing more media appearances and, finally, political movement.

'First we were quoted by an MP in Parliament: then the trade and industry select committee invited CUT to participate in an inquiry into telecoms pricing, and we were invited to meet the minister. Finally, we were invited to join the Oftel forum that regulated pricing, so we were part of the committee that ultimately made the decision to create tariffs that included unmetered internet access.'

CUT is proof that campaigns can have an effect, but they are not easy to run.

'A voluntary campaign will only work if you put in the same commitment as you put into a paid job,' Mailer says. 'It is very hard work, and if you are not prepared to put in the work, then it will not pay off. You can't just have the balloons and the leaflets: to win, you have to do the boring backroom stuff, because most of the time, the people who get involved in the boring backroom stuff are professional lobbyists.

'It gives you credibility. Then to your enemies you become annoyingly credible, and incredibly annoying.'

It is also unlikely that CUT could have succeeded if it were not for the internet – both the subject of its campaign, and the way it could organize itself so successfully. We are now entering the realms of 'digital democracy' – the subject of our next chapter.

Chapter 14

The digital democracy dream

In the previous chapter we met CUT, the Campaign for Unmetered Telecommunications. This determined band of protestors helped bring unlimited internet use to UK homes, allowing us to watch TV, do our shopping, keep in touch with friends and even watch political debate online – well, some of us.

But there is another reason why CUT makes such a good story for this book. Not only was the campaign itself about internet access, it was one of the first to make use of the internet to achieve its aims. Here were early signs of what has been called 'digital democracy' – power to the people, through the power of the internet.

'One of the reasons we wanted unmetered internet use in the first place was for that same ability to bring people together that we used to organize our campaign,' says CUT co-founder Nick Mailer. 'The internet enabled us to find each other, to communicate, to coalesce. We planned everything by email list and online.

'Our research relied on the internet too – we could find out technical information like interconnection charges between companies.

'As we went on, we realized that increasingly, democratic societies would need to be able to access the internet to function – to make use of the network effect to come together, organize, research, debate, campaign.'

This 'network effect' is still growing. Most modern campaigns have a Facebook or Twitter element; in the last chapter we looked at electronic petitions; and sites such as 38degrees.org.uk in the UK and the global site Avaaz.org exist purely to help people come together to build campaigns online – any campaigns.

With Avaaz, for example, users sign up by the millions to vote on new campaign ideas, and then sign up to the campaigns themselves. Such support is often largely symbolic – there is a limit in any case to how far internet users in one country can meaningfully support a campaign in another – but sites like Avaaz demonstrate there is a clear potential to use the internet to bring people together to work towards a single goal.

Politicians have been quick to see this potential – led by the US, birthplace of the internet, where social media campaigning and online campaigning now sit at the heart of all political races.

But are campaigns really any more likely to work, just because they are online?

One academic who has researched this subject extensively is Dr Sandra Gonzalez-Bailon of the Oxford Internet Institute. Her team has found that people have varying thresholds for joining online campaigns, with some – the 'leaders' – willing to join in the early stages, when numbers of other participants are very low, while others – the 'followers' – join only when there are large numbers already taking part.

Dr Gonzalez-Bailon is now researching the role the internet can play in organizing mass action like the Arab Spring, the 'Occupy' movement in the West and the 'Indignados' protests in Spain. The Spanish protests saw millions of people taking to the streets in more than fifty cities to call for social change in the face of a range of social problems, including high unemployment and allegations of political corruption. Movements like this are enabled not just by social networking, but by the rise of smartphones and other mobile internet access devices: now social networks are mobile, people can organize themselves as easily out in the streets as sitting at home on a computer.

'The Indignados movement emerged online, with no formal organization,' she says. 'When it comes to bringing people together like that

243

in a short space of time, online networks like Facebook and Twitter are very efficient.

'Where they are not so efficient is at translating people's demands into specific policy preferences or requests, to make order from this cacophony of voices, so demands can be pushed into institutional channels. Research shows that activity in online networks is very volatile: it is not easy to transform spikes of activity into sustainable political pressure. People disperse as quickly as they come together, and the political momentum disappears.'

New technologies can be designed to try to tackle this problem, says Dr Gonzalez-Bailon. One example that was developed at Princeton University in the US is 'allourideas.org', a 'wiki' style platform – the sort of collaboration tool used by people all around the world to build Wikipedia together. This software allows large groups of people to collect and prioritize social ideas online in an open, democratic way.

'That's an example of an imaginative way that protestors, civic groups or institutions could bring together opinions and ideas to help decision-making,' she says. 'A lot more research needs to be done, but tools like these will be increasingly important for campaigns.'

So the internet is a powerful way for people to come together, urge each other into action and plan a campaign. But it can serve another fundamental role in a democracy, too: as a way of publishing information for anyone to access at any time, the internet can be the ultimate tool for openness and transparency in government.

For many of us, media websites are already our main source of political news. But the internet can offer us more direct access to the corridors of power: more and more democratic bodies, from local councils to the UK and European Parliaments, are letting us watch, listen to or read debates and committee meetings live – or at our convenience.

Parliament Live TV on the web (www.parliamentlive.tv) is the official Westminster web broadcasting service dating back to 2009; and the UK's new devolved bodies all 'webcast' their work. As new bodies, in fact, the Scottish, Welsh and Northern Ireland legislatures had a chance to be digital from the start, variously using the internet for 'webcasting', e-petitions, displaying politicians' voting records, running discussion forums and engaging with people using social media.

A useful 'channel guide' is the BBC's Democracy Live (www.bbc. co.uk/democracylive), which carries live footage, archives and clips from Westminster, all the devolved bodies and Europe. This and similar services offer people unprecedented access to our democratic bodies, giving a real feel for what meetings are actually like.

Ultimately, however, the biggest challenge for these kinds of live-access channels is the same faced by every TV channel: viewing figures. Often, to put it bluntly, no one watches them. While live online access to a council meeting is supposed to make it easier for all sorts of people – single mothers with no childcare, people living in rural areas, people working night shifts – to watch their politicians, in reality more people prefer to keep up with the Kardashians than the Kamerons or Kleggs.

There is a message there for politicians about language, format and presentation. If it is valuable for more people to watch the workings of democracy, perhaps their viewing channels need to be made a bit more watchable, or packaged in a slightly different way – without 'dumbing them down'.

On the other hand, other details of the workings of our democracy that are also available to access online can already be much less dull. For a start, these days – following the MPs' expenses furore – all sorts of information on politicians' salaries, allowances, costs and expenses is published on the web. You can search for your MP's office and business costs and expenses claims at the website of the Independent Parliamentary Standards Authority, for example (www.parliamentary-standards. org.uk/). For some reason, this makes fascinating browsing – never have receipts from medium-priced hotels and claims for whiteboard markers been so compelling.

Local councils have been doing this kind of thing for some time, so you should be able find your councillors' expenses claims online too;

and more recently, some local authority websites are even publishing councillor timesheets. This great innovation means residents of some councils, such as Tower Hamlets in London, can see exactly how many hours each month their councillor spent attending community meetings, and how many at civic receptions.

Also browsable are details of local government spending over £500; government spending over £25,000; public contracts awarded over £10,000; senior civil servants' pay; spending on government credit cards; and all kinds of service information in graphs, tables and spreadsheets – a rising tide of facts and figures gathering into what has become known as the 'open data' movement.

'Open data' refers to the release of data and information generated by organizations, including publicly funded bodies such as councils or government agencies, without them being asked for it – a handy complement to the Freedom of Information laws described in the previous chapter, since if the information is already out there, you don't need to put in a request for it.

Successive recent UK and devolved governments have strongly supported the principle of open data. There is even now a special central 'portal' for releasing data on the web – 'Data.gov.uk' – holding around 9,000 'datasets', and counting.

Much 'open data' is usable only by professionals and others who are used to handling complicated spreadsheets and databases, but some has been released in a format which people can engage with straight away. This includes, for example, the 'Police.uk' website, which allows anyone in England, Wales and Northern Ireland to enter their postcode, town or street name to view maps showing local crime statistics and what action has been taken, and to contact their local neighbourhood police teams. More than 50 million visits have already been recorded to this site, which was recently revamped to allow people to create more detailed customized crime maps of an area such as an estate, village or route to work; compare crime levels in their area with those in similar areas; and view mugshots of convicted criminals.

Also popular is school-performance information placed online by the Department for Education and the devolved governments; details of what sentences have been handed out by the courts for various types of crime; and GP prescribing data by practice (showing the total amounts of each drug prescribed by doctors' practices each month, not individual prescriptions).

Usually, however, data on its own is not enough to give us a clear picture of how our public services are being provided. At least some background information is usually needed to give it context, otherwise, to use a cliché, we are likely to be comparing apples with oranges. For example, in a city one would expect a higher incidence of traffic accidents than in a rural area, so context is important. And some public services might be 'outsourced' to private companies – is that always taken into account when we are looking at information about the cost of staff wages, for instance?

A 2012 report from the National Audit Office, 'Implementing transparency', supported this point, suggesting for example that information about police resourcing should be released alongside crime statistics; and that measures of user satisfaction could be looked at alongside measures of service cost. Overall it described the current state of information release as 'patchy'.

But how much does any of this matter? Do we really need to see all these facts and figures?

One analyst feels there is a huge amount at stake if we are to have the information we need to try to tackle social deprivation, lack of opportunity and exclusion.

'The impact of open data can be massive', says Tom Smith, director of research group Oxford Consultants for Social Inclusion (OCSI).

'The right information about what is happening, for example Census data on migration and how local populations are changing, is vital if we are trying to target services at the right places and the right groups of people. As a practical example, analysis of the open data on GP prescribing of medicines has already pointed to hundreds of millions of pounds of possible savings, simply by making sure all GPs prescribe cheaper, non-branded generic drugs where available.'

Smith offers an example from business to demonstrate the power of information.

'One thing you can do with data is test out ideas,' he says. 'Companies like Tesco with its loyalty cards know what people are buying, and can play with the way their supermarket aisles are laid out, or change their special offers, and get instant feedback.

'They are essentially running a test lab in real time, and responding to actual behaviour.'

An equivalent in the social sector might be to monitor calls coming in to front-line organizations such as social housing associations, Smith says. 'They receive queries all the time, so they have a continuous feed of potential problems in the system. So if for some reason benefit payments didn't arrive for their tenants, for example, they might pick that up before the benefit agencies were aware of problems. The point is that you often only understand a large problem by analysing small pieces of data in a wider way. One person calling in to say their benefit hasn't been paid is one thing. But lots of people calling in points to a possible problem with bank payments or IT systems. It is about looking at the big picture, and spotting patterns.'

So by tracking feedback alongside service data, you can create public services you can test, change, evaluate and tailor closely to people's needs, he says. And making the data open – giving the public a chance to see what is going on – adds transparency to the whole process, helping us to see how decisions are being made and how those decisions are affecting us.

Of course, it may just be possible that some of us have more exciting things to do with our time than pore over spreadsheets of public service data.

If the open data movement is to catch on at all, therefore, much better tools are needed to present, display and explain information, using maps, colours, 3-D landscapes and even virtual worlds similar to the ones we might find in the computer games that many of us do spend our spare time playing.

We need open data websites that are simple, engaging and fun: but with a purpose.

Consider 'Postcode Wars' (www.postcodewars.co.uk), a website developed by six young people from Nottingham aged between fourteen and eighteen. It won top prize at a 2012 event held by 'Young Rewired State', a network of young software developers with a social purpose. The site consists of little more than two empty boxes into which you enter two postcodes – maybe one where you live and one where you want to live, or where a friend lives, or where you grew up. Using several sets of publicly available data – open data – the two postcodes do battle, scoring points for ratings in areas such as house prices, local amenities and crime rates. The one with the most points is the winner.

This approach is not necessarily the best way to compare most types of data, and it is mainly intended as a bit of fun. But it does point the way to how raw facts and figures, if linked to local places and presented in a way that everyone can understand, can become much more compelling.

Various more formal experiments have been launched in this field, from a 'civic dashboard' in Birmingham (http://civicdashboard.org. uk/) – displaying all contacts people make with the council on a map according to where they are made – to the government-backed trial 'Lambeth in Numbers' (http://lambeth-in-numbers.co.uk/), which links together interconnected but previously separate types of data such as obesity statistics, the location of fast-food outlets and people's own records of where they shop for food and eat.

How else can the internet help to engage people with their communities? Among the first websites with a social and democratic purpose in the UK – and the world – are the ones created since 2003 by the pioneering charity 'mySociety'.

Founded a decade ago by former policy analyst in the Prime Minister's Strategy Unit Tom Steinberg, mySociety quickly gained a reputation for developing simple, clear, highly usable websites that opened up the workings of power to mass examination and mass action. Steinberg gathered a small team of volunteer programmers and, among other donations, won some early funding from a government 'e-democracy' grant, showing the government was able to fund such projects, at least, if not create them.

The iconic sites developed by mySociety over the years include 'TheyWorkForYou', allowing anyone to see how their MP votes, receive an email alerting them to whenever their MP speaks in Parliament and see what they said. There is also 'PledgeBank', which lets people promise to take all sorts of action to improve their community or society, providing a certain number of other people pledge to do the same; 'FixMyStreet', letting anyone report problems such as potholes in the road nationwide, instantly, from a mobile device (including sending in an image), without knowing who to contact at which authority; and 'WhatDoTheyKnow', making it easy to log a Freedom of Information Request with any agency and track the results.

These tools – which are also made available for anyone else in any country to adapt for their own systems – mimic the simplicity and power of the world's most successful commercial websites, from Google to Groupon, and harness them for social good.

It seems, however, that public institutions themselves are not always best placed to make the most of these digital tools.

'By 2003, all kinds of services used by large numbers of people – dating, shopping, reading books – were being turned upside down by the internet, so many useful sites were being created, that it seemed very strange that the government and civic sectors were widely unaffected, as if the internet hadn't happened at all,' says Tom Steinberg.

'And it still is a very quiet field compared with many others. The government does now build a lot of websites, but with the possible exception of e-petitions, when was the last time it launched a novel service that made it easier to understand how it works, or helped people work with others to solve a social problem?'

But even if it has taken outside organizations like mySociety to show the way, the internet certainly does have the potential to help people become more active citizens, Steinberg says. 'All the tools we build are about making members of the public more powerful, whether helping them ask their politicians to keep the streets cleaner or complain to a train company about problems with a journey.

'It's to help people understand change isn't just something that happens to them: they can help make change happen.'

Part of the internet's democratic potential is that it is not only able to bring people together or serve people on a large scale – nationally or internationally – but is able at the same time to focus on the smallest community areas such as villages, housing estates or streets.

A 2006 report by academics at Napier University in Edinburgh, 'An e-democracy model for communities', looked at the potential for local community councils – the smallest form of local government (see Chapter 7) – to engage people using the web. It found the internet can 'enable and encourage more people to have their say in local democracy than has previously been the case through . . . public meetings and communications'.

Of course finding the money, and people with the right skills, to use the internet to bond together small community groups is another matter, as this report also pointed out. It suggested that the larger local authorities in each area support community internet projects.

But why leave it to councils? Increasingly, citizens are doing it for themselves.

Consider the story of Nick Booth, a former BBC political reporter who amused delegates at a web engagement conference in 2010 with his tales of 'the rise of the git citizen' – active, online, mobile, and on an extremely short fuse.

Booth lives in Balsall Heath in Birmingham, not far from the Edgbaston cricket ground, and he told how one night traffic managers had placed cones out overnight without warning and the next day threatened the residents with fines for parking on their own street. This sparked him off on a mini rampage with a handheld video camera, confronting the wardens – some of whom had themselves parked illegally – and putting the video online (take a look now, at http://vimeo. com/5855160).

In his talk, Booth admitted: 'I don't think the video shows me in a very good light.' But the fact it was so easy for anyone now to do what he did was an example of what councils might be up against in the digital age, he said.

Public bodies need to recognize that all sorts of messages, conversations and rants will be taking place online and they need to respond, and to share in the enthusiasm, energy and passion of the internet, he said. And they need to help, for example by teaching local people computer skills, sharing technologies with people, and freeing up data.

Above all, they need to show there have been meaningful, tangible consequences to the feedback people offer – to use the new technologies to show people what has happened to their suggestions, says Booth.

An interesting development came in September 2012 when new regulations came into force requiring all local authorities to provide 'reasonable facilities' for members of the public to report on council meetings as they happen, such as a seating area with power to plug in laptops. The government said specifically that this was to 'make it easier for new social media reporting of council executive meetings . . . opening proceedings up to internet bloggers, tweeting and hyperlocal news forums'.

This is a veritable blizzard of techno-speak for an official government statement. And whatever we might think of new words like 'hyperlocal' – used often now to mean very small local areas that create their own internet communities – we can expect to see more of them.

As people get more and more excited about the power of the internet to bring people together, they like to invent new words to show how modern we all are. It's a shame, because techno-jargon can often confuse people and make a fairly simple concept much harder to understand. Consider 'crowdsourcing', for example – a new word often used in places where more familiar words, such as online consultation or asking people to send in comments or ideas over the internet, could be used just as easily.

'Crowdsourcing' is something the Cabinet Office now says it is doing, to invite people to send in new ideas for policy: this is a positive step, as long as people are not put off by the word itself.

A group called the Bristol Manifesto Group also used the 'c' word to invite locals both online and in person to suggest 'three wishes for Bristol' last year; the answers were sifted and distilled into the most popular ideas for improving the city to be presented to its new elected mayor. Could the process have just been called 'asking people for ideas'? You decide.

Whatever we call them, could online tools be woven even more directly into the fabric of democracy?

Ever since people started to think about the possible uses of the internet in politics and government, radical ideas about letting people vote instantly on any issue – and so potentially govern themselves using a form of 'direct democracy' – have been discussed from time to time. In one country, they even seem to be coming to life. In Italy, a citizen network called the Five Star Movement (Movimento 5 stelle, or M5S) has gained widespread support from people fed up with perceived corruption in traditional politics, partly by promoting a concept of 'continual mass consultation' with citizens on policy issues, over the internet.

This experimental system first saw mayors elected in the towns and communes of Sarego, Miro and Comaccio and the city of Parma in northern Italy, and councillors elected in several regions, including a surge in mafia-hit Sicily.

After that, it continued to gather force in local, regional and, in 2013, general elections in Italy, where M5S won an impressive quarter of votes nationwide (while refusing to compromise and form a coalition government). Its controversial leader Beppe Grillo has become a major force in Italian national politics, although time will tell how far the party's experiment with direct democracy online can be taken. Will it turn the Five Star Movement into a true, lasting national force for change, or will direct rule by internet vote become too complex and unmanageable for day-to-day politics? In Parma, for example, the newly elected M5S mayor Federico Pizzarotti, a former IT consultant, had no political experience, but this just seemed to add to his popularity. The movement does need to be seen in an Italian context, but its online mechanics are gripping democrats all over the world.

For some reason, experiments of this kind in the UK have so far been restricted to the world of football: projects such as 'MyFootballClub' and 'FivePoundFootballClub' have allowed people to buy into ownership or control of lower league clubs, giving them a say in issues like player wages and transfers – the chance for fans to do for real what they usually prefer to complain about in the pub: just like politics.

These schemes have generally worked pretty well, though in the early stages of 'MyFootballClub', which controls the English non-league side Ebbsfleet United, plans to allow the fans to actually pick teams for matches had to be dropped after it was realized it was unworkable, and unfair on the manager and players.

The issue with picking teams recalls the potential problems with 'digital democracy' alleged by its detractors in Italian politics – that in its more extreme, 'direct democracy' forms, it might be impossible for professional managers – whether of football teams or public services – to run operations from day to day without unpredictable disruptions.

This is a general problem with any form of 'direct democracy': it feels exciting for citizens to directly control every decision that affects their lives, but the problem with voting on many issues separately is that they may not all work together as a programme of government. Sometimes, electing people to create a whole programme of activity might be the best way. At other times, key individual decisions might be best put directly to the people. Ultimately, a balance must be found.

Another potential problem with any so-called 'e-democracy' project that offers a degree of power to people acting online is that it may be more elitist than democratic, in that it may not be handing power to a very representative cross-section of society.

In 2011, mySociety commissioned an evaluation of the profile of users of two of its websites from Oxford Internet Institute researcher Tobias Escher. Escher found that British internet users who had looked up information on a politician or party in the previous year were very different from the general population, and even from the average internet user. They were better educated (47 per cent had a higher degree compared with 27 per cent of the internet population); and richer (32 per cent have a household income of above £40,000 a year, compared with 22 per cent of British internet users and around 14 per cent of the general population). There was also a male bias of 61 per cent.

There might be various reasons for such imbalance: people on low incomes or with low educational attainment may be less likely to have access to the internet, or the skills and confidence to use it.

Clearly, we need to be careful about using the internet as a formal part of a democratic process. On the other hand, as long as other ways of getting involved are also available, the problem might not be so bad. In any case, says Tom Smith of OCSI, the situation is improving steadily: 'The internet is not representative but it is getting more so, with more and more people coming on all the time.

'It's true that there are still many people who are not online, but it's just the same if you look at who comes to a neighbourhood community meeting, for example – any form of consultation or debate is skewed in some way. And one advantage of the internet is it may be easier to find out about how skewed that group is – who is on there and who is not.'

But there is a third area of concern, and this one is perhaps the most serious. It is that, in the end, the use of the internet and other new communications technologies to enhance our democracy will be only as successful as our underlying democratic processes allow it to be.

Chris Quigley is the founder of Delib, a small company pioneering online techniques to engage people with democratic decision-making.

One of Delib's creations is 'BudgetSimulator', which gives people a chance to understand what it is like to set a budget for a council or another public body, using sliding switches and control panels to show exactly how if you spend more in one area, you have to spend less in another.

Tools like this can work well, Quigley says – they have even been known to increase people's sympathy towards politicians – but only if an authority explains clearly how they will act on the feedback they get.

'Where I think a lot of these "e-democracy" initiatives have gone wrong is to see themselves as a completely new way of doing things,' he says. 'They can be seen as quite romantic projects, and people can fall for the idea that technology can somehow revolutionize democracy on its own.

'But when you start pulling apart how democracy works, and seeing where the internet fits in, you see there are underlying processes you need to fit in to. If an organization is not designed to have the capacity to respond to a large amount of consultation on something like a budget, for example, then the internet will not help it gain value.

'It is about setting expectations, and being transparent about how the whole process will work from beginning to end.'

There is another point to make, too.

'If you don't have an engaged public, no technology exercise is going to work very well,' Quigley says.

This point is key. 'Digital democracy' does not increase anyone's motivation to try to change our society for the better. It can make it easier for people to get involved – if they want to. But do they want to? Will they want to?

The question brings us full circle. Soon it will be time to return to the theme with which this book began, and to think again about the overall state of democracy in the UK – and its future. First, however, we take a quick trip elsewhere: to Brussels, to look at the European dimension of modern British politics.

Chapter 15

Our place in Europe

The plan was audacious but the thief was confident, because – as became clear – he knew his territory. When the guards burst into an upstairs room in the European Parliament buildings, all they found was an overcoat crumpled in a heap on the floor. No other trace remained of the robber who had held up one of the parliament's internal bank branches just minutes before with a fake gun and a wig and escaped with 60,000 euros.

Where to look now? It was impossible. The sprawling maze of offices, corridors and walkways is so vast that the robber did not even need to leave: he just ran away inside the complex and disappeared.

Less than half an hour later, the guards had to reopen the buildings' numerous exits to allow 10,000 staff and visitors to come and go; and somewhere, some time, the robber slipped quietly out with the cash and melted away into the Brussels streets.

This true story – it happened in 2009, and two other similar incidents have happened since – vividly demonstrates at least one aspect of the European Union: it is big.

The European Parliament is just one of several gargantuan modernist building complexes jostling for space in Brussels' European quarter, with more in Strasbourg and in Luxembourg (home of the first European Parliament).

New buildings are always rising, adding acre upon acre of glittering glass, from the sweeping, understated curves of the Berlaymont building, headquarters of the European Commission, to the elegant ant-farms of the European Parliament complex. Some giant blocks house only translators.

The scale of the European enterprise is staggering. Given that there are now some twenty-eight EU member states using twenty-three official and working languages, this is not surprising. But the project did not start off so large.

The first trading partnership was the European Coal and Steel Community, whose six members (France, West Germany, Italy, Belgium, the Netherlands and Luxembourg) came together in 1951 to form a common market for those resources. One aim was to revitalize economies across Europe after the Second World War, but the community had a higher aim as well: that of making a new war between its members impossible. In creating the world's first 'supranational union' – where member states hand over part of their power to a separate higher entity – it laid the foundations for the EU. It was the first step in a new approach: somewhere between traditional international treaties which are agreements between separate states, and a fully fledged federal 'superstate' system like the United States.

Over the past sixty years or so a series of new treaties and waves of new members has seen the organization evolve into a wider economic community and a more powerful European Union with its own Parliament elected by citizens across all member states, and the ability to come up with ideas for its own laws – within the agreed areas of its powers.

In 1957, under the Treaties of Rome, the same six founding members of the coal and steel community added a European Economic Community (EEC) and an atomic energy community to form the European Communities (often just referred to under the EEC). In 1973 they were joined by Denmark, Ireland and the UK. Greece followed in 1981 and Spain and Portugal in 1986, swelling the membership to twelve.

Also in 1986, the twelve countries signed the Single European Act, pledging to form a single market for all goods and workers by 1992, to smooth trade cooperation by stripping away as many barriers as possible. Since this increasingly required member states agreeing to have the same rules and laws as each other, there was also an agreement to work towards closer political union with a bigger role for a European Parliament. And so it was that in 1992, with the signing of the Maastricht Treaty, these states became the modern European Union.

One of the key principles of the Maastricht Treaty was the clunky-sounding but vital concept of 'subsidiarity'. The principle of subsidiarity means decisions should always be taken at the closest practical level to the citizen – in other words, at the lowest possible level of international, national, regional and local community. To support this principle, the treaty also created the Committee of the Regions, a new advisory body representing the interests of local and regional government across Europe.

In 1995 came the accession of three more members: Austria, Finland and Sweden; and in 2004 the fifteen exploded to twenty-five with the addition of Cyprus, the Czech Republic, Estonia, Hungary, Latvia, Lithuania, Malta, Poland, Slovakia and Slovenia. For many of these new member states from Eastern Europe, a key motivation for joining as quickly as possible was to belong to a major group of nations which had opposed the ideologies of the former Soviet bloc. Above all, they wanted to cement their political freedoms. And as smaller nations, they value the EU's power of combination.

The Amsterdam Treaty of 1997 incorporated the 'Schengen' agreement into EU law, strengthening a common travel area across all EU states and one or two outside the EU – but excluding the UK and Ireland. The idea of this is to boost freedom of movement; but the UK and Ireland had security fears, not trusting the strength of common borders as far away as Eastern Europe.

In 1999 came one of the most momentous EU developments, or developments for a large sub-group of EU members: the launch of a single currency. In fact, this had been developing for some time, with a series of agreements about monetary and economic policy stretching back to 1969, partly in a bid to remove problems relating to exchange rates inside what is supposed to be a single market. This culminated in exchange-rate controls and then a single currency (the euro) in 1999 for eleven member states: Austria, Belgium, Finland, France, Germany, Ireland, Italy, Luxembourg, the Netherlands, Portugal and Spain. These were joined subsequently by Greece, Slovenia, Cyprus, Malta, Slovakia and Estonia, bringing a total (so far) of seventeen states into the euro-zone.

The eurozone states have a single monetary policy, set by the European Central Bank. All other member states have committed themselves to joining except Denmark and the UK. In the UK's case, this is partly because the government has not wanted the Bank of England to lose its ability to set interest rates for the UK. Supporters of the euro say it will eventually become a more powerful currency than the pound, and hence attract more business investment; we will come back to the big picture at the end of the chapter.

In 2001 came the Nice Treaty, which mainly reformed internal structures to handle expansion, and in 2007 Bulgaria and Romania acceded, giving twenty-seven member states. In the same year, the most recent EU treaty was signed – the Treaty of Lisbon.

The Lisbon Treaty made many major changes to the way the EU's institutions work, strengthening the European Parliament and reforming the way countries negotiate on policy. It created a common defence policy, expanding the range of possible EU military activity from peacekeeping and humanitarian work to disarmament operations and post-conflict stabilization.

On 1 July 2013 the EU's newest member, Croatia, acceded and there are five other 'candidate countries' lined up for (more or less likely) inclusion at some stage: Iceland, Macedonia, Montenegro, Serbia and Turkey. So from six original predecessor partners, the EU is close to breaking the thirty barrier.

Of other countries that one might have expected to join, the most surprising absences are Norway and Switzerland, neither of which has ever been a member.

Norway has made moves to join the EU or its predecessor bodies four times, or to vote on the possibility, most recently in 1994 when citizens voted against it in a referendum by 52.2 per cent to 47.8 per cent. Both Norway and Switzerland do have various formal agreements with the EU and other European groupings for free trade, and both are part of the Schengen borderless area, so effectively accept to live under many EU regulations, but without the same voting or negotiation rights.

The European Union is still centred on trade rules, including competition laws, food quality and safety at work, with the idea that all businesses in all member states should be faced with the same rules and regulations as all the others. This means fewer unfair advantages or disadvantages for businesses inside the EU, and a standard view of issues such as quality for non-member nations buying EU goods and services.

These basic ideas have expanded over the years to include environmental rules; employment and equality law; harmonization of some taxes such as VAT; consumer issues such as controlling mobile phone 'roaming' charges; some areas of defence; and now monetary and banking union among a core (not including the UK). Citizens of EU member states can travel freely, work and retire anywhere in the EU.

After laws are passed at EU level, member states are then required to pass their own laws transposing EU laws into national laws and tying the levels together. After that, the courts and police forces of the member states uphold EU law like their own – because it is their own.

Not all states are party to all agreements. Where the UK and others have been determined to sit outside certain major European projects, such as Schengen or the single currency, this has so far proved possible. Beyond that, so far, the UK does take part, and accepts the results.

So where is it all heading, and where is the UK headed in relation to it?

Before we enter that turbulent, emotive arena, let's take a step back and look at how some of the EU's main institutions work.

At the heart of the EU are three institutions: the European Commission; the Council of the European Union; and the European Parliament.

The European Commission is generally considered to be the EU's most powerful body, being in charge of the day-to-day running of the EU, including checking to see that the member states are complying with EU laws. The Commission is also the body that generates ideas for new EU laws and treaties, and draws up budgets. It is not, however, a directly elected body – its commissioners are nominated by the member states.

The Council of the EU is made up of government ministers from the member states. It does not have the power to propose new laws, like the Commission. However, for any EU law to be passed or EU budget to be agreed, the Council of the European Union (along with the European Parliament) must vote in favour of it.

The European Parliament is the only directly elected body of the EU. Like the Council, it cannot come up with its own ideas for laws, but can accept, reject or amend laws proposed by the Commission.

Now let us take a more detailed look at each of these institutions, starting with the European Commission.

The commission is divided into more than thirty departments or 'Directorates General' (DGs) covering policy areas such as education and culture; trade; and agriculture and rural development. Most DGs are based in Brussels and are massive organizations, like national government ministries.

In charge of most departments are the European Commissioners – similar to the Cabinet ministers in charge of UK government departments. At the time of writing, there are twenty-eight European Commissioners – the President of the Commission (currently José Manuel Barroso, up to 31 October 2014) and twenty-seven others, one from each member state. As the EU keeps growing, however, it was seen to be impossible to keep adding one new commissioner per member state, and so under new rules passed in the Lisbon Treaty the commission will be reduced to eighteen members from November 2014, with membership rotating between states every five years.

A lot of Eurosceptic anger is directed at the Commission, which is often said to be run by unelected bureaucrats – or 'Eurocrats' – who wield power without ever facing election. This is true compared with national ministries, which are headed by elected politicians; however, the process of appointing the commissioners does pass through the two other main EU institutions, including the elected Parliament.

How this works is that the President of the European Commission is appointed by the Council of the EU, before being approved by the European Parliament; the Council and President then choose all the other commissioners, before the Parliament has the chance to approve or reject them again, all in one go.

Once appointed, the European Commission is the EU's executive arm, acting as the guardian of the EU treaties, and working to make sure that EU policies are correctly implemented. One key area of power is its strong role in making sure there is fair competition in EU markets, with measures to break up cartels and to prevent companies from dominating markets through mergers or takeovers (see also Chapter 12, on the media).

The Commission also initiates proposals for new EU laws and treaties, or ways to shape the development of key EU projects such as the eurozone.

Though the Commission is not elected, it has many lines of communication to member states' elected governments, and all of its work is deeply influenced by politicians. To be passed, any new laws must also pass through the other EU institutions, including the elected European Parliament. This is not to say that there are no problems with the EU and democracy – just that it may be unfair to level the blame for all of these at the door of the Commission; but we will come back to this.

What of the institutions that do actually pass new EU laws – the Council of the EU, and the European Parliament?

The Council of the European Union, also known as the EU Council, is made up of elected politicians – ministers and leaders, including the UK Prime Minister – from the member states. In most cases, new EU laws must pass through the Council as well as through the European Parliament to be accepted.

There is no fixed membership of the Council, which can either be made of up of the heads of state or of the ministers responsible for whatever topic is under debate – when it is often referred to as the 'Council of Ministers'. So, although technically there is only one Council, as it is made up of different people each time the effect is more like a group of different ministerial councils, by topic.

There are currently ten ministerial groupings, ranging from the Economic and Financial Affairs Council (Ecofin) and the Agriculture Council to the Environment Council and the Education, Youth, Culture and Sport Council.

For most issues, a system of 'qualified majority voting' (QMV) is used in the Council, giving more weight to bigger nations by granting them more votes.

Under QMV the UK along with Italy, Germany and France have twenty-nine votes each and all other states have fewer depending on population, from Poland and Spain with twenty-seven down to Malta with three. In all, there are 345 votes and 255 – around 74 per cent – are needed to pass a QMV decision. A majority of member states must also vote for a decision, and they must also represent 62 per cent or more of the EU population – though these other conditions are almost always met once 255 votes are reached.

This system is set to change in November 2014, when a simplified double-majority version set out in the Lisbon Treaty comes into force. This will require votes representing 65% of the EU population, and 55% of all member states to back a proposal: theoretically easier to understand and practice, although in practice most measures are decided by reaching a complete consensus behind the scenes.

Presidency of the Council of the European Union is held by each member state in turn, alphabetically, for six months at a time, taking many years (fourteen at the moment) to rotate back around. The country holding the presidency decides who can speak at each meeting, which order and how much time they have: a delicate matter, since with twenty-eight member states, not everyone can speak at every meeting.

The Council also used to be the forum where the heads of state met to set EU strategy, but since the Lisbon Treaty of 2009 this has been spun off into the confusingly similarly named European Council.

This is a meeting of EU leaders (from the UK, the Prime Minister attends), taking place four times a year, with the President (and chair) not rotating but elected every two and a half years. Currently it is (and so far it has only ever been) Herman Van Rompuy of Belgium, in his second and final permitted term, which runs to the end of 2014.

The other exception to the rotating presidency is the Foreign Affairs Council, also created by the Lisbon Treaty to develop a powerful common approach to EU foreign policy. This is chaired by an elected High Representative for Foreign Affairs and Security Policy, currently the British politician Catherine Ashton, who is also set to stand down at the end of 2014.

Though these councils or high-profile national politicians often steal the headlines, most behind-the-scenes diplomacy, horse-trading and negotiation takes place, long before they fly in to endorse a decision, at a lesser-known body called COREPER.

COREPER is the Committee of Permanent Representatives in the European Union, made up of the member states' ambassadors (or 'heads of mission') and deputy ambassadors to the EU. Together they oversee the work of some 250 committees and working parties of civil servants from the member states, and this is where the real negotiation takes place.

'When you get to the actual economic or environment summit it is mainly for show,' says Frances Robinson, experienced Brussels observer for *Wall Street Journal Europe*. 'Most of the work is done beforehand by the ambassadors at COREPER and their advisers, in consultation with ministers back home. So the conclusions are drafted before anyone flies in – though politicians might sometimes leak these to the press in the hope of getting public support for further, final changes.'

As with all EU institutions, the name of the game behind closed doors is compromise, negotiation, and – usually – consensus. Most agreements in the Council of the EU are not even put to a vote. It is – and to work, it has to be – a consensus culture, though you might not know it from the way EU affairs are often reported and viewed back in the UK and other member states.

'The problem is what the council regards as a good outcome and what the nations think is a good outcome are different,' Robinson says. 'The council always wants a compromise – to say "we agreed" this or that. But member states tend to want to say "we won" – or "we lost".'

And so to the third core EU institution, and the only one that is directly elected by all EU citizens, every five years: the European Parliament.

While this is the institution that is ostensibly 'more democratic' than the others in Europe, there is not a high level of engagement with it by citizens out in member states, such as the UK. Every UK citizen has an MEP, but few of us can say who it is. Can you name yours?

One of the reasons for this is that European constituencies are so large. One European constituency, in fact, can cover the area of some fifty or sixty Westminster constituencies. In all, there are just twelve European constituencies for the whole of the UK, each covering several counties, though each returns several MEPs. They range from the south-east of England constituency, population 8 million, returning ten MEPs, to the Northern Ireland constituency, population 1.7 million, returning three MEPs. Greater London has its own constituency, with eight MEPs. Overall, the UK returns seventy-three out of 754 MEPs, a similar number to France (seventy-four) and Italy (seventy-three). Germany has the most, with ninety-nine; and the other member states in rough proportion to population, with the smallest (Estonia, Cyprus, Luxembourg and Malta) returning just six MEPs each.

Another reason might be the way MEPs are elected in the UK (it is left to each member state to decide on a system of election). The UK has a closed party list system for MEPs, under which parties present lists of candidates for each constituency, in their own order of preference. Citizens then vote for a party, and seats are shared out in each region according to the proportion of votes received by each party. Then after that, candidates are just elected off the list in the pre-agreed order of preference, from the top down. So if a party wins two seats in the region, for example, their top two candidates are elected off the list. It is often difficult, in other words, to be sure exactly which set of candidates your vote might help to elect.

This separation of votes from candidates may add to the separation people feel from their MEP. European election turnouts are very low indeed, at around half the (already worrying) turnouts of UK Parliament elections; in 2009, for example, turnout was 34.7 per cent. This was also lower than 2004, when turnout was 38.5 per cent. However, it was higher than in 1999, when UK turnout plunged to 24.0 per cent, the lowest of any member state.

Because of the party list system, when people do vote for an MEP they vote for a party, not an individual.

Political party groupings, however, are understandably completely different in the European Parliament than in the UK Parliament. There are connections, however, because all the UK parties have affiliations to European party groupings.

Across Europe, there are more than 160 parties who return MEPs to the European Parliament – far too many to fight their corner alone, and in any case this would make no sense in an international Parliament. So the parties cluster into groupings: currently, seven groupings, each with at least twenty-five MEPs from at least seven states.

The largest by far of these groupings is the European People's Party (EPP), with some 270 affiliated MEPs – more than a third of the European Parliament. However, although it is the largest, and although the EPP is a centre-right grouping, there are no UK MEPs affiliated with it, as it is viewed by UK Conservatives as too 'pro-European'. So the UK MEPs are gathered in the other six groupings.

At the time of writing, the breakdown and UK affiliations of all the groupings was as follows:

Party	Affiliated MEPs	UK MEPs
European People's Party	270	0
Progressive Alliance of Socialists and Democrats/ Party of European Socialists (PES)	190	13 (Labour Party)
Alliance of Liberals and Democrats	85	12 (Liberal Democrats)
Greens/European Free Alliance	58	5 (Green Party, Plaid Cymru and Scottish National Party)
European Conservatives and Reformists Group	53	26 (25 Conservative, 1 Ulster Conservatives and Unionists)
Europe of Freedom and Democracy Group	36	11 (UK Independence Party)
European United Left – Nordic Green Left	34	1 (Sinn Féin)

There were also twenty-six 'non-attached' or unaffiliated MEPs, including five from the UK, mainly from the Eurosceptic fringe. All these numbers shift continually, however, and by the time you read this it will all have changed following the 2014 European Parliament elections, so these numbers are for illustration only, by way of an example, and the best way of gaining an up-to-date picture is from the European Parliament website. Why not take a look now?

The equivalent of the Speaker in the European Parliament is the President, elected every two years (so twice in each five-year Parliament). In recent years, an unofficial deal has been struck between the two largest party groupings – the EPP and the PES – to take turns to share this role.

The European Parliament's party groupings do not always match the political leanings of the Council of Ministers – unlike in Westminster or most other national parliaments, which are controlled by government – so it tends to be independent-minded, adding to the spice of EU politics.

It does have a fair amount of power these days, as well. In fact, following the Treaty of Lisbon, the European Parliament has 'co-decision' or joint lawmaking powers with the Council of the European Union in most policy areas. 'Co-decision' can follow a complicated path, rather like lawmaking in the UK between the government, the House of Commons and the House of Lords, with laws being proposed by the European Commission and then passing backwards and forwards between the EU Council and the European Parliament for discussion, amendment and approval. But on the whole, both the Council and the Parliament need to approve a new EU law.

The work of the European Parliament is largely carried out in more than twenty committees (currently twenty-three) in subject areas from foreign affairs to women's rights and gender equality. Each handles law in its field, with committee chairs, sub-chairs and rapporteurships set proportionately and by negotiation between the groupings. The 'rapporteur' – literally, the committee's reporter – is a powerful role, helping to steer the committee's work and liaising between the committee and the other EU institutions.

When a new EU law is debated there are usually dozens and some-times hundreds of amendments to be voted on in committee, before the law goes back to the full plenary of the Parliament, where amendments can be reintroduced.

The plenary sessions are huge affairs: the second-largest democratic chamber in the world, after the Parliament of India. MEPs of all nations and party groupings sit round a vast, funnel-shaped chamber or hemi-cycle, with representatives from the European Commission and other institutions also there to defend their proposals.

As a vote approaches, party group leaders will work to achieve a common position, meaning laws do need a broad consensus from all sides to pass. As in the Council, negotiation and diplomacy are key.

When the electronic votes finally come, hundreds of amendments can be taken at a time, with MEPs usually being led along by their groupings using tried and tested hand signals from party officials: thumbs up or thumbs down. The amended law is then forwarded to the Council of the EU.

One side-issue for the European Parliament is that it has two (or three) homes. Its main monthly plenary meetings and all votes of the Parliament are held in its 'official' and earlier home of Strasbourg. However, occasional other plenary meetings and all its committee work – taking up more of MEPs' time – take place in a second massive complex in Brussels, the mammoth home of the bank robbery described at the start of the chapter. So it is that the whole weary mass of MEPs, officials, translators and reporters shuttle expensively between Brussels and Strasbourg. Some further administration work for the Parliament is also carried out in a third location – Luxembourg, home of the Parliament's General Secretariat. France in particular is keen to maintain the Strasbourg tradition, which according to the EU treaties would require unanimity to undo – so France would have to agree to any change.

In March 2012 a huge majority of MEPs themselves – 429 to 184, with thirty-seven abstentions – voted to express their support for the creation of a single seat for the Parliament in Brussels. For the moment, however, there is no way through the deadlock.

The European Parliament has, over the history of the EU, become steadily more powerful. Step by step, it has gained a new right to veto here, a new right to be consulted there – partly as a way of narrowing what is widely seen as a democratic gap in EU decision-making. This process is likely to continue, as the stronger it gets, the harder it pushes for more powers.

Before we look a bit more closely at these vital issues of democracy in Europe – and whether or not a 'gap' exists – there is one other institution in the EU family that may deserve a quick mention: the European Court of Auditors (ECA).

This is an independent body scrutinizing the EU budget, which now runs at well over 100 billion euros a year (a level representing roughly one eighth of the UK's total annual public spending). Around 80 per cent of this is sent back down into the member states, mostly as development and social funding to help the poorest regions in projects from road-building to encouraging entrepreneurship, or as agricultural and fishing subsidies. A fair chunk (more than 7 billion euros a year in recent years) is spent supporting research by international groups of universities and companies that is seen to benefit European policy goals.

All this spending is scrutinized by the auditors, a group of experts with one member from each state.

Since 1994, the court has not been able to issue a 'declaration of assurance' on the EU budget, leading many to say that EU finances are so corrupt that its auditors can never 'sign off the accounts'.

This is not quite the case, however. The main problem here lies with the fact that the EU spending accounts are made up from returns handed in by the member states, and it has proven impossible for the auditors to verify all the controls put in place in every country to the required standard.

This sounds bad, and it is not good, but it is also the case that in a House of Lords inquiry into the EU budget in 2007, the then Auditor General Sir John Bourn stated that if the same system operated in the UK, he might well be unable to issue a declaration of that kind. There were 500 separate accounts for the UK, he said, and 'in the last year, I qualified thirteen of the 500. If I had to operate the EU system, then, because I qualify thirteen accounts, I might have to qualify the whole British central government expenditure.'

As with much relating to the European debate, it seems the truth is more complicated than the black-and-white picture that is often painted in the media or in political debate.

Those on the ground understand this: the staff of the UK Representation to the EU working quietly away amid all the growing noise, heat and turbulence of life at the interface between the UK and Brussels.

In a discreet modern office block in the heart of the European Quarter of Brussels, the UK Representation is home to 100 staff in ten teams, with three ambassador–level diplomats. It is similar to other British embassies overseas, with one key difference: the mission here is not just to observe, talk or negotiate but forms a direct part of a policymaking body: COREPER.

'The thing that distinguishes us from the classic British embassy in Mongolia or wherever is we are also here to directly deliver British policy through the Council of the European Union in all its levels,' says one diplomat posted to the office. 'This means we are also part of the policymaking community, working with officials and ministers in the UK and at the European Parliament.

'We are always talking to all the European institutions – asking them what they are thinking about, how they are thinking of handling a policy issue such as a new way of regulating businesses on pollution. Then we relay the news to London, agree a position and try to influence the policy's development.'

How does this fit in with the widely held British perception of EU politics as a confrontational battleground?

'Clearly the nature of our positions on the EU means that sometimes we are in defensive mode,' notes the diplomat, diplomatically. 'But often, the best form of engagement and influence is to be shaping change rather than just resisting it.'

The fact that democratic links are much closer between citizens and national politicians than between citizens and Europe does lie at the heart of much of the conflict that arises, the diplomat says.

'One of our challenges is that when you are looking at policy development in the UK, the relationship between parliament and government is more clear cut because everyone comes up for election.

'In the EU the relationships are not so clear, and so one of the roles we have as a member state is to remind European institutions that we are all here in different ways to serve our publics.'

Ideally, the result of most EU activity and cooperation will be to achieve tasks that simply cannot be carried out so well by the UK or other member states acting alone, the diplomat says. 'The way the UK would see it is that there are things we would do nationally and there are things we would see an advantage in doing alongside each other, in a co-ordinated fashion or through EU institutions.

'So if you look at foreign policy, for example, there are a series of revolutions and protest movements still developing in the Middle East. How do you make sure we support democratic change in those countries, and oppose oppression?

'For some activities, such as making sure British people in those countries are safe for example, we will act nationally. But other areas such as applying sanctions, or supporting UN observer missions, are a good example of something that is more effective when done together.'

The UK's devolved administrations have representation in Brussels as well: the Scottish government, for example, has an office within the UK Representation, and ministers and officials from Wales, Scotland and Northern Ireland are consulted and attend meetings in policy areas which have been devolved or where there is strong devolved interest, such as agriculture, fishing or economic development.

The Scottish National Party has a vision for direct Scottish membership of the EU as part of its plan for independence, but if this does not happen some in Scottish politics would still like to see Scotland being given more influence within the UK set-up at Brussels. For now, however, it is ultimately the UK minister who has a place at the top table in Europe.

So much for the UK's presence in Brussels. But how about back at home? How does the UK's Parliament interact with the EU, injecting national democracy back out into the international process?

When it comes to EU policy and law, the UK Parliament has a triple role: to scrutinize draft EU legislation before it is passed; to change UK law to implement EU law and treaties; and to hold the UK government to account on its EU policies and negotiating positions.

It is an accepted principle that UK government ministers should not usually agree to any EU proposals that have not first been scrutinized by Parliament.

If, for example, the EU foreign affairs council is pushing to set up a peacekeeping mission in a conflict area, the UK will give assent only when the plan has passed parliamentary scrutiny back in Westminster (some other member states such as Sweden have similar procedures, but not all).

In the House of Commons, this job is done by the European Scrutiny Committee, which may recommend further debate in a European Legislation Committee or in the Commons chamber; and in the Lords by the European Union Select Committee, which reviews more general issues.

One potentially interesting new development was contained in the Lisbon Treaty, which came into force in 2009. This offers national parliaments the new power to raise a 'yellow card', football-referee-style, if they think a proposed new EU law violates the principle of subsidiarity – the need for decisions to be taken as much as possible at local or national level. Proposals for new laws are now sent to parliaments, which have eight weeks to wave the yellow card, offering a 'reasoned opinion' why it should be rethought. If enough national parliaments object to a proposal (a third or more for most types of new law), the Commission can decide to amend or withdraw it – or it can just carry on regardless.

So far, however, the new power has had little or no impact. A 2012 report by the House of Commons library found that in the first year of the system, of eighty-two proposed new laws that had been sent out to parliaments for opinions, just thirty-four had received a 'yellow card' (including two from the UK – one on a proposed law change for seasonal workers, and one for financial workers) – and only five had received more than one yellow card. In all cases, the threshold for possible action was 'far from being reached'.

The truth is that subsidiarity breaches do not seem to be much of an issue with EU law, a fact which led the European Scrutiny Committee to comment drily on the yellow-card system: 'There is, in our view, less to the provisions . . . than meets the eye.'

In principle, however, if it can be made to work more effectively than this, more participation by national parliaments in the EU lawmaking process could be an interesting area to consider, in light of the ongoing antagonism from some in the UK to all things European. Some people claim that the pooling of powers that has taken place bit by bit over the years to form the modern EU has amounted to an unacceptable 'loss of sovereignty' to what is perceived as a remote, less democratic body than our national government.

Those who hold such views, to one degree or another, are often referred to as 'Eurosceptics'.

In fact, Euroscepticism covers a very wide range of views, from those who want the UK to withdraw from most EU activity, to those who see the EU as worthwhile but in need of some reform. 'Eurobarometer' polls run by the European Commission to gauge people's views on the EU across Europe show the UK is by no means the only member state with pockets of Euroscepticism, either.

According to the French academic Cécile Leconte, these views shift and interact over time and are underpinned by many different lines of reasoning, including utilitarian views (a cost/gain analysis on issues such as the economy and security); issues of national identity; the perception in some regions or industries that they might lose out from EU membership; dissatisfaction with incumbent governments; and lack of knowledge of how the EU works.

In her book *Understanding Euroscepticism*, Leconte writes: 'By focusing disproportionately on the final stages in decision-making, the media fail to expose the close co-operation between national administrations and the Commission in the drafting of legislative proposals, as well as the multiple arenas where proposals are negotiated and compromises elaborated.

'This might reinforce the widespread perception that Brussels forces decisions upon member states, instead of presenting the EU as a constant search for compromises and consensus.'

Public views of the UK's EU membership have risen and fallen over the years. In 1973, the time of a referendum on the nation continuing in the EU, results were that 67.2 per cent said 'yes' and just 32.8 per cent 'no'. In the 1980s, polls saw UK support for EC membership rising even higher, to around 80 per cent.

Nowadays, however, views seem to have soured: one poll carried out in December 2013 by Opinium for the *Observer* newspaper found that just 26% of British voters at that time regarded the EU as, overall, a 'good thing' compared with 42% who say it is a 'bad thing'.

The UK government has already passed legislation committing it to hold a referendum on future EU treaty changes judged to represent 'significant' transfers of power from Westminster to the EU. The Conservative Party has now also pledged to hold an 'in–out' referendum on EU membership if it is elected in 2015, based on negotiation of 'a new settlement with our European partners'.

Whether or not this happens, it seems clear that many if not most UK politicians will continue to push for at least some further reform to the EU, both to improve the way it works and to help people connect with it.

Simon Hix, Professor of European Politics at the London School of Economics and Political Science, thinks more steps could be taken right away to energize EU democracy.

In his book *What's Wrong with the European Union and How to Fix It*, he suggests introducing a 'winner takes more' system of power within the European Parliament, meaning the larger party groupings would have more powers to push through the amendments they want. This would make the European Parliament more like the kind of parliament we all recognize, where it matters far more which party is in charge.

Hix also suggests a more open contest for Commission President, with manifestos and debates. Both these changes could lead to more public recognition and hence a stronger democratic mandate, he says.

Other possible reforms could build on the 'open method of co-ordination' – a system of 'soft law' already in place for some policy areas under which the Council of the EU sets broad policy goals and the European Commission develops guidelines. Member states use these in their own national laws, and the results are monitored by the Commission, but they are simply indicators, not laws. There is no legal compulsion on anyone to take part or comply, though peer pressure alone does seem to play a part in galvanizing states into action.

In recent years this method has been applied in employment strategy, social inclusion, pensions, immigration, asylum, education, and culture and research, and its use has also been suggested for health and environmental affairs.

Other possible deeper changes could see the EU developing into an organization of concentric or overlapping circles or tracks, with each state able to opt in or out of each, as it sees fit. The UK is one of several states that has already opted out from various sections of the EU treaties, including from the Schengen free movement zone and from the eurozone.

Could this flexible approach be expanded to almost every EU policy area?

This 'pick-and-choose' style of vision might mean that a more enthusiastic core of countries could carry on collaborating and working together in more and more areas, while other nations could expand collaboration in some areas but step back from others.

Such a vision might suit some in the UK, but whether it could ever become a reality would depend on whether enough other member states share it. Ultimately, the UK cannot force through any treaty changes on its own: a choice of 'in or out' will never be purely on the terms of the UK or any single member state, since the EU is forged from treaties agreed among many nations.

To put it another way, once a group of nations signs a treaty, they are all tied into it more deeply than they are to laws passed in their own countries. This can be seen as a bad or 'undemocratic' situation – but of course there were always reasons for signing the treaty in the first place, when it was considered that acting together would be better than acting alone.

And many Eurosceptic UK citizens and politicians agree that whatever happens, there will always remain many areas where it is better for European countries to act together. Most feel, for example, that it will be essential for the UK economy to remain as part of the single market at the core of the EU. Other areas where benefits seem clear are in its foreign policy work, where a bigger block of power is much stronger and more effective.

In environmental policy and scientific research, too, there would seem to be clear advantages of collaboration. At the beginning of 2013, for example, the European Commission announced the investment of up to 1 billion euros each for research into two cutting-edge areas of scientific research: the mapping of the human brain and uses for the ground-breaking new material graphene. In both projects UK research institutes will benefit, from both funding and working with other leading EU scientists.

As well as clear benefits such as these, the UK has also been an active partner in helping to shape the whole of the EU ever since it joined. In fact, the UK has played a major role in the development of this unique international body, according to one long-term observer of EU affairs.

'Britain has always been much more important in the EU than you would know from back home,' says Brussels-based academic and writer Aubrey Silberston, Emeritus Professor of Economics at Imperial College London. 'We have had some very strong commissioners, and a lot of pull. Britain has also been very important in the Parliament, chairing many key committees, and in the EU Council.'

The situation for Britain in Europe has shifted in recent times, however, Silberston says. 'Now, perhaps, British influence is rather less, partly because the accession of new member states has somewhat diluted the influence of the earlier members. More seriously, the opt-outs that Britain has obtained since Maastricht, as well as its absence from the eurozone, have caused other member states to regard Britain as not fully engaged in Europe.

'Now there is all this talk in the press running down the importance of the EU, and the general impression in Britain is that Europe is a bloody nuisance. What some people don't realize is what a miracle the EU is if you think of the centuries of warfare in Europe.

'I suppose the prospect that there could be another war is now so distant in people's minds they don't recognize what a fantastic achievement it is.'

It is true that nowadays the emergence of war within Western Europe seems so remote a possibility that most people do not think it is a sufficient reason to continue expanding the powers of the EU. What we are left with is a more complicated set of decisions.

How do we build on the good things we have in Europe, while making sure the EU is not too remote and too inflexible to allow its member states to control their own affairs, as far as possible? Do we try to engage citizens more with Europe, or try to change the basis on which the EU operates?

Whatever happens in the coming years, a storm is brewing. The question of how, how far and when the UK can, will and should engage in both the core and surrounding elements of the European Union will play a massive part in shaping the future of democracy in the UK, Europe – and the world.

Debate will be fierce, and that is a good thing. Democracy is about debate, and the stage is set for one of the most dramatic political debates of our time.

Chapter 16

Over to you – the future of UK democracy

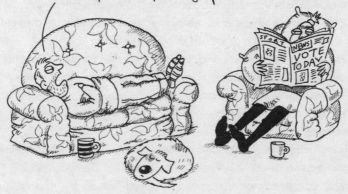

As we near the end of this book, it is time to think back over the ground we have covered.

We've looked at struggles and reforms across centuries, in all corners of the UK. We have examined rights, laws, debates, parties, parliaments, assemblies, monarchs, special advisers, ministers, bloggers, a man called Mr Chicken and a mayor who was once a monkey.

This book has tried to describe how the various elements of democracy fit together, and how they work, in the hope that simply to understand a bit more might inspire people, in some small way, to see the point of getting more involved themselves. That is to say, yourselves.

It is striking that not one of the areas we have covered – from freedom of the press to devolution; from human rights to Europe; from election turnout to internet campaigning – is fixed but all are undergoing a process of change, and more often than not, big change, controversial change, and change whose final outcome is not yet clear.

Is that what you expected, at the beginning of the book? Isn't democracy in the UK supposed to be solid, stable, historic and strong? But how can that be, if all these platforms on which it stands are shifting, breaking apart and re-forming year by year? What does this mean for us? Where is it all heading? Can we help to shape that change?

In the first part of the book we saw the scale of people's disengagement from some key aspects of democracy – people not voting; people not joining political parties. These might seem like small issues, but they are symptomatic of a much deeper problem.

According to figures from the parliamentary democracy charity the Hansard Society in its annual audit of political engagement, the percentage of people who say they would definitely vote in an election if one were held tomorrow has been falling for some time. In 2012 it dropped below 50 per cent (to 48 per cent) for the first time in the decade or so the survey has been run, and in 2013 was recorded as just 41 per cent.

Does this mean that everyone else simply doesn't care about politics? Isn't rejecting the mainstream political system in protest or disgust just as valid a way of 'being political' as voting, or signing a petition?

Professor Colin Hay of the University of Sheffield considers this possibility in his book *Why We Hate Politics*. He accepts that for some people non-participation in politics is felt to be a political act in itself. This might be combined with 'direct action', sometimes illegal, such as attacks on GM crops or the sometimes (though by no means always) violent demonstrations that have erupted around recent G8 summits of the world's richest (and democratic) economies.

However, says Hay, while such protest actions do often show that people care about society, they are 'neither a substitute for, nor incompatible with, formal political participation'.

In other words, there is no reason why people who protest cannot also vote or take part in more formal activities. In a sense, 'formal' politics is all that we have to run our lives as an organized, collaborative and cooperative group of people. It runs our schools, our courts, our social services, our healthcare, our legal aid, our emergency services – our whole society. How meaningful is it simply to reject all this, rather than trying to make it work better, to improve it?

One pointer to a way to engage more people in helping to improve our democracy is provided by that same Hansard Society 'audit' of how people feel about democracy.

Although only 16 per cent in the Hansard survey said they believe their direct involvement in national politics could bring about change, some 57 per cent feel they have influence in local decision-making.

This feels significant. When it comes to driving engagement, the answer – or a big part of the answer – is local.

In Chapter 7, we saw the impact the UK's local authorities can have on people's lives. There are many ways to get involved, and most councils hold open meetings and consult local residents on new policies or plans. Some are now moving further and looking for new ways to involve local people more directly in running the services they use.

We have already heard about West Lothian council's teams of 'citizen inspectors'; another example can be found in the London Borough of Lambeth, which has launched a bid to become the country's first 'co-operative council', involving residents directly with running as wide a range of services as possible.

Its inspiration came from a piece of local research similar to the one the Hansard Society carries out for the country as a whole. Lambeth politicians noticed from a residents' survey that around 2 per cent of people said they were already actively involved in some way in local decision-making, which turned out to be comparable to the national average. What caught politicians' interest, though, was that around 9 per cent of people on top of that said they would already like to be more actively involved, given the chance – if they knew how, or had the means. Still not a big percentage, perhaps – but a huge increase on the numbers already active (it is also a lower figure than the 56 per cent of people in the Hansard Society survey who felt local involvement could make a difference, but that is because this question was stronger – it was asking whether local people were actually prepared to get involved, right now).

Inspired by these figures, the borough has encouraged the development of a wide range of projects involving citizens in running local services. Projects up and running so far include the Young Lambeth Cooperative, allowing anyone over the age of eleven to join a group running the council's youth clubs. The Lambeth Resource Centre, a day-care centre for people with disabilities, is about to become a mutual society run jointly by staff, disabled people and their carers. Residents have set up Brixton Energy Solar 1, the UK's first inner-city, cooperatively owned energy project on a housing estate; and other activities feed into library services and mental-health services.

Diarmid Swainson, an assistant director at Lambeth, says the initiative is aimed at rebalancing the relationship between citizens, politicians and public services, which is perceived as unequal, even in a democracy.

'How it is usually seen is that citizens have needs and demand services, and we provide those services to meet those needs, but this creates a dependency culture that is negative for both the citizen and the public sector.

'For council officers, it means we are constantly rationing services, becoming seen as cold-hearted because we are always waiting for people to be in crisis before we help them.'

To change this, the council is hoping to move away at least partly from needs-based assessments – identifying problems – to focus on cooperative working to enhance the positive aspects of people's lives.

Of course, it is important to retain the overall control of public services by politicians elected by all people to serve all people, Swainson says – a democratic and legal requirement. But that does not mean to say there are not many meaningful ways where local people can work alongside public bodies to improve their communities.

'We are very clear that we are not trying to remove or undermine or change the structure of democracy locally – we are still going to have councillors elected by all citizens who take most of the big decisions about allocation of resources across the borough. But we are trying to blend that with a system where individuals or groups of people have more of a say over how money is allocated within the services they use, and feel like they are being heard.'

Many other councils, including Edinburgh, Oldham and York, are now experimenting with similar projects.

So what about nationally? How might we be able to improve the ways people engage with the UK Parliament, the national devolved bodies, and all the machinery of national government?

Some feel the answer to changing citizens' views of the state lies with changing what can be seen as the UK's unstructured approach to enshrining citizens' basic rights. Perhaps what we need, they say, is a 'written constitution'.

Clearly, as this book has shown, UK citizens do already enjoy many powers and rights, and there are many laws and conventions governing how the country's democracy operates. So it is not that we do not have constitutional rules, or even that most of them are not written down. What people mean when they say we don't have a 'written constitution' is that, as we heard in Chapter 11, the UK does not have a single, central statement of citizens' rights.

A constitution is so-called because it is usually written when a state is founded – but the UK was never founded. Parts of it were brought together by law, but there was never a day where the whole nation came together. It just happened, over time.

One result of not having a constitution might be that the fundamental rules of how the UK is run are easier to change than they would otherwise be.

In his 2009 book *The New British Constitution*, the leading analyst Professor Vernon Bogdanor listed some fifteen major constitutional reforms that had taken place in the previous twelve years alone, from setting up the devolved national bodies to the passing of the Human Rights Act; reform of the system of hereditary peers; changes to our legal system; freedom of information laws; and changes to the rules on political parties.

'This is a formidable list,' Bogdanor says. 'It is scarcely an exaggeration to suggest that a new constitution is in the process of being created before our eyes. But, because the reforms have been introduced in a piecemeal, unplanned and pragmatic way, rather than in one fell swoop, we have hardly noticed the extent of the change.

'It is much easier to notice change in the United States, or indeed in any country with a codified constitution than it is in Britain, with its peculiar, uncodified constitution.'

This might not be such a bad thing – notice that Bogdanor uses the word 'pragmatic' to describe what happens in the UK – and the ability to make changes and reforms could be positive.

However, some see the possibility of creating a new – or first ever – constitution for the UK as an opportunity to engage ordinary citizens in radical new ways.

One prominent campaigner for a UK constitution, the public law barrister Richard Gordon QC, says as part of any new settlement a new 'citizen's branch' of the constitution could be added in. Under this concept a 'third chamber' of Parliament, whose members would be selected annually at random from the electoral register – just like court juries – would be created with some powers to propose new laws, launch public inquiries and help to uphold the constitution. A body like this would make the UK a much more participatory democracy – 'people would feel more involved in the process of politics,' Gordon says.

However, the formation of any constitution would be likely to take a very long time, he acknowledges, with constitutional conventions formed of specialists and citizens to draw it up bit by bit, with public voting on each part.

Such a possibility, or something like it, is already being looked at by the House of Commons Political and Constitutional Reform Committee – though the committee is looking first at whether any action is needed at all.

The creation of a UK constitution would certainly not be an easy path: to gather together all the UK citizen's most important rights and principles – from systems of election, to the role of the monarch, devolution, and core values of equality and human rights – and write them all into a single document would be a hundred times harder than reforming one part of the constitution, such as the House of Lords – and look how hard that has been.

And whether or not any constitution could ever realistically be drawn up and agreed on by everybody, there are some reasons why we might not want to develop a single new UK constitution in the first place.

For one, we may not want to restrict Parliament in this way. Can we really predict the future well enough to understand now exactly where we should or should not allow the position to be set solid for a long time to come? (It is true that constitutions can be changed if enough people want to do so, but this usually requires much larger parliamentary majorities than it takes to pass ordinary laws, or other legal hurdles.)

Some feel it is more pragmatic to continue with our 'unwritten constitution'. Janet Seaton, former head of information services at the Scottish Parliament, says it is the UK's legal flexibility that makes devolution so possible to achieve, for example: 'It's precisely the ability of our unwritten constitution to accommodate such changes that makes it the envy of countries where it is all laid down in black and white.'

In any case, how could we decide exactly who should write the new constitution? Politicians? Judges? People who are specially elected or appointed? And how would they be elected or appointed, and by whom?

These problems might not be impossible to solve, but they are tough. Perhaps it would be easier simply to set out in more detail the underlying values of UK society. After all, most constitutions are based on human rights law.

As we have seen in Chapter 11, the UK has already written a Human Rights Act into law, implementing the European Convention on Human Rights, a treaty signed by forty-seven states including all EU members. Some feel the UK could go further than this and write its own British Bill of Rights, as an extra layer of commitment in some key areas and a deeper setting of the rights into the UK context.

Such a Bill – which would have to be supported by all three major parties, and could be a possible precursor to a constitution – was recommended by a Parliamentary Joint Committee on Human Rights. On the other hand, as Vernon Bogdanor writes in *The New British Constitution*, a UK Bill of Rights would have to both align with and go further than the European Convention. It would have to align with it, or risk legal (and moral) clashes; and it would have to go further, or what would be the point?

If it does go further, however, it would risk a different kind of fall-out: that it would be too restrictive on the UK Parliament's freedom to pass other laws it wants, at a time when some people already complain that the Human Rights Act is too restrictive in areas such as votes for prisoners.

The task of solving these overlapping problems was handed in 2011 to a Commission on a Bill of Rights, an independent group set up by the Ministry of Justice to see what kind of new law might be desirable – and possible. The difficulty of this task was made clear when the Commission reported late in 2012 that it could not reach agreement on the way forward. In a further complication, it reported that many in the devolved parts of the UK do not want a new UK-wide Bill.

In Northern Ireland, in any case, the 1998 Belfast Agreement proposed the development of a separate Northern Ireland Bill of Rights, embedding non-discrimination for all communities, in addition to European rights. As yet, however, none has been enacted.

Whether or not the UK does one day have a single written constitution or a Bill of Rights, there may be other, more easily achievable actions that would boost people's feelings of identification with the UK's democratic institutions.

For one thing, they could be more representative: if there were more women, people from minority ethnic communities and people with disabilities in political office or positions of public leadership, more ordinary citizens would feel there was a place for people like them in politics and public service. Currently, all these groups of people are heavily under-represented both in appointments to the boards of public bodies and in elected office; disabled people, for example, make up only around 8 per cent of appointments to public boards, even though 14 per cent of the working-age population are disabled.

To help close the gaps, the government has launched an 'Access to elected office' strategy, combining guidance for political parties on their responsibilities and powers under the Equalities Act 2010, including the ability to use women-only electoral shortlists with exemption from discrimination law; a new fund to support disabled people running for elected office; and an online training course for potential political candidates with disabilities.

All these activities are worthwhile, but more effort is surely needed in this area to try to ensure the UK's politicians and public boards are more representative of the whole population. The subject of 'quotas' – setting aside places for certain types of candidate – is highly controversial, but it is not the only method to consider: encouragement, support and training for all types of candidate, as well as innovations such as job-sharing or flexible working could all help to redress the balance.

Another area that may need a boost is education – teaching children about how our society works, from as young an age as possible.

'Citizenship' is already a core curriculum subject in secondary schools in England (age 11–16), and an optional subject in primary schools (age 5–11) as part of a joint framework with Personal, Social and Health Education (PSHE). Citizenship Studies is also available at GCSE and A-level.

Elsewhere in the UK the position varies, with Citizenship taught either as a cross-curriculum theme spanning several subjects (the basis in Scotland) or as part of a wider topic such as Personal and Social Education (as in Wales, and there is something similar in Northern Ireland). For an excellent overview of the position across the UK and Ireland, see the website of Citizenship teaching forum the Five Nations Network (www.fivenations.net).

So most UK state-school pupils will be offered basic teaching of topics such as how elections work, or what it means to sit on a jury. But with greater knowledge so important to greater engagement in a democracy – and greater engagement desperately needed – more could always be done.

UK citizens, from the youngest children at school to college and university students and adults throughout their lives, could have more opportunities to learn about every aspect of democracy, from simple reading and discussion to active training in politics, social or community work. The best aspects of UK Citizenship teaching – teaching it across the curriculum as part of other subjects, as well as on its own – could be combined to increase its effect.

Why is knowledge important? Try this trick on yourself.

First, ask yourself the question – do you trust politicians generally to tell the truth? If the answer is 'yes', then that's fine – you are halfway to political engagement. But you will also be in a small minority: according to a 2013 poll by Ipsos MORI, only 18 per cent of people answer 'yes' to this question. If the answer is 'no', or involves various kinds of swearing, next think of a politician you have some personal connection with – your local MP, perhaps, if you have spoken to them, or a local councillor you have met or whom you have approached to help you with a problem. How do you feel about them?

Of course, it will depend on the politician – and your second answer might involve even more swearing than the first. But in general, people's views of politicians whom they know and perhaps for whom they vote is usually more positive than their general view of politicians, despite the fact that all politicians are local to somebody.

'When you ask people about politicians, they say they don't trust them,' says Andy Williamson, a fellow of the Hansard Society. 'But when you ask them about their local MP, the level of trust goes up. It's about familiarity – you tend to trust people you know, and distrust people you don't know.'

In the same way, people distrust things they do not understand, Williamson says. 'And one problem with democracy is people are not familiar enough with how it works.'

There is no single big easy answer to this problem, he says, but 'a lot of small incremental things to do.

'The first is to improve our education system so we improve our teaching of political literacy. We have got to start with people understanding why we have the systems we have, and how they work.'

Then there need to be awareness-raising campaigns out in local communities to explain how our system works and engage people's imagination, he says. 'For really hard to reach groups, you have got to look at using intermediaries – the answer is for people to go out to schools, youth groups, community centres, to build little hubs of democratic knowledge. And we need to use local people to do it – the people we trust are the people we know.'

In arguing for education, some people will always object that what is being taught is just one-way, is biased, is questionable, is just a matter of opinion. They will point to what are, in their opinion, the bad things that democratically elected governments have done over the years, or that democratically elected politicians have done, and ask why should we teach children about that?

But pointing out problems, in itself, is not constructive. There are problems with all forms of government, all people and all things, but does this mean they should be rejected, or does it mean we should continue to discuss, and debate, and improve?

In the end, as Churchill implied, anyone who says we should get rid of democracy altogether, or that it is not worth taking part in democracy, has first to say what better system there is.

Because democracy is simply, at its heart, a practical system for running human society, based on everyone working together to ensure fair treatment for as many people as possible.

The election – a free, fair and private vote – is where it all starts. Election, quite simply, is the best way of changing a country's leadership. What way that actually exists or has ever existed, here or in another country, is better?

When people vote, everyone is equal. When a person – when you – walk into that private booth, take your ballot paper and put a cross on it, at that moment, in carrying out that choice, you have the same power as anyone else in the country.

People who live without democracy understand the importance of the vote. In many countries, for example, the decisions made by their politicians affect not how well their schools or health services are run, but whether they have clean water or whether their children can go to school. But if their politicians never have to worry what people think about them, then this is unlikely to change.

The value of what UK citizens often take for granted can be seen in the desperate lengths to which people are prepared to go to win the same freedoms for themselves. Think of the hundreds of thousands of people who took to the streets in Ukraine in 2004 in bitter, freezing weather, day after day, to protest against rigged elections: and the new battles being fought in that country today to hold on to as much as possible of the national power they thought they had clawed back, and once more thrown into doubt by Russian intervention. Or think of Zainab Al-Khawaja, a Bahraini activist who according to Amnesty International was assaulted by security officials four times in 2011 for peaceful protests against the ruling regime. She was at various times punched in the head, kicked, dragged along the ground and shot in the thigh with a tear-gas canister resulting in seventeen stitches and a bone fracture. Each time she picked herself up and carried on the struggle for the kinds of basic democratic rights that we in the UK often take for granted.

But it is not all about the vote. Once a democratic government is elected, it is about building a society for all people – about people helping each other, about collective action.

'There are problems, like environmental damage that no one can solve on their own,' writes Colin Hay. 'And when it comes to companies, it is not fair to expect each one to place rules and restrictions on how it trades: everyone needs there to be the same rules for everyone, and so we need at least some kind of politics.'

This vision is developed by a colleague of Colin Hay's at the University of Sheffield, Professor Matthew Flinders, in his book *Defending Politics: Why Democracy Matters in the Twenty-first Century*.

'When all is said and done, politics does make a positive difference to people's lives,' Flinders writes. 'It provides healthcare, education, and social protections; it protects basic human rights and freedoms; it provides clean water, electricity, and sanitation; it allows us to talk and to challenge and to protest, and most of all it provides a way of negotiating between our different viewpoints and demands without resorting to violence and fear.'

Reading these lines, we come back to the puzzle – how is it then that people can have become so disengaged from the UK system? How has it come to be seen by so many people as something rotten, untrustworthy or under threat? And as something separate from us, rather than something drawn from us, chosen by us and supported by us?

Part of the answer may lie in people's perception that politicians say one thing and do another, says Flinders. They promise the world, and deliver peanuts. But, he points out, voters can be just as unrealistic.

'If we want to attack politics and politicians for failing to deliver, we need to be aware that the public are also capable of creating rhetoric–reality gaps. The public demand better services but are not willing to pay higher taxes. The public want to address climate change but they don't want to give up their energy–intensive lifestyles. They want to eat cake but not get fat. They care about dwindling fish stocks, just not enough to make them stop eating fish.'

Partly, therefore, our expectation of what politicians can realistically achieve in a few short years, in the face of continuous debate and op-position, needs to be cut back – they do not just represent us personally, and they will always have to compromise.

Democracy is not about perfection, it is about doing the best we can using cooperation and debate, not fear and force.

Reform will always be needed: our society will always have to adapt to suit our changing situation and beliefs, and we can and must always try to improve how it works. But we must not allow its democratic heart to stop, or our system really will begin to rot from the inside out.

Significantly, like many other analysts, Flinders traces the roots of social disengagement within the UK and other established democracies to a lack of political literacy and understanding – and so we come back to education, and the purpose of this book.

Because now, at the end of our journey, it is over to you.

How much do you know now about how democracy works? How much more might you be interested in finding out? How can you make sure your views are heard? Can you sign a petition? Read about your council's latest plans? Might you be able to work for your community in some way – with a voluntary group, a charity or a political party? How much can you change? How much can you help? If you did not vote at the last election, might you change your mind?

The best way to understand the huge, messy problems our politicians face is to walk up to the edge of them – and take the plunge. Not everyone will want to be active in politics, but that does not mean you cannot be a more active citizen. You will never be able to make things perfect, because things can never be perfect. But one of the most precious things that democracy brings is the freedom to think, talk, persuade and act in a way that might make things better.

The rest is up to you.

A democratic world?

This book set out to describe some of the basic elements of how democracy works in the UK, with the hope of inspiring more people to join in. So apart from a quick trip to Europe, we have not looked towards the rest of the world.

But democracy is a topic of vital interest to all nations: arguably, the most important topic that exists. In some countries where people have lived for decades or centuries without most of the rights and freedoms enjoyed in developed democracies, the foundations are now finally being laid for stronger societies based around elections and the rule of law. But it is a hard struggle.

The US-based non-profit organization Freedom House assesses every country annually as 'Free', 'Partly Free' or 'Not Free'. The mere fact of holding elections does not make a country free: in fact, 60 per cent of all countries now hold elections, and plenty of these (such as Russia) are designated as Not Free. Instead, Freedom House considers a country's record in twenty-five areas, such as freedom of the press and the right to peaceful protest – the sorts of elements described in this book as vital to a functioning democracy.

The reports depict a world where, as of 2014, only eighty-eight of 195 states are Free (down from ninety in the previous year). In all, 2.8 billion people live in these free nations, or 40 per cent of the world's population. A further fifty-nine nations qualify as Partly Free, home to a further 1.8 billion people.

Most disturbingly, however, some forty-eighty countries are still Not Free. In these societies, there are few basic rights. Some 35 per cent of the population of the 'modern' world, or 2.5 billion people, live under these conditions. Of these, more than half live in one state: China.

The ruling elites in countries which are 'Not Free' do not much like this description of their handiwork. But invariably, while they all speak the language of justice, development and democracy, their actions tell a different story.

At the outset of the series of popular uprisings in 2011 that became known as the Arab Spring, Freedom House reported: 'In China, the authorities responded to events in Cairo's Tahrir Square with a near-hysterical campaign of arrests, incommunicado detentions, press censorship, and stepped-up control over the internet. The Chinese Communist Party's pushback, which aimed to quash potential pro-democracy demonstrations before they even emerged, reached a crescendo . . . with the sentencing of a number of dissident writers to long terms in prison. In Russia, the state-controlled media bombarded domestic audiences with predictions of chaos and instability as a consequence of the Arab protests, with a clear message that demands for political reform in Russia would have similarly catastrophic results.'

Non-democratic governments must always be oppressive, because they are focused on one task as their first, second and third priorities: to hold on to power, which for the elite few also brings with it unimaginable personal wealth.

What can anyone do about any of this? Clearly, regimes like those in control of Russia and China are much too big and powerful to pay attention to any other nation. From time to time since the Second World War the US, European nations and others have intervened in smaller undemocratic nations, though this is a hugely controversial area. In any case, there are far too many smaller undemocratic regimes for direct intervention by other single states or small groups of states to be possible, even if it were desirable – or effective.

What about the people of the world acting together? What about international law, and the UN?

It is true that the UN was originally conceived as a kind of 'world government', in the aftermath of two world wars which had caused death, devastation and misery on an unimaginable scale and pitted countries against each other across the entire globe.

To try to make sure this could never happen again, fifty-one nations gathered at the San Francisco Opera House in 1945 to sign a charter for a new organization with four overarching aims: 'to save succeeding generations from the scourge of war . . . to reaffirm faith in fundamental human rights, in the dignity and worth of the human person, in the equal rights of men and women and of nations large and small . . . to establish conditions under which justice and respect for the obligations arising from treaties and other sources of international law can be maintained, and to promote social progress and better standards of life in larger freedom.'

Since then, membership of the UN's General Assembly – its main policymaking body, within which all nations have an equal vote – has grown to 193 states (some disputed states such as Kosovo have yet to be formally recognized internationally).

Though the structure of the UN is notoriously complex – author and former UN employee Maggie Black has described the job of understanding it as 'mind-bendingly difficult' – the organization and its many agencies do a huge amount of work that is essential for the world to function smoothly. In areas such as trade, peacekeeping (though see below), human rights, shipping, copyright, cultural protection and humanitarian aid, the UN allows nations and global regions with different goals, governments and outlooks to work together, design technical rules and – at the very least – to talk to each other.

When it comes to political action, however, its powers are severely limited. One of the most controversial institutions of the UN is the Security Council, which sits at its core. This is a small group of nations which decides on the stronger or more direct actions the UN is able to take or to support to uphold international peace and security, such as peacekeeping operations, sanctions and even the endorsement of direct military action against states.

The most powerful five military nations at the time the UN was set up – Britain, China, France, the USSR (now the Russian Federation) and the US – are permanent members of the Security Council, and they each have the unlimited right to veto or block any action proposed. There are also ten other members of the council elected for two years at a time by the General Assembly. These changing or temporary members have an equal vote to the big five, but no veto. Some other powerful modern nations such as Germany, Brazil, India and Japan are now pushing to be admitted as permanent members, but would be unlikely to be awarded a veto either.

At the time the UN was founded, the permanent five Security Council members had all fought alongside at least one of the other members as allies. Afterwards, however, the Cold War split the USSR and China apart from the others as the ideological enemies of democracy (in fact, to begin with China was represented at the UN by the nationalists of Chiang Kai-shek, forced to withdraw to Taiwan by the communist forces of Mao Zedong; but in 1971 the 'People's Republic of China' became the nation's accepted UN representative). Now the Soviet Union has fallen and Russia holds elections, but the fairness of those elections is widely questioned; many basic human rights do not appear to be upheld; corruption in the country is rife; and Russia still prefers to align itself with China and against the US and Europe on many human rights issues.

One problem that arises from this is that UN peacekeepers can only enter a country either if they are invited by that nation's government to help keep peace or oversee a transition, or if the Security Council, including all five permanent members, votes in favour of intervention.

All too often, however, the council that was supposed to unite the world's military forces to promote 'larger freedom' has been deadlocked over intervention. There is a sense that China and Russia in particular, with their undemocratic regimes, are keen above all to protect the principle that governments must be able to do what they like inside their own borders. Or in the case of Crimea, sometimes beyond their legal borders as well.

Sometimes the Security Council does support direct military action by UN forces or by 'coalitions of the willing' – groups of member states or regional bodies like NATO, backed by UN resolutions. This usually happens to protect civilians, but tends to be in more extreme situations where there is civil war raging, or a genocide seems imminent. Even then, intervention can be weak and ineffective, as in Rwanda and Somalia.

Some observers are optimistic that UN-backed action within states is becoming more frequent and more positive, however. The Canadian diplomat and author David Malone, writing in *The Oxford Handbook on the UN*, has argued that the Security Council has appeared less deadlocked since the end of the Cold War. He points to an increasing number of UN or UN-backed interventions inside states such as Angola, Bosnia, Cambodia, East Timor, Kosovo, Kuwait, Mozambique, Namibia and Somalia in recent decades – and in 2013 he might have added Mali as well.

'While the future is uncertain, cumulatively the Council's decisions in the post-Cold War era have proved immensely influential,' writes Malone. 'By asserting the UN's responsibility to intervene, even in internal conflicts – where human rights and the humanitarian interests of populations are severely affected – Council decisions, arising from evolving interpretations of the [UN] Charter, have deeply affected the meaning of sovereignty at the international level. This is no small legacy for the Council in the post-Cold War era.'

Even this progress must surely have been plunged back into doubt in 2014, however, given events in Syria and Ukraine which appear to be pitting Cold War enemies directly against each other once more, exposing once again the weakness of the UN Security Council.

It is not just by supporting military action that the UN tries to promote human rights: it has also drawn up a bewildering array of conventions, treaties, codes, statements and declarations – at the last count, 100 or more on human rights topics from equality to the elimination of torture and slavery.

The most famous of these is the Universal Declaration of Human Rights, a totemic statement of thirty articles adopted by the UN General Assembly in 1948 to add depth to the mention of human rights in the UN's founding charter. The declaration is not a treaty or a law but has been used as the foundation for many countries' own national constitutions and laws, and for other UN treaties such as the International Convention on Civil and Political Rights.

One problem, however, is that no one has to sign up to any of these documents, and even if they do, there is no meaningful enforcement mechanism, so countries can just sign up as if to sign a piece of paper is a meaningful action in itself – they are never compelled to do anything else about it. The International Covenant on Civil and Political Rights, for example, has been ratified by 167 countries – observant readers will notice this is seventy-nine more than the number of free countries in the world, as defined by Freedom House.

Regimes that are particularly flagrant in ignoring conventions can be reported to the UN Human Rights Council, and denounced by officials there known as 'rapporteurs' – but if they are comfortable with torturing their own people, they can probably live with a ticking off from an obscure dignitary.

The development of democracy is also linked to the UN's extensive development work, which helps tackle hunger and poverty and build basic social support structures such as schools and hospitals. 'Building democratic societies' is listed alongside key themes such as fighting poverty and empowering women as an explicit working theme of the UN Development Programme.

The UN has also established a Democratic Governance Thematic Trust Fund, to which countries are invited to donate: since it was set up just over ten years ago this has spent more than 100 million US dollars on about 800 projects. The projects it supports have been worthwhile: in

Bangladesh, for example, it has funded the development of digital tools allowing citizens to report on the quality of public services over the web and using mobile phones, with public officials pledging to respond. However, at an average of about £80,000 per project, it seems unlikely to have a major impact on its own. And none of this stops any government from violating human rights within its own borders. So are there any legal sanctions that could be taken against such states?

The UN does have a judicial branch: the International Court of Justice, presided over by fifteen judges of different nationalities elected jointly by the General Assembly and the Security Council.

Individuals cannot sue governments in this court, however, nor can governments sue each other without the permission of the accused. So it can adjudicate only on disputes where both parties to the dispute agree to bring the case, and to abide by the result, before it starts: not a great way to force any government to do anything it does not want to do.

The court cannot review decisions made by the Security Council, either, so effectively whatever the Security Council does is legal.

What about the International Criminal Court (ICC) in The Hague? Could oppressive regimes ever face any sanctions there?

The ICC, set up in 2002, is an independent entity established to prosecute former national and military leaders for genocide, crimes against humanity, war crimes and crimes of aggression. It is separate from the UN, though the two bodies cooperate and the UN Security Council can refer cases to the ICC.

However, not all countries are signed up to its jurisdiction: 122 states have done so, but many, including China, Russia and the US – three of the five permanent members of the Security Council – have either not signed or not ratified the treaty (the UK has done both). Furthermore, as the ICC (like the UN) has no police force of its own, it is not a body with any power to stop events from taking place, such as governments killing their own people; it can act only against individuals with the cooperation of individual states, when the conditions are right. States who sign up to the court do pledge to cooperate with it in investigating and prosecuting crimes, but there is no formal sanction if they do not act. If a case is referred to the court by the UN Security Council, all UN member states have a duty to cooperate – but again, without sanction.

International law, then, is patchy at best, and largely voluntary. It would be wrong to say that the UN, international courts and other elements of the international diplomatic and legal system are pointless, as they could be part of the vital first stages of a journey towards a fairer and freer world. But it is hard to see how true globally enforced law will ever be possible without first having governments in place in all or most countries that share similar values. Until this happens, not only will most oppressive governments simply be able to opt out or ignore international law, but many democracies will also remain wary of signing over jurisdiction of their actions to a body or bodies which could be influenced by undemocratic nations.

Membership of the UN Human Rights Council, for example, includes such systemic human rights violators as China, Russia and Saudi Arabia. At least it is an improvement on its predecessor body, the UN Commission on Human Rights, which in 2003 was chaired by Colonel Gaddafi's Libya – like putting a starving polar bear on drugs in charge of rights for baby seals.

Properly to promote universal human rights worldwide, all nations would have to agree on a form of closer and more direct collaboration of which it is almost impossible to conceive unless, at the very least, all five of the permanent members of the UN Security Council become free nations. In other words, this would mean the establishment of functioning democracies in China and Russia.

At the moment, this seems some way off, but you never know. Might there be anything citizens of the UK and other free nations can do to try to help speed up the arrival of greater freedoms and rights for people everywhere in the world?

Usually, when this subject is discussed, people shrug their shoulders and start to talk about 'the real world'. However much we might like everyone in the world to live free from dictatorship and the fear of violence and oppression from their own governments, they say, the truth is that alliances between democratic and undemocratic nations are often needed to underpin essential activities such as trade, energy, or our own security. Unpleasant as it might be, we cannot afford not to do business with the non-democratic governments that rule over a third of the modern world with all its space, people and resources.

This might well be true, some of the time – but it does not mean we cannot do anything at all. Democratic governments already make great play of the pressure they supposedly put on non-democratic regimes like China to 'improve their human rights record' – glossing over the inconvenient truth that their very existence is a human rights violation.

Such pressure, however weak, is a start, but there is more we can do, as a country and as individuals.

In 'Ten critical human rights challenges for the next American President', a paper written in 2012 by a cluster of human rights groups, the US government was urged to do more in several areas. These include providing political support, technical assistance and aid to new and developing democracies such as Tunisia, Egypt, Libya and Yemen; spending more on support for civil society and the development of independent media in other nations, not just on trade, aid and military links; and ensuring the US government does not ignore human rights in striking deals with undemocratic regimes that are perceived to help protect the interest of US citizens, such as fighting terrorism.

These same points could be taken as a blueprint for all democratic nations. As the report points out, ultimately such actions are in everyone's interest, not just because they are morally right, but because 'governments that abuse human rights make unstable and unreliable partners'.

This is worth remembering. Undemocratic governments may seem strong but they can also crumble quickly and are quirky, unpredictable and have no accountability. Are these the best partners?

The UK's activity in promoting democracy and human rights abroad has been monitored in recent years by Democratic Audit, a research organization based at the University of Liverpool. Every few years the organization scrutinizes UK democracy across seventy-five areas, from elections to the justice system, including asking the question: 'Do the country's international policies contribute to strengthening global democracy?'

The answer to this key question, taken from the organization's fourth survey published in 2012, is broadly positive. 'The UK is in principle committed to human rights and their international promotion as a matter of policy', Democratic Audit says.

This is important, because human rights and democracy are two sides of the same coin, the organization says. 'Human rights and democracy, two interdependent sets of values, apply not only to individual countries, but universally – or at least they should do. In this sense a truly democratic state must seek to further democracy on an international scale.'

It welcomes the publication by the UK's Foreign Office of annual international human rights and democracy reports, and notes that human rights are also mentioned as part of a five-point strategy for UK foreign policy between 2011 and 2015 adopted by the Foreign Office in 2010. Point number five is to 'use "soft power" as a tool of UK foreign policy; expand the UK Government's contribution to conflict prevention; promote British values, including human rights; and contribute to the welfare of developing countries.'

There is some criticism in the audit too, however.

While welcoming the mention in this strategy of human rights, Democratic Audit points out that they are not considered worth being an item in their own right, being presented instead as a subset of 'British values'. This, it says, is 'arguably a curious categorization, given that the UK is committed to human rights under international conventions, and as universal values.'

The audit also warns that the UK does not always seem to pay enough attention to human rights when it comes to countries which might be important to us in other ways.

'There is evidence that [the UK] has softened its approach or lessened its criticism when faced by violations perpetrated by countries which may be important trading powers or strategic allies of the UK, or both,' the report says. 'The universal nature of human rights makes this inconsistency problematic and unacceptable.'

A similar finding emerged from a recent House of Commons Foreign Affairs Committee review of the human rights and democracy work of the Foreign Office.

Like Democratic Audit, while welcoming the government's commitment to continue publishing annual reports on its work in this area, the committee had major concerns about human rights violations by the UK's 'friends', such as Bahrain, a military and political ally of the US and the UK whose own government has been widely reported to have attacked dissidents, as well as doctors and nurses in hospitals where protestors were being treated.

While it is inevitable that the UK will have strategic, commercial or security-related interests which have the potential to conflict with its human rights values, 'in pursuing these alongside its human rights work overseas, the UK runs the risk of operating double standards, and our view is that it would be in the government's interest for it to be more transparent in this respect and for ministers to be bolder in acknowledging that there will be contradictions', the committee said.

'Rather than trying to assert that the two can co-exist freely, part of the government's role should be publicly to set out and explain its judgments on how far to balance them in particular cases'.

Other recommendations from the committee included for the government to consider linking the awarding to UK businesses of lucrative public sector contracts, investment support and export credit guarantees to the human rights records of those businesses overseas; and for the government to introduce new accountability measures for its human rights programmes, such as benchmarks, targets or indicators.

The UK is also now part of human rights work undertaken by the new foreign policy arm of the European Union, the European External Action Service (EEAS). The EU has placed the spread of democracy at the heart of its development aid policies; and the EEAS recently adopted its first ever Strategic Framework on Human Rights and Democracy with an action plan (no less) for putting it into practice.

The key messages of the framework include embedding human rights in all EU external policies 'without exception'. This comprehensive approach will integrate promotion of human rights into 'trade, investment, technology and telecommunications, internet, energy, environmental, corporate social responsibility and development policy as well as into common security and defence policy and the external dimensions of employment and social policy and the area of freedom, security and justice, including counter-terrorism policy. In the area of development cooperation, a human rights based approach will be used to ensure that the EU strengthens its efforts to assist partner countries in implementing their international human rights obligations.'

These kinds of principles are sometimes easier said than done. When it comes to trade with other countries, in particular, individual EU member states are often worried that if they do not trade with any one particular undemocratic nation, another EU member will.

How will the EU principles be monitored and audited? Who will make sure no member state breaks ranks? There is some way to go before we live in a world where even policies like these, which we already have, are properly implemented.

But clearly there are many areas of activity that the UK could develop and expand to help promote freedom and democracy worldwide, both within its own policies and in the framework of the EU.

The simple spread of information can have an impact: consider, for example, the BBC World Service.

The World Service radio and now internet service has the largest worldwide audience of any international news provider, at about 240 million people, or just under 3.5 per cent of the entire global population. Providing a balanced and independent service, it broadcasts and publishes in thirty-two languages on web and radio, including Arabic, Burmese, Chinese (Cantonese) and Russian.

In recent years, some cuts have been made in the service's funding, as it has shifted from Foreign Office grant support towards funding mainly out of the BBC licence fee by 2014. But it has retained its unique vision. In the words of its 2011–12 annual review, 'one of our core public purposes [is] addressing the shortfall in international news from a trusted, impartial global news provider.' So the UK is producing a public service for the entire world – a situation of which we can be proud, and look to build on.

As the internet takes over from TV and radio as the news source of choice for many across the world, as well as a platform for free speech, other dangers loom.

Even with the radio service, several countries, including China and Iran, have long been accused of systematic jamming of World Service radio signals. Countries like these are also renowned for controlling citizen access to the internet within their borders. Now, however, they are also pushing for control of the routing systems that coordinate the internet globally to be switched from US control to UN control.

On the face of it, this request sounds fair enough – international control over the internet rather than US or Western 'domination'. What many observers fear, however, is that the countries pushing for this 'internationalization' – such as Russia, Saudi Arabia and China – have a hidden agenda to build in greater ease of censorship and control to the fabric of the internet. The US, on the other hand, has built and promoted the internet as a free global platform, and has built a structure of quasi-independent bodies to defend this freedom. So while many agree that more work is required to 'internationalize' oversight of the internet's basic functions and to encourage non-US companies to take more advantage of its commercial potential, it will be vital to retain the internet's free and open nature.

At the heart of this battle are two organizations: the Internet Governance Forum and the International Telecommunications Union.

The Internet Governance Forum (IGF) was set up by the UN to

provide an informal global framework for governments, business, parliamentarians and civil society to share ideas about how to run the internet. It is an advisory body, working not by formal international treaties but by informal exchanges. Now, however, countries such as the ones mentioned above – China, Russia, Saudi Arabia – are pushing for internet control to be brought within the formal remit of the International Telecommunication Union (ITU), a UN agency which oversees global coordination of telecommunications.

The UK government is among many opposing this move, arguing that formal UN control is both unnecessary and potentially damaging to the unique innovative qualities of the internet. But the battle continues. And so it seems as if the future of the internet is closely tied to the future of democracy.

Not everyone would agree that the encouragement of democratic government and civil liberties in other countries is a valid goal for the UK or any democratic nation. What such people ignore, however, is that most people who actually live under governments which are not democratic would dearly love to be free. They ignore the many non-Western democracies that now exist. And they ignore the fact that in most countries with authoritarian regimes many of the biggest problems, such as corruption, a lack of freedom of speech and rigged elections, take place in violation of these countries' own existing laws, constitutions and public statements.

Most of all, they ignore the fact that to argue against democracy openly and fairly, you need democracy in the first place. In a sense, it is impossible to argue against democracy: because to argue against it is to express yourself, to join a debate and expect to be taken seriously – for which you will need freedom of expression, and hence (in the real world) democracy.

There is another deep illogicality in attacking a 'Western' democratic nation for doing something that is perceived to be undemocratic or contrary to the rule of law – say, Guantanamo Bay – and then using that as a reason to attack democracy itself. This is nonsensical. If you object to any nation doing something that you feel violates human freedom, then you must support human freedom.

In the end, if we believe that all people are of equal value and are born deserving the same rights and chances as everyone else, then we believe in freedom of knowledge, freedom of thought and freedom of expression for everybody, as we expect for ourselves.

Time and again, it has been proven that only democracy can bring these freedoms.

As Aung San Suu Kyi – the rightfully elected and then deposed leader of an Asian country, next door to China – has made clear, for the people of Burma the struggle against oppression is inseparable from the struggle for democracy. In her moving Nobel Peace Prize acceptance speech in Oslo in June 2012, Aung San Suu Kyi – whose political party is named the National League for Democracy – could not have been clearer on this point.

'If I am asked why I am fighting for democracy in Burma,' she said, 'it is because I believe that democratic institutions and practices are necessary for the guarantee of human rights.'

Every country's struggle for freedom, she said, is everybody's business: 'The peace of our world is indivisible. As long as negative forces are getting the better of positive forces anywhere, we are all at risk.'

Aung San Suu Kyi ended her speech with a vision: 'Ultimately, our aim should be to create a world . . . of which each and every corner is a true sanctuary, where the inhabitants will have the freedom and the capacity to live in peace. Every thought, every word, and every action that adds to the positive and the wholesome is a contribution to peace. Each and every one of us is capable of making such a contribution.'

This appeal is to every one of us, as individuals.

Why should freedom be only for some countries and some people, and not others? Are they somehow lesser people, who do not deserve what we have?

Aung San Suu Kyi's message is that, as human beings across the world, we have more in common than we might realize, and we can and ought to show solidarity and support for each other. At a higher level, she is saying, above nationality, comes humanity. This realization is at the heart of the concept of human rights. Could it now be extended into a related concept of human citizenship?

One of the main messages of this book was that, as a citizen of the United Kingdom, if you don't like the way things are, you are at least able to think about ways of getting involved to change them.

Is this not also true as a citizen of the world? What could be more important than using your freedom to fight for the freedom of others, whoever and wherever they are? As with improving society inside the UK, finding out more about life in other countries might be a good place to start. The rest, once again, is up to you.

Acknowledgements

I hugely appreciate the support, help and advice given to me by so many people in the course of writing this book.

To my wife Gillian, and my children Ezra and Frida – thanks with all my heart for your love and support throughout a long period when I was even more cantankerous than usual.

Invaluable early and ongoing guidance and help were provided by close friends and colleagues Jenny Wilson, Thames & Hudson; Kelly Falconer, *Asia Literary Review*; Rupert Carter; Paul Bowen QC, Doughty Street Chambers; my agent Piers Blofeld of Sheil Land Associates; Doug Young, my publisher at Transworld; and Henry Vines, my thorough and perspicacious editor.

For interviews, comments, guidance and encouragement across the many chapter subject areas, I am indebted to so many people, including Stephen Baker, Suffolk Coastal District Council and Waveney District Council; Jonathan Baume, Civil Service Commissioner; Councillor Paul Bettison, Bracknell Forest Council; Catherine Bochel, University of Lincoln; Keith Bush, National Assembly for Wales; Martin Callanan MEP, Conservative Party; Tamasin Cave, Alliance for Lobbying Transparency; Lynda, Baroness Chalker of Wallasey, Conservative Party; Bruce Crawford MSP, former Minister for Parliamentary Business and Government Strategy, Scottish Government, Scottish National Party; Michael Cross, *Law Society Gazette*; Peter Cruickshank, Napier

University; James Curran, Goldsmiths, University of London; Susan Dalgety, independent communications adviser; Anna Daniel, National Assembly for Wales; diplomatic staff at the UK Representation to the EU in Brussels; Chris Dodwell, AEA; Professor Jonathan Drori, University of Bristol; Glyn Evans, Warwick University; Carole Ewart, Campaign for Freedom of Information in Scotland; Peter Facey, Unlock Democracy; Lynn Featherstone MP, Parliamentary Under-Secretary of State for International Development, Liberal Democrats; Alex Feeney, National Assembly for Wales; Richard Forsdyke, Herbert Smith; John Fox, Socitm Insight; Dr Ruth Fox, Hansard Society; Maurice Frankel, Campaign for Freedom of Information; Angela Frodin, Socitm Insight; Richard Gartner, King's College London; Dr Sandra Gonzalez-Bailon, Oxford Internet Institute; Richard Gordon QC, Brick Court Chambers; Martin Greenwood, Society of Information Technology Management; Justin Griggs, National Association of Local Councils; Zoe Gruhn, Institute for Government; Dr Non Gwilym, National Assembly for Wales; Richard Gwyn Jones, National Assembly for Wales; Greg Hadfield, Open Data Cities; Christopher Hall, sculptor and online campaigner; William Hardy, Open University; Mike Harris, Index on Censorship; Lord Toby Harris, Labour Peers' Group; Patrick Harvie MSP, Scottish Green Party; Tracey Hill, Labour Party; Michael Hocken JP, Magistrates' Association; Stephen Jakobi OBE, Fair Trials International; Gethin Jones, National Assembly for Wales; Professor Richard Keeble, University of Lincoln; Rebecca Kelly, West Lothian Council; Councillor Jason Kitcat, Brighton and Hove City Council; Caroline Lucas MP, Green Party; Eric MacLeod, Scottish Parliament; Nick Mailer, Positive Internet; Martin Moore, Media Standards Trust; Dr Roger Mortimore, Ipsos MORI; Dan Mount, Civic Agenda; Dr David Newman, e-consultation.org; Quintin Oliver, Strategem; Anne Peat, Scottish Parliament; Fred Perkins, Information TV; Helia Phoenix, National Assembly for Wales; Chris Quigley, Delib; Dr Matt Qvortrup, Cranfield University; Professor Colin Rallings, University of Plymouth; Mary Reid, Liberal Democrat Voice; Frances Robinson, *Wall Street Journal*; Dr Meg Russell, University College London; Professor

Acknowledgements

Richard Sambrook, Cardiff University; Richard Sarson, freelance journalist; Janet Seaton OBE, Parliamentary Information and Research Services consultant; Professor Aubrey Silberston CBE, Imperial College London; Nigel Smith, VoxScot; Dr Tom Smith, Oxford Consultants for Social Inclusion; Martin Stanley, civilservant.org.uk; Tom Steinberg, mySociety; Ian Stuart, Mayor of Salford; Diarmid Swainson, London Borough of Lambeth; Ian Taylor, former Science and Technology Minister; Ella Taylor-Smith, Napier University; John Thompson, journalism.co.uk; Judith Townend, City University London; John Turner, Association of Electoral Administrators; Gene Webb, Socitm Insight; Iwan Williams, National Assembly for Wales; Dr Andy Williamson, Future Digital; Sir Robert Worcester, Ipsos MORI; Derek Wyatt, Digital Strategy Consultant; Sir George Young MP, Chief Whip and former Leader of the House of Commons; Anthony Zacharzewski, Democratic Society; and Nadhim Zahawi MP, Conservative Party.

Finally, thanks to Harry Venning, for managing to illustrate so many tough and thorny subjects so powerfully and amusingly. And thanks to Vicky Sargent and Pete Willis at Boilerhouse Media for building my website.

Thanks so much to all of you – and apologies to anyone I have left out or whose details I have misrecorded.

Index

Index